ENCYCLOPEDIA OF MAMMALS

ENCYCLOPEDIA OF MAMMALS

VOLUME 17
Index

MARSHALL CAVENDISH

NEW YORK • LONDON • TORONTO • SYDNEY

Published by Marshall Cavendish Corporation
99 White Plains Road
Tarrytown, New York 10591-9001

The material in this series was first published in the English language by Marshall Cavendish Limited, of 119 Wardour Street, London W1V 3TD, England.

Library of Congress Cataloging-in-Publication Data

Encyclopedia of mammals.
   p. cm.
   Includes index.
   ISBN 0-7614-0575-5 (set)   ISBN 0-7614-0599-2 (v. 17)

   Summary: Detailed articles cover the history, anatomy, feeding habits, social structure, reproduction, territory, and current status of ninety-five mammals around the world.
   1. Mammals—Encyclopedias, Juvenile. [l. Mammals—Encyclopedias.]   I. Marshall Cavendish Corporation.
   QL706.2.E54 1996
   599'.003—dc20
                              96-17736
                                CIP
                                AC

Printed in Malaysia
Bound in U.S.A.

CONTENTS

GENERAL INDEX

A

aardvarks, *1*, 2–27
  see also hyraxes
  anteaters, *1*, 4
  behavior, *1*, 10–23
  body heat, *1*, 10
  breeding programs, *1*, 27
  burrowing, *1*, 12–14
  captivity, in, *1*, 27
  classification of, *1*, 7, 9
  enemies of, *1*, 13, 15
  family tree, *1*, 6–7
  farming pest, as, *1*, 24–5
  food and feeding, *1*, 4, 16–9
  habitats, *1*, 12–15
  hunting of, *1*, 24
  mating, *1*, 21
  names for, *1*, 5–6
  physical description, *1*, 8–9
  profile, *1*, 3–9
  rainfall, effect on, *1*, 14
  reproduction, *1*, 22–3
  social structure, *1*, 20–1
  survival, *1*, 24–6
  temperature, effect on, *1*, 14
  termites, feeding on,
    1, 4, 12, 16–7, 23, 24
  warthogs, similarity to,
    11, 1633
aardwolves
  behavior, *7*, 1051
  family tree, *7*, 1046
  food and feeding, *3*, 291
  habitats, *7*, 1052–3, 1061
  physical description, *7*, 1048
  survival, *7*, 1066
  territory, *7*, 1061
Abbot's duikers
  habitats, *6*, 766
  survival, *6*, 780
Aborigines
  bandicoots, hunting of,
    16, 2444
  dogs, introduction by,
    16, 2428

  kangaroos and, *8*, 1142
  koalas and, *8*, 1168, 1170
Abyssinian genets
  habitats, *4*, 506
  survival, *4*, 519–20
Abyssinian wolves
  see Simien jackals
acid rain
  badgers, effect on, *1*, 129
  hamsters, effect on, *7*, 937
acouchis
  profile, *6*, 889
  social structure, *6*, 902
adaptations see specific animal
addaxes
  food and feeding, *1*, 69
  habitats, *1*, 65–6
  life cycle, *1*, 73
  survival, *1*, 75, 77–8
African brush-tailed
  porcupines
    behavior, *12*, 1700
African buffalo
  defenses, *3*, 432–3
  diseases, *3*, 442
  domestication of, *3*, 442
  evolution, *3*, 419–20
  family tree, *3*, 423
  food and feeding, *3*, 431
  habitats, *3*, 428, *7*, 1055
  herds, *3*, 434–5
  life cycle, *3*, 437
  male aggression, *3*, 434
  physical characteristics,
    3, 424–5
  social structure,
    3, 434–5
  spotted hyenas, prey of,
    7, 1059
  survival, *3*, 438
  water parasites, removal of,
    3, 426–7
African civets
  habitats, *4*, 506
  life cycle, *4*, 514

African clawless otters
  behavior, *11*, 1571
  family tree, *11*, 1567
  habitats, *11*, 1573
  hunting by, *11*, 1570
African crested porcupines
  adaptations, *12*, 1706
African crocodiles
  habitats, *5*, 742
African desert cats
  see sand cats
African dormice
  life cycle, *7*, 928
African elephants
  behavior, *5*, 660–71
  evolution, *5*, 656
  family tree, *5*, 657
  food and feeding, *5*, 664–5
  habitats, *5*, 654, 662–3
  physical description,
    5, 655, 658–9
  survival, *5*, 672–7
  tusks, *5*, 654–5
African genets
  life cycle, *4*, 515
African golden cats
  habitats, *14*, 2015
  hunting by, *14*, 2020
  profile, *9*, 1253–4,
    14, 2005, 2007
  survival, *14*, 2028
African hedgehogs
  behavior, *7*, 972
  habitats, *7*, 974
  profile, *7*, 966–7
African hunting dogs
  pack hunting, *4*, 576
  teeth, *4*, 577
African leopards
  physical description, *8*, 1096
African linsang
  habitats, *4*, 507
African lions
  habitats, *9*, 1234
  survival, *9*, 1245–9

African lynx **see** caracals
African mole rats
  habitats, *9*, 1364
  profile, *9*, 1355–6
African palm civets, *4*, 498
  domestication, *4*, 521
  family tree, *4*, 501
  habitats, *4*, 507
  hideouts of, *4*, 504–5
  physical description,
    4, 502–3
African polecats
  profile, *15*, 2214
African porcupines
  defenses, *12*, 1708
  family tree, *12*, 1697
  food and feeding, *12*, 1710
  physical description, *12*, 1698
African rock squirrels
  life cycle, *14*, 2103
  social structure, *14*, 2099
African root rats
  profile, *9*, 1357
African small cats
  family tree, *14*, 2009
  habitats, *14*, 2015
  survival, *14*, 2028
  territory, *14*, 2022
African swamp rats
  family tree, *13*, 1905
  habitats, *13*, 1912
African swine fever
  bushpigs, *11*, 1638
  forest hogs, *11*, 1638
  giant forest hogs, *11*, 1637
  warthogs, *11*, 1638
African tree pangolins
  social structure, *1*, 96
African wild asses
  family tree, *7*, 1021
  food and feeding, *7*, 1030–1
  habitats, *7*, 1027–8
  life cycle, *7*, 1034–5
  social structure, *7*, 1033
  survival, *7*, 1038

African wildcats
  behavior, *14*, 2012
  habitats, *14*, 2014–5
  hunting by, *14*, 2018, 2020
  life cycle, *14*, 2025
  profile, *14*, 2005, 2008
  rabies, *14*, 2028
  survival, *14*, 2026, 2028
African wild dogs, *5*, 600–25
  alpha pairs,
      5, 608, 616–7, 619
  behavior, *5*, 608–19
  breeding, *5*, 618
  camouflage, *5*, 603
  canine distemper, *5*, 622
  conservation measures,
      5, 622–3
  diseases, *5*, 621–3
  DNA, *5*, 605
  dominant males, *5*, 616
  drinking water and, *5*, 610
  family tree, *4*, 527, 579,
      5, 604–5, 708, *8*, 1072
  habitats, *5*, 610–11, *7*, 1003
  hunting by, *5*, 612–5
  hunting of, *5*, 603
  life cycle, *5*, 618–9
  pack hunting, *5*, 602, 604,
      608, 610, 613, 615,
      617, 621, 624
  performers, as, *5*, 624
  persecution of, *5*, 622
  physical description,
      4, 526, *5*, 606–7
  profile, *5*, 601–7
  rabies, *5*, 621, 623, 625
  radio tracking, *5*, 625
  rinderpest, *5*, 622
  satellite tracking, *5*, 625
  social structure,
      5, 616–7
  survival, *5*, 620–4
  teeth, *5*, 602, 604
  thumb, *5*, 605
  viciousness of, reputation,
      5, 609
African yellow-winged bats
  hunting, *2*, 197
  reproduction, *2*, 202
agile gibbons
  habitats, *6*, 792–3

physical description, *6*, 784,
      785–6
  singing, *6*, 798–9
agoutis
  behavior, *6*, 895
  food and feeding, *6*, 902–3
  habitats, *6*, 897
  hunting of, *6*, 910
  profile, *6*, 889
  reproduction, *6*, 905
Alaskan seals
  see northern fur seals
albino ferrets
  survival, *15*, 2236–7
Alexander, Richard, *9*, 1370
Alexander's mongooses
  profile, *9*, 1332
Algerian hedgehogs
  habitats, *7*, 974
Allen's galagos
  food and feeding, *5*, 747
  habitats, *5*, 742
  locomotion, *5*, 744
  social structure, *5*, 749
Allen's swamp monkeys
  food and feeding, *10*, 1474
  profile, *10*, 1461
alpacas
  domestication, *3*, 342, 348
  family tree, *3*, 345
  survival, *3*, 364
alpine ibexes
  hunting of, *6*, 859
  physical description, *6*, 841
Alpine marmots
  social structure, *14*, 2096
  survival, *14*, 2106
Altai weasels
  habitats, *4*, 587
Amami rabbits
  habitats, *12*, 1806
  survival, *12*, 1820
Amargosa voles
  survival, *15*, 2210
Amazon dolphins
  habitats, *5*, 636
Amazonian manatees
  behavior, *9*, 1284
  family tree, *9*, 1281
  food and feeding, *9*, 1290–1
  habitats, *9*, 1286–8

hunting of, *9*, 1300
  life cycle, *9*, 1294–5
  physical description,
      9, 1279–80, *9*, 1283
  profile, *9*, 1278
  survival, *9*, 1297–1300
  territory, *9*, 1292
American badgers
  burrowing, *1*, 114, 124–5
  food and feeding, *1*, 120–1
  habitats, *1*, 116–7
  life cycle, *1*, 127
  profile, *1*, 109
  protection of, *1*, 131
  social structure, *1*, 124–5
American bighorn sheep
  behavior, *6*, 842
  diseases, *6*, 856
  food and feeding, *6*, 849
  habitats, *6*, 852, 859
  social structure, *6*, 850, 853
  survival, *6*, 855–6, 858
American bison
  family tree, *3*, 397
  food and feeding, *3*, 406–7
  habitats, *3*, 402–3
  physical characteristics,
      3, 396, 398–9
  population, *3*, 417
  reproduction, *3*, 410
  survival, *3*, 412–6
American black bears, *2*, 236–61
  aggression, *3*, 297
  behavior, *2*, 244–55
  blue bears, *2*, 239
  conservation measures,
      2, 258–9
  creamy white bears, *2*, 238–9
  cubs, *2*, 254–5
  dawn bears, *2*, 240
  denning, *2*, 252–3
  Everglades bears, *2*, 259
  evolution, *2*, 238
  family tree, *2*, 241, 267,
      3, 293, *11*, 1592, 1670
  food and feeding,
      2, 238, 250–1
  glacier bears, *2*, 239
  habitats, *2*, 239, 246–9,
      3, 298, 326
  hibernation, *2*, 252–3

Kermode bears, *2*, 239
  life cycle, *2*, 254–5
  mating, *2*, 244–5, 254–5
  national parks and, *2*, 259–61
  profile, *2*, 240–3
  satellite tracking of, *2*, 261
  size, *2*, 247
  sloth bears, *2*, 241, 266
  smell, sense of, *2*, 240
  spectacled bears, *2*, 240, 266
  sun bears, *2*, 241, 266
  survival, *2*, 256–60
  temperature, effect of, *2*, 248
  territories, *2*, 244, 247–8
  timber trade and, *2*, 258
  tree-climbing, *2*, 245
  walking, *2*, 239
American martens
  habitats, *7*, 950
  profile, *9*, 1305
  trapping for fur, *9*, 1326–7
American minks
  behavior, *9*, 1311
  family tree, *9*, 1306
  habitats, *9*, 1312, 1314
  mating, *9*, 1322
  physical description, *9*, 1309
  Pyrenean desmans,
      as prey of, *10*, 1391
  sea minks compared, *9*, 1307
  survival, *9*, 1325, *10*, 1404
  trapping for fur, *9*, 1327
American opossums
  family tree, *10*, 1514, *16*, 2425
  habitats, *10*, 1521
American pikas
  family tree, *7*, 942
American pine voles
  habitats, *15*, 2197
American river otters
  behavior, *11*, 1571
  family tree, *11*, 1566
  food and feeding, *11*, 1578
  habitats, *11*, 1572–3
  physical description, *11*, 1568
  profile, *11*, 1564–5
  survival, *11*, 1582, 1585–6
American shrew-moles
  burrowing, *10*, 1389
  food and feeding, *10*, 1399
American water voles

habitats, *15*, 2196

Amur leopards
family tree, *8*, 1203
survival, *8*, 1221–2

Anatolian leopards
family tree, *8*, 1203
survival, *8*, 1221

Andean bears
see spectacled bears

Andean condors
habitats, *3*, 300

Angolan lions
profile, *9*, 1228

Angolan mongooses
profile, *9*, 1332
survival, *9*, 1352

angwantibo
captivity, *5*, 755
food and feeding, *5*, 747
habitats, *5*, 740, 742
locomotion, *5*, 745

anoas
habitats, *3*, 428
life cycle, *3*, 436–7
lowland anoas
see lowland anoas
mountain anoas
see mountain anoas
survival, *3*, 438, 441

Antandroy tribe
lemurs and, *8*, 1195

Antarctic fur seals
habitats, *13*, 1962–3
life cycle, *13*, 1971

anteaters, *1*, 28–53
see also aardvarks; giant
anteaters; silky anteaters;
tamanduas
behavior, *1*, 36–47
borderline species, *1*, 38
breeding, *1*, 42
conservation measures,
1, 50–1
erosion of habitats, *1*, 50
evolution, *1*, 29–32
family tree, *1*, 32–3, 84
floods and, *1*, 48
food and feeding, *1*, 40, 44–5
great horned owl, as prey of,
1, 41
habitats, *1*, 38–41, 53

hazardous waste production
and, *1*, 52
jaguars, as prey of, *1*, 41
physical description, *1*, 34–5
pollution and, *1*, 52
predators, *1*, 49
profile, *1*, 29–35
rainfall, effect on, *1*, 40
rain forests, *1*, 40, 50–1
reproduction, *1*, 46–7
survival, *1*, 48–52
temperature, effect on, *1*, 40
territory, *1*, 42–3

antelope jackrabbits
physical description, *7*, 945

antelopes, *1*, 54–79
behavior, *1*, 62–73
communication, *1*, 63
conservation measures,
1, 76–7
danger, reaction to, *1*, 62
droughts, effect on, *1*, 66
family tree, *1*, 58–9, *3*, 396,
422–3, *6*, 761
food and feeding, *1*, 68–9
four-horned antelopes,
3, 396, 422
grasslands, *1*, 66
grazing antelopes, *3*, 423
habitats, *1*, 64–7
hunting of, *1*, 78
life cycle, *1*, 72–3
lions, as prey of, *1*, 67
mating, *1*, 72
noises of, *1*, 63
profile, *1*, 55–61
Serengeti, *1*, 74
signaling systems, *1*, 62
social structure, *1*, 70–1
spiral-horned antelopes,
3, 397, 423
survival, *1*, 74–8
termites and, *1*, 67
woodlands, *1*, 64

Antillean manatees
family tree, *9*, 1281
habitats, *9*, 1286–7
survival, *9*, 1296, 1299–1300

ape forms
family tree, *11*, 1541

apelike forms

family tree, *6*, 787

apes
family tree, *5*, 735, *6*, 787, 865,
10, 1462, 1488, *11*, 1541

apes, great
see also chimpanzees;
gorillas; orangutans
family tree, *11*, 1541

aquatic rats see fish-eating rats

aquatic tenrecs
family tree, *7*, 968
habitats, *7*, 975

Arabian oryx
food and feeding, *1*, 69
habitats, *1*, 65
Jiddat al Harasis herd,
1, 76–7
life cycle, *1*, 73
Operation Oryx, *1*, 76–7
profile, *1*, 57
social structure, *1*, 71
survival, *1*, 76–7
tournaments, *1*, 71

Arabian tahrs
habitats, *6*, 859
survival, *6*, 857

Arabian wolves
survival, *16*, 2417

arctic foxes
camouflage, *5*, 686
color, *5*, 689
family tree, *5*, 683, 708
fur, *5*, 687
habitats, *5*, 688, 690, 714, 716,
11, 1679, *15*, 2199, 2207
hunting by, *5*, 693–4
physical description,
5, 680, 684–5
profile, *5*, 681
reproduction, *5*, 698–9
survival, *5*, 700–2
temperature, effect on,
5, 686
territory, *5*, 696–7, 722

arctic hares
behavior, *7*, 946–7
habitats, *3*, 327, *15*, 2198
physical description, *7*, 945

arctic lemmings
habitats, *15*, 2197

arctic terns

habitats, *15*, 2251

Arctic wolves, *4*, 584

Arfak ring-tailed possums
population, *12*, 1743

argalis
habitats, *6*, 859

Argentine gray foxes
habitats, *5*, 689–90
hunting by, *5*, 693, 695
reproduction, *5*, 698
survival, *5*, 701–2
territory, *5*, 696

Ariegeois
habitats, *7*, 1028

Arizona jaguars
survival, *8*, 1117

armadillos, *1*, 80–105
behavior, *1*, 88–99
burrowing, *1*, 88–9
classification, *1*, 85
conservation measures,
1, 102–3
diseases, *1*, 104
family tree, *1*, 33
food and feeding, *1*, 91, 94–5
foraging, *1*, 94–5, 98
grasslands, *1*, 90–1
habitats, *1*, 82, 90–3
hunting of, *1*, 100
leprosy research, *1*, 104
life cycle, *1*, 98–9
mating, *1*, 98
medicine, use in, *1*, 100, 104
physical description, *1*, 86–7
profile, *1*, 81–7
rainfall, effect on, *1*, 92
scent marking, *1*, 97
social structure, *1*, 96–7
survival, *1*, 100–4
temperature, effect on, *1*, 92
termites, feeding habits,
1, 91–2
threats to, *1*, 89

armored shrews
physical description,
14, 2037

Asian black bears, *2*, 240, 266
aggression, *3*, 297
denning, *3*, 296
description, *3*, 295
family tree, *3*, 293,

11, 1592, 1670
food and feeding, *3*, 297,
   302, 304–5
habitats, *3*, 290, 298–9,
   4, 586
life cycle, *3*, 306–7
migration, *3*, 298
names for, *3*, 292
survival, *3*, 309, 311–3
Asian buffalo
   family tree, *3*, 422
   profile, *3*, 419
Asian dholes
   physical description, *4*, 526
Asian elephants
   behavior, *5*, 660–71
   calls, *5*, 668
   conservation measures,
     5, 674–5
   evolution, *5*, 656
   family tree, *5*, 657
   food and feeding, *5*, 664–5
   habitats, *5*, 654, 662–3
   physical description,
     5, 655, 658–9
   survival, *5*, 673–7
   tusks, *5*, 654
Asian painted bats
   mating, *2*, 228
Asian small-clawed otters
   behavior, *11*, 1570–1
   family tree, *11*, 1567
   food and feeding, *11*, 1579
   habitats, *11*, 1572, 1574
   physical description,
     11, 1568
Asian water buffalo
   habitats, *3*, 428
   survival, *3*, 439
Asiatic chevrotains
   behavior, *12*, 1753
Asiatic golden cats
   behavior, *9*, 1259
   habitats, *9*, 1261
   hunting by, *9*, 1265
   life cycle, *9*, 1268
   profile, *9*, 1253–4
   survival, *9*, 1272–3
Asiatic lions
   habitats, *9*, 1234
   profile, *9*, 1228

survival, *9*, 1244,
   1246–7, 1249
Asiatic shrew-moles
   burrowing, *10*, 1389
   food and feeding, *10*, 1399
Asiatic wild asses
   behavior, *7*, 1025
   family tree, *7*, 1021
   food and feeding, *7*, 1031
   habitats, *7*, 1019, 1026–8
   life cycle, *7*, 1034–5
   social structure, *7*, 1033
   survival, *7*, 1037–9
Aspinall, John, *6*, 885
asses
   conservation measures,
     7, 1039
   family tree, *7*, 1021, *16*, 2451
   physical description, *7*, 1020
   profile, *16*, 2447
   social structure, *7*, 1033
   survival, *7*, 1036
Attenborough, David, *3*, 426
Auckland sea lions
   see New Zealand sea lions
Australasian marsupials
   profile, *12*, 1721
Australian bandicoots
   food and feeding, *16*, 2435
Australian dingoes
   conservation measures,
     4, 596–7
   domestication, *4*, 597–8
   evolution, *4*, 578
   family tree, *4*, 579
   habitats, *4*, 584–6
   life cycle, *4*, 593
   pack hunting, *4*, 582–3
   survival, *4*, 594–9
Australian echidnas
   habitats, *11*, 1652
Australian forest possums
   survival, *12*, 1743
Australian fur seals
   habitats, *16*, 2433
Australian hopping mice
   life cycle, *13*, 1916
   survival, *13*, 1922–3
Australian National Strategy for
   the Conservation of Species
     and Communities,

16, 2442–3
axis deer
   habitats, *4*, 560
aye-ayes
   behavior, *8*, 1181
   evolution, *8*, 1175
   family tree, *5*, 734, *8*, 1177
   food and feeding, *8*, 1186–7
   habitats, *8*, 1183
   physical description,
     8, 1178–9
   profile, *8*, 1174–6
   social structure, *8*, 1188
   survival, *8*, 1196
Azara's fox
   hunting by, *5*, 693
   survival, *5*, 702

B

babirusas
   family tree, *11*, 1619
   food and feeding, *11*, 1629
   habitats, *11*, 1618, 1626
   shelter, construction of,
     11, 1622
   survival, *11*, 1636, 1638
   tusks, *11*, 1630
baboons
   behavior, *10*, 1440
   family tree, *10*, 1437
   habitats, *8*, 1211
   leopards, prey of, *8*, 1213
   physical description,
     10, 1464
   social structure,
     10, 1470, 1473
back-striped weasels
   habitats, *15*, 2222
   survival, *15*, 2235
Bactrian camels
   family tree, *3*, 344
   habitats, *3*, 341, 348, 350–1,
     356, 360, 365, *7*, 1029
   life cycle, *3*, 359
   social structure, *3*, 356
   speed of, *3*, 349
   survival, *3*, 360, 363, 365
badgers, *1*, 106–31
   behavior, *1*, 114–27
   burrowing, *1*, 114–5, 122–5

diseases, *1*, 124, 128–30
earthworms, feeding habits,
   1, 120
family tree, *1*, 110–1, *11*,
   1566, *15*, 2216, *16*, 2372
food and feeding, *1*, 120–1
forestry and, *1*, 130
grooming, *1*, 126
habitats, *1*, 116–9
hibernation, *1*, 124–5
hunting of, *1*, 129–30
life cycle, *1*, 126–7
mating, *1*, 126–7
odor, *1*, 116
physical description,
   1, 112–3
profile, *1*, 107–13, *16*, 2370
protection of, *1*, 131
rainfall, effect on, *1*, 118
scent marking, *1*, 122
social structure, *1*, 122–5
survival, *1*, 128–30
temperature, effect on, *1*, 118
tuberculosis, *1*, 124, 128–30
Baird's tapirs
   habitats, *16*, 2458
   survival, *16*, 2470
baleen whales
   behavior, *15*, 2247
   family tree, *5*, 631, *15*, 2242,
     2269, 2295, *16*, 2321, 2347
   food and feeding, *16*, 2330
   habitats, *5*, 627, *15*, 2300
   profile, *15*, 2239–40, 2242,
     2293, *16*, 2319
   survival, *16*, 2336
Bali cattle, *3*, 443
Bali tigers
   profile, *15*, 2164
   survival, *15*, 2181, 2183
Balkan snow voles
   survival, *15*, 2210
bamboo bats
   reproduction, *2*, 229
bamboo lemurs
   food and feeding, *8*, 1186
banded anteaters
   profile, *1*, 31
banded hare wallabies
   profile, *8*, 1150
   survival, *8*, 1169

banded linsangs
  physical description, *4*, 503
banded mongooses
  behavior, *9*, 1336
  profile, *9*, 1332
  social structure, *9*, 1346
banded palm civets
  family tree, *4*, 500
  food and feeding, *4*, 511
  habitats, *4*, 507–8
  species, *4*, 498
  survival, *4*, 520
bandicoots
  behavior, *16*, 2428
  diseases, *16*, 2442
  family tree, *14*, 2138
  food and feeding, *16*, 2434–5
  habitats, *14*, 2146
  hunting of, *16*, 2440, 2444
  life cycle, *16*, 2438-9
  physical description,
    16, 2427
  profile, *12*, 1722, *16*, 2421–3
  survival, *16*, 2440, 2442
  territory, *16*, 2436
bank voles
  food and feeding, *15*, 2200
  habitats, *15*, 2197–8
  life cycle, *15*, 2204
  profile, *15*, 2190
  survival, *15*, 2208
banteng
  described, *3*, 422
  domestication, *3*, 443
  food and feeding, *3*, 431
  habitats, *3*, 428
  survival, *3*, 441
Barbados raccoons
  habitats, *12*, 1832
  survival, *12*, 1846–7
Barbary leopards
  family tree, *8*, 1203
  survival, *8*, 1221
Barbary lions
  profile, *9*, 1228
  survival, *9*, 1245–6
Barbary macaques
  habitats, *10*, 1468
  life cycle, *10*, 1477
  physical description, *10*, 1465
  social structure, *10*, 1473

Barbary sheep
  survival, *6*, 855–6
barracuda
  habitats, *5*, 638
Barrallier, Ensign, *8*, 1148
bat-eared foxes
  behavior, *5*, 686
  evolution, *5*, 682
  family tree, *5*, 683, 708
  food and feeding,
    3, 291, *5*, 681
  habitats, *5*, 688–9, 714,
    9, 1341
  hunting by, *5*, 680, 693–5
  meerkats and, *9*, 1346
  survival, *5*, 702
  termites, feeding on, *3*, 291
  territory, *5*, 686–7
bats *see also* fruit bats;
  leaf-nosed bats; small bats;
    vesper bats
  classification, *2*, 133–4
  described, *1*, xx
  echolocation,
    2, 174, 193, 196–8
  family tree, *2*, 136, 162–3
  fear of, *2*, 178–80, 204, 233–4
  folklore, in, *2*, 178–9
Bavarian pine voles
  survival, *15*, 2209–10
Bawean warty pigs
  survival, *11*, 1638
bay cats
  habitats, *9*, 1262
  profile, *9*, 1253
  survival, *9*, 1271, 1273
  territory, *9*, 1267
beach voles
  survival, *15*, 2210
beaked whales
  breaching, *16*, 2358
  family tree,
    5, 631, *16*, 2347
  food and feeding, *16*, 2356
  habitats, *16*, 2353
  migration, *16*, 2355
  profile, *16*, 2343–5
  social structure, *16*, 2359
bearded pigs
  food and feeding, *11*, 1629
  habitats, *11*, 1618, 1626,

16, 2459
  social structure, *11*, 1631
bearded sakis
  habitats, *10*, 1417
  social structure, *10*, 1421
  survival, *10*, 1429
bearded seals
  family tree, *13*, 1982
  hunting by, *13*, 1990, 1992
  polar bears, prey of, *11*, 1680
  profile, *13*, 1980
bear parts, trade in, *3*, 310–11
bears *see also* American black
  bears; Asian black bears;
    brown bears; grizzly bears;
      Malay bears; polar bears;
        sloth bears; small
          bears; spectacled
            bears; sun bears
  evolution, *2*, 240
  family tree, *4*, 500, *11*, 1592
  habitats, *4*, 561
  intelligence, *2*, 272
  short-faced bears, *2*, 240
beavers, *3*, 314–39
  activities of, *3*, 322–3
  agriculture and, *3*, 339
  behavior, *3*, 322–35
  broad-tail beavers
    see broad-tail beavers
  burrowing, *3*, 322–3
  Canadian beavers
    see Canadian beavers
  dams, *3*, 325–6, 330
  European beavers
    see European beavers
  evolution, *3*, 316–7
  family tree, *14*, 2086, 2112–3
  food and feeding,
    3, 325, 332–3
  habitats, *3*, 324–7, *4*, 535,
    16, 2380
  hoarding, *3*, 333
  hunting of, *3*, 336–7
  kits, *3*, 334–5
  life cycle, *3*, 334–5
  lodge-building, *3*, 330–1
  mating, *3*, 334
  Mongolian beavers
    see Mongolian beavers
  mountain beavers

see mountain beavers
  North American beavers
    see North American
beavers
  pelts of, *3*, 336–7
  Point Arena mountain
beavers *see* Point Arena
    mountain beavers
  Point Reyes mountain
    beavers *see* Point Reyes
      mountain beavers
  profile, *3*, 315–21
  rainfall, effect of, *3*, 326
  Rio Grande beavers
    see Rio Grande beavers
  scent, *3*, 317, 328
  smell, sense of, *3*, 318
  survival, *3*, 336–8
  swamp beavers
    see capybaras
  swimming, *3*, 317, 322
  temperature, effect of, *3*, 326
  territory, *3*, 317, 328–9
  tree-felling beavers, *3*, 323
  true beavers
    see true beavers
  wolves, as prey of, *16*, 2409
behavior
  see specific animal
beiji
  see Yangtze dolphins
Belding's ground squirrels
  behavior, *14*, 2090
  life cycle, *14*, 2103
beluga whales
  behavior, *16*, 2350
  facial expressions, *16*, 2359
  food and feeding, *16*, 2356
  habitats, *16*, 2352–3
  life cycle, *16*, 2361
  migration, *16*, 2354–5
  polar bears, prey of, *11*, 1681–2
  profile, *16*, 2345
  survival, *16*, 2364, 2367
Bengal foxes
  family tree, *5*, 708
  habitats, *5*, 714–5
  hunting by, *5*, 719
Bengal tigers
  behavior, *15*, 2168
  habitats, *4*, 508, *15*, 2170–1

hunting by, *15*, 2176
life cycle, *15*, 2178–9
physical description,
   15, 2167
profile, *15*, 2164
survival, *15*, 2181, 2183
Bennett's tree kangaroos
   habitats, *8*, 1157–8
Bernhard, Prince of
   Netherlands, *15*, 2184
bettongs
   behavior, *13*, 1856
   habitats, *13*, 1858
   profile, *13*, 1850
   survival, *13*, 1871–2
Biet's snub-nosed monkeys
   habitats, *10*, 1443
   hunting of, *10*, 1454
   survival, *10*, 1455
big cats
   family tree,
     8, 1098, *15*, 2165
big-headed flying foxes
   habitats, *2*, 142
bighorn sheep
   habitats, *2*, 249
big thicket hog-nosed skunks
   survival, *16*, 2392
bilbies
   behavior, *16*, 2428–9
   diseases, *16*, 2442
   family tree, *16*, 2425
   food and feeding,
     16, 2434–5
   habitats, *16*, 2430–1
   life cycle, *16*, 2438
   physical description,
     16, 2427
   profile, *16*, 2421–3
   survival, *16*, 2440–2, 2445
binturongs
   climbing by, *4*, 504
   life cycle, *4*, 515
   pets, as, *4*, 520
   physical description, *4*, 503
birch mice
   family tree, *13*, 1878, 1905
   life cycle, *13*, 1916
bison, *3*, 392–417
   American bison
     see American bison

behavior, *3*, 400–11
breeding, *3*, 410
breeding programs, *3*, 415–6
bulls, *3*, 408–9, 411
calves, *3*, 410
conservation measures,
   3, 414
evolution, *3*, 394–6
family tree, *3*, 396–7, 423
food and feeding, *3*, 406–7
habitats, *3*, 402–5, *16*, 2405
hunting of, *3*, 416
natural selection, *3*, 409
profile, *3*, 393–9
rainfall, effect of, *3*, 404
reproduction, *3*, 410–1
social structure, *3*, 408–9
survival, *3*, 412–6
temperature, effect of,
   3, 404
wood bison
   see wood bison
black-backed jackals
   evolution, *8*, 1071
   family tree, *8*, 1073
   habitats, *8*, 1076, 1078–9
   hunting by, *8*, 1083–5
   life cycle, *8*, 1088
   physical description,
     8, 1070, 1074–5
   social structure,
     8, 1086–7
   survival, *8*, 1090
black bears
   see American black
     bears; Asian black bears
   description, *3*, 294
   physical description,
     11, 1672
blackbucks
   family tree, *6*, 760–1
   populations, *6*, 781
   survival, *6*, 779–80
   territory, *6*, 774
blackcap whales
   profile, *15*, 2292
black flying foxes
   survival, *2*, 152
black-footed cats
   habitats, *14*, 2014–5
   hunting by, *14*, 2020–1

life cycle, *14*, 2024–5
physical description,
   14, 2010–1
profile, *9*, 1254, *14*, 2007–8
territory, *14*, 2023
black-footed ferrets
   habitats, *15*, 2223–4
   survival, *15*, 2234–7
black-footed rock wallabies
   habitats, *8*, 1131
   survival, *8*, 1145
black-handed spider monkeys
   social structure, *10*, 1420–1
   survival, *10*, 1427
black-legged mongooses
   physical description, *9*, 1335
   profile, *9*, 1332
black lemurs
   behavior, *8*, 1180
   habitats, *8*, 1184
   survival, *8*, 1195, 1197
black mambas
   habitats, *1*, 93, *4*, 457
black panthers
   family tree, *8*, 1203
   habitats, *8*, 1209
   physical description, *8*, 1205
black rats
   behavior, *13*, 1882, 1908
   bubonic plague, *13*, 1920–2
   habitats, *13*, 1910
   survival, *13*, 1896–8
black rhinoceroses
   behavior, *13*, 1934
   family tree, *13*, 1930
   food and feeding, *13*, 1940–1
   habitats, *13*, 1936–7
   horns, *13*, 1928
   life cycle, *13*, 1944–5
   poaching, *13*, 1946
   profile, *13*, 1927
   social structure, *13*, 1942
   survival, *13*, 1946–7, 1949–50
black spider monkeys
   family tree, *10*, 1411
   food and feeding, *10*, 1419
black-spotted cuscuses
   survival, *12*, 1741
black-tailed jackrabbits
   habitats, *7*, 948
   physical description, *7*, 945

survival, *7*, 961
black-tailed prairie dogs
   behavior, *14*, 2090
   life cycle, *14*, 2103
   physical description,
     14, 2089
   social structure, *14*, 2096
   survival, *14*, 2104–5
black tamarins
   behavior, *10*, 1492
   calls, *10*, 1500
   profile, *10*, 1488
black vultures
   habitats, *4*, 509
black wildebeests
   habitats, *1*, 66
   noises of, *1*, 63
   profile, *1*, 56
   survival, *1*, 74
Blainville's beaked whales
   profile, *16*, 2344
Blanford's foxes
   food and feeding, *5*, 712
   habitats, *5*, 689, 714
   profile, *5*, 708
   survival, *5*, 728
blesbok
   behavior, *1*, 62
   habitats, *1*, 66
blind mole rats
   behavior, *9*, 1363
   family tree, *9*, 1358
   food and feeding,
     9, 1368–9
   habitats, *9*, 1366
   profile, *9*, 1357–8
   reproduction,
     9, 1375
Blixen, Karen, *5*, 620
blue bears
   habitats, *2*, 239
bluebirds
   habitats, *2*, 249
blue duikers
   life cycle, *6*, 777
   profile, *6*, 758
bluefin tuna
   habitats, *5*, 639
blue foxes
   habitats, *5*, 689
   reproduction, *5*, 698

blue whales
  behavior, *16*, 2324
  family tree, *15*, 2242,
    2294, *16*, 2321
  food and feeding,
    16, 2330–1
  habitats, *16*, 2327–8
  life cycle, *16*, 2334–5
  physical description,
    16, 2322–3
  profile, *16*, 2317
  social structure, *16*, 2332
  survival, *16*, 2338–41
blue wildebeests
  life cycle, *1*, 73
  physical description, *1*, 61
  survival, *1*, 74
bobcats
  behavior, *12*, 1778–9
  habitats, *4*, 535, 561,
    12, 1772, 1780, *16*, 2405
  hunting by, *12*, 1784
  life cycle, *12*, 1788–9
  territory, *12*, 1786–7
bog lemmings
  profile, *15*, 2190
bondegezou
  discovery of, *8*, 1171
bongos
  habitats, *1*, 65
  life cycle, *1*, 72
bontebok
  behavior, *1*, 62
  habitats, *1*, 66
  survival, *1*, 75–76
Bontebok National Park
  1, 76
bottle-nosed dolphins
  habitats,
    5, 627, 636, *15*, 2274
  hunting by, *5*, 643
  social structure, *5*, 642
  swimming, *5*, 628, 634
bottlenose whales
  food and feeding, *16*, 2356
Bougainville's bandicoots
  habitats, *16*, 2430
bovids
  family tree, *3*, 344,
    6, 812, 838–9, *11*, 1618
bovine tuberculosis

common brush-tailed
  possums, *12*, 1742
bowhead whales
  behavior, *15*, 2298–9
  family tree, *15*, 2243, 2295
  food and feeding, *15*, 2304–5
  habitats, *15*, 2301
  physical description, *1*
    5, 2297
  reproduction, *15*, 2309
  social structure, *15*, 2306–7
  survival, *15*, 2311–4
Brazilian shrew mice
  habitats, *13*, 1885
  profile, *13*, 1878
Brazilian tapirs
  behavior, *16*, 2454–5
  habitats, *16*, 2457–8
  profile, *16*, 2449
  survival, *16*, 2470
breeding
  see specific animal
breeding farms
  coypus, *3*, 369, 378, 388–91
breeding programs
  bison, *3*, 415–6
  cheetahs, *4*, 469
  chimpanzees, *4*, 491, 493
  civets, *4*, 516–8
  tamaraus, *3*, 440–1
Brelich's snub-nosed monkeys
  food and feeding, *10*, 1444
  survival, *10*, 1455
bridled dolphins
  habitats, *5*, 636
bridled nail-tailed wallabies
  survival, *8*, 1141, 1143, 1145
brindled bandicoots
  food and feeding, *16*, 2434
  habitats, *16*, 2430
bristly rabbits
  see hispid hares
broad-faced potoroos
  habitats, *13*, 1858–9
  profile, *13*, 1849
  survival, *13*, 1872
broad-striped mongooses
  survival, *9*, 1352
broad-tail beavers
  survival, *3*, 338
brown bats

survival, *2*, 233, 235
brown bears, *2*, 262–87
  see also grizzly bears
  aggression, *2*, 271, 277
  anger, displays of, *2*, 279
  behavior, *2*, 270–81
  conservation measures,
    2, 284, 286
  Cree tribe and, *2*, 284
  cubs, *2*, 280–1
  denning, *2*, 279
  evolution, *2*, 264–5
  family tree, *2*, 266–7, *3*, 293,
    11, 1592, 1670
  fights, *2*, 278–9
  food and feeding,
    2, 270–1, 276–7
  habitats, *2*, 272–5, *3*, 298,
    6, 847, *16*, 2381
  hibernation, *2*, 279
  hunting by, *2*, 276
  hunting of, *2*, 283
  Kodiak bears, *2*, 265
  life cycle, *2*, 280–1
  mating, *2*, 270, 280–1
  migration, *2*, 274
  nomadic life, *2*, 278
  physical description,
    11, 1672
  profile, *2*, 240, 266–9
  satellite tracking of, *2*, 261
  smell, sense of, *2*, 266
  street entertainers, as,
    2, 282–3
  survival, *2*, 282–6, *16*, 2390
  territories, *2*, 278–9
  vegetation zones, *2*, 274
  worship of, *2*, 284, 286
brown capuchins
  behavior, *10*, 1414
  family tree, *10*, 1411
  habitats, *10*, 1417
  life cycle, *10*, 1425
brown-eyed Swiss cattle
  vampire bats, as prey of,
    2, 172
brown hares
  behavior, *7*, 946
  family tree, *7*, 943
  food and feeding, *7*, 952
  habitats, *7*, 924, 948

life cycle, *7*, 959
  molting, *7*, 947
  physical description,
    7, 944–5
brown hyenas
  behavior, *7*, 1050
  family tree, *7*, 1047
  habitats, *7*, 1051, 1052–4
  hunting of, *7*, 1067
  life cycle, *7*, 1063
  physical description,
    7, 1048–9
  scavengers, *7*, 1045
  social structure, *7*, 1056–7
  survival, *7*, 1064–6
brown lemmings
  profile, *15*, 2190
  reproduction, *15*, 2230
brown lemurs
  behavior, *8*, 1180–1
  food and feeding, *8*, 1186
  profile, *8*, 1175
brown mongooses
  survival, *9*, 1352
brown rats
  behavior, *13*, 1882, 1908–9
  defenses, *13*, 1925
  family tree, *13*, 1905
  food and feeding, *13*, 1915
  habitats, *13*, 1910
  physical description,
    13, 1906–7
  profile, *13*, 1901–2
  survival, *13*, 1894, 1898, 1920
brown spiny bandicoots
  habitats, *16*, 2430
brown-throated
  three-toed sloths
    behavior, *14*, 2065
    family tree, *14*, 2061
    food and feeding,
      14, 2072
    habitats, *14*, 2066
    life cycle, *14*, 2077
    survival, *14*, 2080
brumbies
  survival, *7*, 1036, 1038–9
brush-tailed bettongs
  behavior, *13*, 1856
  food and feeding, *13*, 1867
  habitats,

13, 1858–9, 1873
survival, *13*, 1872
territory, *13*, 1862–3
brush-tailed porcupines
adaptations, *12*, 1706
behavior, *12*, 1701
habitats, *12*, 1704
profile, *12*, 1696
brush-tailed possums
family tree,
8, 1124, 1151, *12*, 1723
habitats, *12*, 1729
profile, *12*, 1722
social structure, *12*, 1734
survival, *12*, 1742
brush-tailed rock wallabies
survival, *8*, 1145
Bryde's whales
behavior, *16*, 2325
family tree, *16*, 2321
food and feeding,
16, 2330
habitats,
16, 2326, 2328–9
life cycle, *16*, 2335
profile, *16*, 2317
social structure, *16*, 2332
survival, *16*, 2339
bubonic plague
black rats,
13, 1920–2
buffalo
bull fights, *3*, 442
family tree, *3*, 397
buffy-headed marmosets
habitats, *10*, 1495
survival, *10*, 1507
bulldog bats
family tree, *2*, 163
hunting by, *2*, 174–5
life cycle, *2*, 177
bull fights, *3*, 442
bull moose
behavior, *4*, 557
food and feeding, *4*, 563
bumblebee bats
see Kitti's hog- nosed bats
Burchell's zebras
profile, *16*, 2449
survival, *16*, 2468
burrowing

aardvarks, *1*, 12–13
American badgers,
1, 114, 124–5
armadillos, *1*, 88–9
badgers, *1*, 114–5, 122–5
beavers, *3*, 322–3
coypus, *3*, 374–5, 385
European badgers,
1, 114, 124–5
European rabbits,
12, 1806, 1812
gophers, *14*, 2091
ground squirrels,
14, 2087, 2090, 2093
marsupial moles, *14*, 2144
meerkats, *9*, 1339
mole rats,
9, 1364–5, 1371
mountain beavers, *3*, 331
pangolins, *1*, 92, 99
pocket gophers, *14*, 2099
susliks, *14*, 2093
voles, *15*, 2201
wombats,
16, 2423–4, 2428, 2437
burrowing bettongs
behavior, *13*, 1856
food and feeding, *13*, 1866
habitats,
13, 1858–60, 1873
life cycle, *13*, 1868
survival, *13*, 1870–2
territory, *13*, 1862
burrowing mice
family tree, *13*, 1878
food and feeding,
13, 1889
burrowing pikas
habitats, *7*, 950
bush babies
see galagos
bushbucks
behavior, *1*, 63
food and feeding, *1*, 68
bush dogs
family tree, *4*, 527
habitats,
4, 532–3, 547, *6*, 898
hunting by, *4*, 531, 536
pack hunting, *4*, 576
physical description,

4, 523–4, 526, 533
sociability, *4*, 531
teeth, *4*, 577
territory, *4*, 539
bush hyraxes
activeness of, *1*, 10
climate changes and, *1*, 26
communication, *1*, 10
family tree, *1*, 7
feeding habits, *1*, 18–9
habitats, *1*, 13
reproduction, *1*, 22
social structure, *1*, 20
bushman rabbits
family tree, *7*, 943
bushpigs
African swine fever,
11, 1638
family tree, *11*, 1619
fighting, *11*, 1633
habitats,
6, 872, *11*, 1618, 1624–5
male dominance, *11*, 1632
sleeping sickness, *11*, 1638
social structure, *11*, 1630
bushy-tailed mongooses
captive breeding, *9*, 1353
survival, *9*, 1352

C

cacomistles
behavior, *12*, 1830
habitats, *12*, 1833
profile, *12*, 1824–5
survival, *12*, 1846
caddis flies, *2*, 225
Calamian deer
survival, *4*, 571, 572
California gray whales
migration, *15*, 2254–5
survival, *15*, 2260, 2263
Californian pronghorns
survival, *12*, 1767, 1769
California sea lions
behavior, *13*, 1960
family tree, *13*, 1957
food and feeding,
13, 1966, 1968
habitats, *13*, 1962
life cycle, *13*, 1971

profile, *13*, 1954–5
survival, *13*, 1976
Camarguais
survival, *7*, 1040
Cambodian forest oxen
see kouprey
camels, *3*, 340–65
Bactrian
see Bactrian camels
behavior, *3*, 348–9
body temperature, *3*, 348–9
conservation measures,
3, 362–3
diseases, *3*, 358
dromedaries
see dromedaries
evolution, *3*, 344
family tree,
3, 344–5, *6*, 760, 813,
7, 995, *11*, 1618
food and feeding, *3*, 354–5
gait, *3*, 343–4
guanacos
see guanacos
habitats, *3*, 350–3, *7*, 924
life cycle, *3*, 358–9
mange, *3*, 358
manhus, *3*, 358
mating, *3*, 358
physical characteristics,
3, 346–7
profile, *3*, 341–7
social structure,
3, 356–7
spitting by, *3*, 349
survival, *3*, 360–4
temper, *3*, 349
tourism and, *3*, 362–3
vicuñas see vicuñas
water conservation,
3, 354
white camels
see white camels
camouflage
see specific animal
Canadian beavers
dams, *3*, 326
description, *3*, 320–1
family tree, *3*, 319
range, *3*, 324
reintroduction programs,

3, 339
  survival, *3*, 337
cane rats
  family tree, *3*, 371
canids
  family tree, *4*, 578–9
canine distemper
  African wild dogs, *5*, 622
Cape foxes
  grooming, *5*, 721
  habitats, *5*, 714
  physical description, *5*, 706
  profile, *5*, 708
Cape fur seals
  behavior, *13*, 1960
  food and feeding,
    13, 1967–8
  habitats, *13*, 1963
  survival, *13*, 1976
Cape hares
  habitats, *7*, 949, 961
Cape hyraxes
  feeding habits, *1*, 18
Cape lions
  profile, *9*, 1228
  survival, *9*, 1246
Cape mole rats
  behavior, *9*, 1363
  food and feeding, *9*, 1368
  habitats,
    9, 1362, 1364–5
  reproduction, *9*, 1374
Cape mountain zebras
  survival, *16*, 2468
Cape pangolins
  family tree, *1*, 85
  habitats, *1*, 91–2
  life cycle, *1*, 99
  survival, *1*, 103–4
Cape porcupines
  habitats, *12*, 1703
  survival, *12*, 1716
caprines
  see goats;
    sheep captivity
  see specific animal
capuchins, *10*, 1406–31
  behavior, *10*, 1414–25
  conservation measures,
    10, 1428–9
  family tree, *10*, 1410–1

food and feeding, *10*, 1418–9
habitats, *1*, 41, *10*, 1416–7
life cycle, *10*, 1424–5
physical description,
  10, 1412–3
profile, *10*, 1407–13
social structure, *10*, 1420–3
survival, *10*, 1426–30
zoos, *10*, 1431
capybaras, *3*, 366–91
  agriculture and, *3*, 390
  behavior, *3*, 374–87
  breeding, *3*, 386
  coypus
    see coypus
  evolution, *3*, 367–8, 370
  family tree, *3*, 370–1
  features of, *3*, 372–3
  food and feeding, *3*, 380–1
  habitats, *3*, 376–9
  hunting of, *3*, 388
  jaguars, prey for, *8*, 1108–9
  life cycle, *3*, 386–7
  male dominance, *3*, 383
  morrillos and, *3*, 384–5
  pelts, *3*, 388
  profile, *3*, 367–73
  rainfall, effect of,
    3, 376, 378
  scent marking, *3*, 384
  size, *6*, 887
  social structure, *3*, 382–3
  survival, *3*, 388–90, *6*, 910
  swimming, *3*, 374
  temperature, effect of,
    3, 378
  territory, *3*, 384–5
  vocalization, *3*, 383
  wetlands, *3*, 374–5, 391
caracals
  captivity, *14*, 2029
  family tree, *14*, 2008
  habitats, *14*, 2014–5
  hunting by, *14*, 2020–1
  life cycle, *14*, 2024–5
  physical description,
    14, 2010–1
  profile, *14*, 2007–8
  survival, *14*, 2026–7
  territory, *14*, 2022
caracaras

habitats, *6*, 899
caribou
  behavior, *4*, 556–7
  calves, *4*, 566
  fighting, *4*, 564
  habitats, *4*, 558–9
  life cycle, *4*, 565–6
  social structure, *4*, 568
carnivores
  family tree, *16*, 2373
Caspian tigers
  profile, *15*, 2164
  survival, *15*, 2181, 2183
cats
  domestication, *4*, 518
  evolution, *4*, 498
  family tree,
    4, 449, 501, *8*, 1098,
    15, 2165
cattle
  antelopes
    see antelopes
  bison
    see bison
  wild cattle
    see wild cattle
cave-dwelling bats
  fruit bats, *2*, 147
  leaf-chinned bats, *2*, 168–9
  small bats, *2*, 194–5, 200
  vesper bats, *2*, 232–3
cave fish
  habitats, *2*, 168
cave swiftlets
  echolocation, *2*, 198
cavies
  behavior, *6*, 894–905
  colonies, *6*, 894–5
  family tree, *6*, 890–1
  food and feeding,
    6, 902–3
  habitats, *6*, 896–9
  rainfall, effect on, *6*, 898
  reproduction, *6*, 904–5
  social structure, *6*, 900–1
  temperature, effect on,
    6, 898
caviomorphs
  habitats, *6*, 896
  survival, *6*, 906
cavylike rodents

evolution, *12*, 1694
family tree, *3*, 301, 371,
  6, 891, *7*, 917, *12*, 1697,
  15, 2190
habitats, *6*, 896
size, *6*, 887
vocalization, *6*, 900
cebid monkeys
  behavior, *10*, 1414
  family tree, *10*, 1411
  food and feeding, *10*, 1419
  habitats, *10*, 1416–7
  life cycle, *10*, 1424
  profile, *10*, 1407–9
  survival, *10*, 1429
Celebes wild pigs
  habitats, *11*, 1618, 1626
centipedes
  habitats, *2*, 169
Central American water mice
  adaptations, *13*, 1883
  physical description,
    13, 1881
Chacoan peccaries
  diseases, *11*, 1637
  food and feeding, *11*, 1629
  habitats, *11*, 1624
  hunting by, *11*, 1622
  profile, *11*, 1618
  social structure, *11*, 1630
  survival, *11*, 1636–9
chacos
  habitats, *6*, 898–9
chamois
  climbing skills, *6*, 845
  family tree, *6*, 839
  food and feeding, *6*, 848
  habitats, *2*, 274, *6*, 846
  social structure, *6*, 851
  survival, *6*, 856
cheetahs, *4*, 444–69
  behavior, *4*, 452–65
  captive breeding, *4*, 469
  current distribution, *4*, 467
  death, causes of, *4*, 456
  facial markings, *4*, 463
  family tree, *4*, 448–9, *8*, 1098,
    1203, *9*, 1228, *12*, 1774
  genes, vulnerability, *4*, 448
  habitat loss, *4*, 467
  habitats, *4*, 452, 454–7,

9, 1237, 1367

hunting by, *4*, 452, 455–6, 458–9, 465, *9*, 1236

hunting of, *4*, 466–8

immune system, *4*, 448

kopjes, *4*, 454

life cycle, *4*, 464–5

males, *4*, 462–3

mating, *4*, 461

miombo, *4*, 454

19th century distribution, *4*, 467

physical description, *4*, 450–1

profile, *4*, 445–51, *12*, 1772

rainfall, effect of, *4*, 456

reserve management, *4*, 469

scent, *4*, 461

siblings, *4*, 462

social structure, *4*, 460–3

speed of, *4*, 446–7, 452–3

survival, *4*, 466–8

temperature, effect of, *4*, 456

territory, *4*, 463

zoos, *4*, 468–9

chevrotains

behavior, *12*, 1753

evolution, *12*, 1745–6

family tree, *3*, 344, *6*, 813, *11*, 1618, *12*, 1748

food and feeding, *12*, 1760–1

habitats, *12*, 1746, 1754–6

physical description, *12*, 1751

profile, *12*, 1747–8

territory, *12*, 1759

zoos, *12*, 1769

chimpanzees, *4*, 470–95

affection, displays of, *4*, 485

aggression, *4*, 484–5

behavior, *4*, 478–89

breeding programs, *4*, 491, 493

captive breeding, *4*, 491

captivity, *4*, 491, 493

conservation measures, *4*, 492–3

described, *4*, 472

destruction of environment and, *4*, 490

diseases, *4*, 492

DNA (deoxyribonucleic acid), *4*, 474, 495

evolution, *4*, 473–4

facial expressions, *4*, 483

families, *4*, 482–3

family tree, *4*, 474–5, *6*, 865

food and feeding, *4*, 486–7

foraging, *4*, 486

habitats, *4*, 480–1

HIV virus, *4*, 492

humans, similarity to, *4*, 474, 495

hunting of, *4*, 492, 494–5

intelligence of, *4*, 478

language of, *4*, 478–9

life cycle, *4*, 488–9

male dominance, *4*, 482–3, 488

manipulative skills, *4*, 486

nests, *4*, 482–4

pets, as, *4*, 493

physical characteristics, *4*, 476–7

profile, *4*, 471–7

rain forests, *4*, 480

rights of, *4*, 495

sanctuaries, *4*, 494

scientific research, use in, *4*, 479, 492

sexual behavior, *4*, 488–9

social structure, *4*, 482–5

sounds made by, *4*, 478–9

subordinate males, *4*, 485

survival, *4*, 490–4

territory, *4*, 482

tourism and, *4*, 494

chinchilla-rats

habitats, *6*, 898

survival, *6*, 910

chinchillas

colonies, *6*, 895

conservation measures, *6*, 911

family tree, *6*, 891

food and feeding, *6*, 903

grooming, *6*, 901

habitats, *6*, 897–8

hunting of, *6*, 909

reproduction, *6*, 905

size, *6*, 889

social structure, *6*, 900–1

survival, *6*, 907, 909–10

Chinese desert cats

habitats, *9*, 1261

survival, *9*, 1272–3

Chinese Eastern Railway, *7*, 932

Chinese hamsters

physical description, *7*, 914

Chinese shrew-moles

profile, *10*, 1383

species, *10*, 1389

Chinese tigers

survival, *15*, 2181

Chinese water deer

behavior, *4*, 556

habitats, *4*, 558

chipmunks

family tree, *14*, 2087

habitats, *14*, 2093

profile, *14*, 2084

survival, *14*, 2106

Chiriqui olingos

survival, *12*, 1847

chital deer

see, axis deer

Chlamydia psittaci

koalas, *8*, 1170

civets, *4*, 496–521

anal-dragging, *4*, 512

behavior, *4*, 504–15

breeding, *4*, 514–5

breeding farms, *4*, 516–8

camouflage, *4*, 500

captivity of, *4*, 521

conservation measures, *4*, 518–9

defenses, *4*, 513

deforestation, effect of, *4*, 519

domestication, *4*, 518–20

evolution, *4*, 497–8

food and feeding, *4*, 510–1

habitats, *4*, 506–9

handstanding, *4*, 512

life cycle, *4*, 514–5

mating, *4*, 514–5

nighttime and, *4*, 504–5

perfume, use of secretions,

4, 516–8

profile, *4*, 497–503

rainfall, effect of, *4*, 508

rain forests, *4*, 498

scent marking, *4*, 512–4

secretion, *4*, 516

solitariness, *4*, 504–5

sounds, *4*, 505

survival, *4*, 516–20

teat-ownership, *4*, 515

temperature, effect of, *4*, 508

territory, *4*, 512–3

Clara bandicoots

survival, *16*, 2443

clawless otters

habitats, *11*, 1574

climate

anteaters and, *1*, 40

hyraxes and, *1*, 26

small bats and, *2*, 192

climbing shrews

physical description, *14*, 2036

clouded leopards

behavior, *8*, 1206–7

evolution, *8*, 1200

family tree, *8*, 1098, 1202

habitats, *8*, 1208, 1210, *11*, 1600

hunting by, *8*, 1215

life cycle, *8*, 1216–7

physical description, *8*, 1205

profile, *8*, 1199, *12*, 1772

survival, *8*, 1221

coastal dolphins

family tree, *5*, 630

coatis

behavior, *12*, 1830

family tree, *12*, 1827

food and feeding, *12*, 1836

grooming, *12*, 1838

habitats, *12*, 1833, 1834

life cycle, *12*, 1842–3

profile, *12*, 1825

social structure, *12*, 1838

cochito

see Gulf of California porpoises

coendous

adaptations, *12*, 1707
profile, *12*, 1694
collared lemmings
  behavior, *15*, 2194–5
  life cycle, *15*, 2204
  profile, *15*, 2188–90
  survival, *15*, 2208
  territory, *15*, 2203
collared peccaries
  behavior, *11*, 1622–3
  family tree, *11*, 1618
  food and feeding, *11*, 1629
  habitats, *11*, 1624, 1626
  hunting by, *11*, 1622
  profile, *11*, 1617
  sounds of, *11*, 1632
  survival,
    11, 1636, 1638
collared pikas
  habitats, *7*, 950
Collie, Alexander, *8*, 1137
colobines, *10*, 1432–57
  behavior, *10*, 1440–51
  captive breeding, *10*, 1457
  conservation measures,
    10, 1454–5
  evolution, *10*, 1433–6
  family tree, *10*, 1436–7
  food and feeding,
    10, 1444–5
  habitats, *10*, 1442–3
  hunting of, *10*, 1453–4
  life cycle, *10*, 1450–1
  profile, *10*, 1433–9
  social structure, *10*, 1446–7
  survival, *10*, 1452–6
  territory, *10*, 1448–9
colobus monkeys
  family tree, *10*, 1436
  food and feeding, *10*, 1445
  fur trade, *10*, 1454
  habitats, *10*, 1442
  life cycle, *10*, 1451
  physical description,
    10, 1439
  survival, *10*, 1452
  territory, *10*, 1448–9
Colombian weasels
  habitats, *15*, 2224
  survival, *15*, 2235
colpeo foxes

family tree, *5*, 682
habitats, *5*, 690
hunting by, *5*, 693
reproduction, *5*, 698
Columbia ground squirrels
  behavior, *12*, 1778
Columbus, Christopher,
  9, 1277, *13*, 1979, *14*, 2052
common brush-tailed possums
  artificial nest boxes,
    12, 1743
  bovine tuberculosis,
    12, 1742
  reproduction, *12*, 1737
  social structure, *12*, 1734–5
  survival, *12*, 1740–2
common chimpanzees
  family tree,
    4, 474, *11*, 1541
  habitats, *4*, 481
  physical characteristics,
    4, 477
  social structure, *4*, 485
common dormice
  habitats, *7*, 920, 937
  life cycle, *7*, 931
common European hamster
  family tree, *7*, 916
common frogs
  habitats, *2*, 275
common genets
  habitats, *4*, 506
common gibbons
  see lar gibbons
common hamsters
  habitats, *7*, 922–3
  life cycle, *7*, 931
  squeaking, *7*, 923
  survival, *7*, 933–5
common hippopotamuses
  evolution, *7*, 992
  habitats, *7*, 1001
  profile, *7*, 991
common jackals
  habitats, *7*, 1055
common kestrels
  habitats, *7*, 925
common long-eared bats
  habitats, *2*, 219–20
  profile, *2*, 214
common marmosets

family tree, *10*, 1488
left-right preferences,
  10, 1493
life cycle, *10*, 1502
physical description,
  10, 1490–1
profile, *10*, 1486
common mole rats
  behavior, *9*, 1362–3
  eusocial behavior, *9*, 1371–2
  family tree, *9*, 1359
  food and feeding,
    9, 1368–9
  habitats, *9*, 1364
  physical description, *9*, 1361
  reproduction, *9*, 1374–5
common pipistrelle bats
  habitats, *2*, 219
  profile, *2*, 213
  reproduction, *2*, 229
common raccoons
  family tree, *12*, 1826
  food and feeding,
    12, 1836
  habitats, *12*, 1832–3
  life cycle, *12*, 1842–3
  physical description,
    12, 1828–9
  profile, *12*, 1823
  survival, *12*, 1844
common rats
  behavior, *13*, 1882
  food and feeding,
    13, 1915
  survival, *13*, 1894
common ring-tailed possums
  artificial nest boxes,
    12, 1743
  social structure, *12*, 1734
common seals
  family tree, *13*, 1982
  habitats, *13*, 1988
  life cycle, *13*, 1996
  physical description,
    13, 1984–5
  profile, *13*, 1981
  survival, *13*, 2002
  territory, *13*, 1994
common shrews
  behavior, *14*, 2038
  food and feeding, *14*, 2044

physical description,
  14, 2033–7
common tenrecs
  food and feeding, *7*, 979
  habitats, *7*, 975
  life cycle, *7*, 982
common terns
  habitats, *4*, 534
common voles
  habitats, *15*, 2196
  territory, *15*, 2203
common wasps
  habitats, *2*, 221
common weasels
  family tree, *15*, 2217
  habitats, *15*, 2222–3
  physical description,
    15, 2219
  survival, *15*, 2232
common wombats
  behavior, *16*, 2428
  habitats,
    16, 2430, 2432
  life cycle, *16*, 2439
  physical description,
    16, 2426–7
  profile, *16*, 2424
  survival, *16*, 2442
common zebras
  profile, *16*, 2449
concolor gibbons
  habitats, *6*, 793
  life cycle, *6*, 800
  singing, *6*, 799
  survival, *6*, 805
Cope, Edward,
  15, 2247
Coquerel's sifakas
  habitats, *8*, 1183
Corbett, Colonel Jim,
  8, 1222
Corbett, Major Jim,
  4, 508
corsac foxes
  habitats, *5*, 715
  survival, *5*, 727–8
coteries
  life cycle, *14*, 2103
  social structure,
    14, 2096, 2098–9
cotton rats

food and feeding,
13, 1888–9
life cycle, 13, 1892
survival, 13, 1898
cottontail rabbits
habitats, 4, 535
life cycle, 7, 958
cottontails
behavior, 12, 1804
family tree, 12, 1800
habitats, 12, 1806
life cycle, 12, 1814
cotton-top tamarins
behavior, 10, 1492
family tree, 10, 1489
profile, 10, 1486
survival, 10, 1504,
1506–7
courtship
see specific animal
coyotes, 4, 522–47
alpha (dominant) pair,
4, 540–1
behavior, 4, 530–43
coydogs, 4, 546
diseases, 4, 542
distemper, 4, 542
family tree, 4, 527, 578,
5, 709, 8, 1072, 16, 2398
fur of, hunted for, 4, 544
habitats,
4, 532–5, 561, 7, 951,
12, 1705, 1757, 1834
hunting by,
4, 530–1, 536–7
hunting of, 4, 544
life cycle, 4, 542–3
mating, 4, 541, 542
pack hunting,
4, 537, 541
physical description,
4, 523, 529, 534
profile, 4, 523–9, 5, 708
pronghorns, enemies of,
12, 1755
rabies, 4, 542
rainfall, effect of, 4, 534
scent marking, 4, 538–9
social structure, 4, 540–1
survival, 4, 544–6, 8, 1090
temperature, effect of,

4, 534
territory, 4, 538–9
coypus
behavior, 3, 374–87
breeding farms,
3, 369, 378, 388–91
burrowing,
3, 374–5, 385
evolution, 3, 370
family tree, 3, 370–1
features of, 3, 372–3
feral population,
3, 389, 391
food and feeding,
3, 380–1
fur trade and, 3, 369
habitats, 3, 376–9
hunting of, 3, 388
life cycle, 3, 386–7
nest building, 3, 369
nutria, 3, 369, 377, 389
protection measures,
3, 390
social structure, 3, 383
survival, 6, 908–9
swimming, 3, 377
territory, 3, 385
water and, 3, 376–7
wetlands,
3, 374–5, 391
Cozumel Island coatis
habitats, 12, 1832
survival, 12, 1846–7
crabeater seals
behavior, 13, 1987
family tree, 13, 1983
habitats, 13, 1988
hunting by, 13, 1990–3
survival, 13, 2002
crab-eating foxes
habitats, 5, 689
hunting by, 5, 692
reproduction, 5, 699
territory, 5, 696
crab-eating raccoons
habitats, 12, 1832–3
creamy white bears
habitats, 2, 239
crescent nail-tailed wallabies
survival, 8, 1143
crested African porcupines

survival, 12, 1717
crested porcupines
see Old World
crested porcupines
crocodiles
habitats, 2, 142
nile crocodiles, 1, 93
predator, 1, 67
crowned lemurs
behavior, 8, 1180
habitats, 8, 1184
Cuban flower bats
survival, 2, 181
Cuban solenodons
habitats, 14, 2040, 2042
survival, 14, 2051–3
Cultural Properties
Protection Act (Japan),
7, 937
Cuming's slender-tailed
cloud rats
profile, 13, 1902
survival, 13, 1923
cuscuses
family tree, 8, 1124, 1151,
12, 1723, 16, 2424
habitats, 12, 1729
profile, 12, 1722
social structure, 12, 1734
Cuvier's beaked whales
habitats, 16, 2353
Cyrenaica voles
survival, 15, 2211

D

Dama gazelles
food and feeding, 6, 773
survival, 6, 778, 780
Damaraland mole rats
social structure, 9, 1371
dams
beavers, 3, 325–6, 330
Canadian beavers, 3, 326
Darwin, Charles,
3, 352, 4, 473–4, 5, 681–2,
8, 1143, 10, 1467
dasyures
behavior, 14, 2143
habitats, 14, 2145
life cycle, 14, 2152–3

profile, 14, 2136, 2138
survival, 14, 2154–5
Daubenton's bats
habitats, 2, 221
hunting by, 2, 224
David, Père Armand,
10, 1454
dawn bears
evolution, 2, 240
family tree,
2, 241, 11, 1670
dawn dogs
family tree, 5, 709
profile, 5, 707
dawn horses
evolution, 7, 1020
Day, Michael, 15, 2185
DDT
small bats and, 2, 204
vesper bats and,
2, 232, 235
Decken's sifakas
habitats, 8, 1184
deer, 4, 548–73
antlers, 4, 550–2, 556, 569
behavior, 4, 556–69
digestion, 4, 562
diseases, 4, 560
domestication of, 4, 573
evolution, 4, 550–1
family tree,
4, 552–3, 6, 761, 813,
11, 1619
farming of, 4, 573
fighting, 4, 569
food and feeding, 4, 562–3
habitats, 4, 558–61
hunting of, 4, 570, 572
life cycle, 4, 564–7
Lyme disease, 4, 560
males, 4, 551–2
mating, 4, 564
mud wallowing, 4, 567
pampas deer, 4, 569
pests, as, 4, 572
profile, 4, 549–55
rainfall, effect of, 4, 560
social structure, 4, 568–9
speed, 4, 557
spirochete, 4, 560
survival, 4, 570–2

temperature, effect of,
4, 560
deer mice
behavior, 13, 1883
food and feeding,
13, 1888
habitats, 13, 1884, 1886
life cycle, 13, 1892–3
nesting, 13, 1891
physical description,
13, 1880–1
profile, 13, 1876–7
survival, 13, 1895, 1897–8
defenses
see specific animal
deforestation
hyraxes and, 1, 26
degus
colonies, 6, 895
profile, 6, 890
Demidoff's dwarf galagos
captivity, 5, 755
habitats, 5, 742
denning
American black bears,
2, 252–3
Asian black bears, 3, 296
brown bears, 2, 279
desert foxes
habitats, 5, 714
desert gundis
reproduction, 9, 1375
survival, 9, 1377
desert hedgehogs
family tree, 7, 969
habitats, 7, 975
profile, 7, 966–7
desert rat kangaroos
behavior, 13, 1857
habitats, 13, 1858–60
profile, 13, 1849
desmans
evolution,
10, 1381, 1383
family tree,
7, 969, 10, 1385
food and feeding,
10, 1398
habitats, 10, 1390–2
hunting of, 10, 1403–4
life cycle, 10, 1401

physical description,
10, 1387
Desmoulins, Antoine,
15, 2293
devilfish
see gray whales
dholes, 4, 574–99
alpha (dominant) pair,
4, 590–1, 593
behavior, 4, 582–93
conservation measures,
4, 596
evolution, 4, 577
family tree,
5, 605, 8, 1072
habitats,
4, 584–7, 11, 1601,
15, 2171, 16, 2458
hunting by, 4, 588–9
life cycle, 4, 592–3
mating, 4, 592–3
pack hunting,
4, 576, 582–3, 589, 591
physical characteristics,
4, 580–1
profile, 4, 575–82
rainfall, effect of, 4, 586
social structure, 4, 590–1
survival, 4, 584, 595
teeth, 4, 577
temperature, effect of,
4, 586
territory, 4, 591
whistling hunters, as,
4, 578
diadem sifakas
survival, 8, 1195
diana monkeys
survival,
10, 1480–1
dibatag gazelles
behavior, 6, 765
size, 6, 758
dibblers
family tree, 14, 2139
survival, 14, 2157
dik-diks
profile, 6, 757
survival, 6, 779
territory, 6, 774
dingoes

behavior, 16, 2428
family tree,
5, 708, 16, 2373, 2398
habitats, 8, 1133, 1159
hunting by, 4, 588
physical characteristics,
4, 581
disc-winged bats
profile, 2, 188, 214
sucker-footed bats,
similarity to, 2, 206
diseases
see specific animal
distemper
coyotes, 4, 542
Djakarta Jim, 11, 1538
DNA (deoxyribonucleic acid)
African wild dogs, 5, 605
chimpanzees, 4, 474, 495
dog bears
see Malay bears
dog-faced fruit bats
social structure, 2, 146
dog foxes
reproduction, 5, 724
doglike bats
reproduction, 2, 202
dogs
bears, evolution from, 2, 240
family tree,
2, 267, 4, 500, 578,
5, 605, 709, 16, 2399
dolphins, 5, 625–51
behavior, 5, 634–45
breathing, 5, 630
communication, 5, 643
conservation measures,
5, 648–9
described, 1, xxi
echolocation,
2, 198, 5, 641
evolution, 5, 628–9
family tree, 5, 628, 630–1,
15, 2242–3, 2268, 2295,
16, 2320
food and feeding,
5, 640–1
habitats, 5, 636–9
hunting of, 5, 646
intelligence, 5, 634–5
lactation, 5, 645

mating, 5, 644
physical description,
5, 632–3
pollution, effect of,
5, 648–9
profile, 5, 627–33
reproduction, 5, 644–5
social structure, 5, 642–3
sounds made by, 5, 640
survival, 5, 646–50
tuna fisheries and,
5, 646–7, 650
United Nations Resolution,
5, 650
X-ray vision, 5, 641
domestication
African buffalo, 3, 442
African palm civets, 4, 521
alpacas, 3, 342, 348
Australian dingoes,
4, 597–8
banteng, 3, 443
cats, 4, 518
cattle, 3, 440–3
civets, 4, 518–20
deer, 4, 573
genets, 4, 518–20
guanacos, 3, 360
llamas, 3, 342, 348
vicuñas, 3, 360
yaks, 3, 422, 443
domestic cats
population, 9, 1274–5
domestic dogs
family tree,
5, 708, 16, 2398
profile, 16, 2397
wolves, as prey of,
16, 2409
Doppler method of location
small bats, 2, 196
dorcas gazelles
food and feeding,
6, 771
survival, 6, 780
Doria's tree kangaroos
survival, 8, 1169
dormice
adaptability, 7, 913
behavior, 7, 920–31
diseases, 7, 934

evolution, *7*, 915–6
family tree,
 7, 917, *13*, 1878, 1904
food and feeding,
 7, 921
foraging, *7*, 920
habitats, *7*, 922–5
hearing, *7*, 921
hibernation,
 7, 923, 928, 930–1
life cycle,
 7, 928–31, *13*, 1916
mating, *7*, 928–9
survival, *7*, 932–6
doucs
 captive breeding,
  10, 1457
 survival,
  10, 1453–5
douroucouli
 see night monkeys
drills
 studies of, *10*, 1483
 survival, *10*, 1481
dromedaries
 family tree, *3*, 344
 food and feeding, *3*, 355
 habitats, *3*, 350–1
 humps, *3*, 342
 life cycle, *3*, 359
 physical characteristics,
  3, 346–7
 social structure,
  3, 356–7
 speed of, *3*, 349
 survival, *3*, 360–1, 364
 white breeds, *3*, 343
droughts
 antelopes, effect on,
  1, 66
du Chaillu, Paul, *6*, 880
duckbilled platypuses
 survival, *11*, 1664
dugongs
 family tree, *9*, 1280
 food and feeding, *9*, 1291
 habitats, *9*, 1287–8
 life cycle, *9*, 1295
 mermaids, mistaken as,
  9, 1278
 physical description,

9, 1279–80, 1282–3
 profile, *9*, 1278
 studies on, *9*, 1301
 survival, *9*, 1299–1300
 swimming, *9*, 1285
duikers
 behavior, *6*, 764–5
 camouflage, *6*, 769
 captivity, *6*, 773
 defenses, *6*, 768–9
 family tree,
  1, 58, *6*, 760, 839
 food and feeding,
  6, 770–1
 habitats, *6*, 766–7
 life cycle, *6*, 776–7
 profile,
  6, 758, 759–60
 survival, *6*, 778–9
 territory, *6*, 774–5
dune mole rats
 behavior, *9*, 1363
 family tree, *9*, 1358
 food and feeding, *9*, 1368
 habitats, *9*, 1365
 reproduction, *9*, 1375
 survival, *9*, 1379
dunnarts
 profile, *12*, 1722
Durrell, Gerald,
 10, 1440, 1508
dusky antechinuses
 behavior, *14*, 2143
 hunting by, *14*, 2150–1
dusky dolphins
 swimming, *5*, 628
dusky langurs
 behavior, *10*, 1441
 captive breeding,
  10, 1457
dusky titi monkeys
 food and feeding,
  10, 1418
 habitats, *10*, 1417
dwarf antelopes
 behavior, *6*, 764–5
 camouflage, *6*, 769
 family tree, *1*, 59, *6*, 761
 food and feeding,
  6, 770–1, 773
 habitats, *6*, 766–7

life cycle, *6*, 776–7
 profile, *6*, 758–9
 survival, *6*, 778–9
 territory, *6*, 774–5
dwarf cuscuses
 habitats, *12*, 1728
dwarf galagos
 habitats, *5*, 741
 locomotion, *5*, 744
dwarf hamsters
 habitats, *7*, 924
dwarf lemurs
 behavior, *8*, 1181
 family tree, *8*, 1177
 life cycle, *8*, 1191
 profile, *8*, 1175–6
dwarf mongooses
 behavior, *9*, 1336
 life cycle, *9*, 1348–9
 profile, *9*, 1331, 1332
 social structure,
  9, 1345, 1347
dwarf siamangs
 see kloss gibbons
dwarf sperm whales
 habitats, *16*, 2352
 life cycle, *16*, 2361
 migration, *16*, 2354
 profile, *16*, 2344
 survival, *16*, 2365, 2367

E

eagle owls
 habitats, *7*, 1029
eared seals, *13*, 1952–77
 behavior, *13*, 1960–73
 evolution,
  13, 1953–4, 1956
 family tree,
  13, 1956–7, 1983
 fasting, *13*, 1966
 food and feeding,
  13, 1966–9
 habitats, *13*, 1962–5
 hunting of, *13*, 1974–6
 life cycle, *13*, 1970–1
 mating, *13*, 1971
 physical description,
  13, 1958–9
 profile,

 13, 1953–9, 1980–1
 rainfall, effect on,
  13, 1964
 survival, *13*, 1974–6
 temperature, effect on,
  13, 1964
early cats
 family tree, *8*, 1202
early hyenids
 family tree, *7*, 1047
earthworms
 badgers, feeding habits,
  1, 120
eastern barred bandicoots
 family tree, *16*, 2425
 survival, *16*, 2443
Eastern cottontail rabbits
 habitats, *12*, 1807
eastern gray kangaroos
 habitats, *8*, 1130–1
 survival, *8*, 1140
eastern gray squirrels
 habitats, *5*, 717
eastern hare wallabies
 survival, *8*, 1169
eastern lowland gorillas
 family tree, *6*, 864
 habitats, *6*, 871–2
eastern Mexican jaguars
 survival, *8*, 1117
eastern needle-clawed galagos
 survival, *5*, 754
eastern pocket gophers
 habitats, *14*, 2094
 life cycle, *14*, 2103
eastern pygmy possums
 artificial nest boxes,
  12, 1743
 food and feeding,
  12, 1731
 reproduction,
  12, 1737
eastern quolls
 behavior, *14*, 2142
 habitats, *16*, 2433
 hunting by, *14*, 2150
 profile, *14*, 2138
 survival, *14*, 2155
eastern tree hyraxes
 hunting of, *1*, 25
echidnas

albino, *11*, 1659

convergent evolution, *12*, 1696

food and feeding, *11*, 1656–7

habitats, *11*, 1650–1

mating, *11*, 1658

pouch, *11*, 1658–9

profile, *11*, 1642–4

rainfall, effect on, *11*, 1652

reproduction, *11*, 1658

temperature, effect on, *11*, 1649, 1652

echolocation

cave swiftlet, *2*, 198

dolphins, *2*, 198, *5*, 641

oilbirds, *2*, 198

small bats, *2*, 193, 196–8

solenodons, *14*, 2044

true seals, *13*, 1990

vesper bats, *2*, 174

edentates

aardvarks, *1*, 4

anteaters, *1*, 29–32

armadillos, *1*, 84

evolution, *14*, 2060

family tree, *1*, 85, *14*, 2060–1

edible dormice

see fat dormice

Egyptian fruit bats, *2*, 134

family tree, *2*, 137

Egyptian mongooses

food and feeding, *9*, 1343

life cycle, *9*, 1348

elands

family tree, *1*, 59

food and feeding, *1*, 69

habitats, *7*, 1054

noises of, *1*, 63

social structure, *1*, 70

survival, *1*, 78

elephants, *5*, 652–77

aggression, *5*, 670

behavior, *5*, 660–71

conservation measures, *5*, 674–5

described, *1*, xx

drinking, *5*, 665

family tree, *5*, 657

food and feeding, *5*, 664–5

habitats, *1*, 92, *5*, 662–3

hearing range, *5*, 667

herds, *5*, 667–8

hunting of, *5*, 672

ivory trade, *5*, 672–7

life cycle, *5*, 670–1

mating, *5*, 670

musth, *5*, 670

physical description, *5*, 658–9

profile, *5*, 653–9

sirenians, similarity to, *9*, 1279

skin, *5*, 669

social structure, *5*, 666–9

survival, *5*, 672–7

trunks, *5*, 653–4, 664

tusks, *5*, 672

elephant seals

family tree, *13*, 1983

habitats, *15*, 2251

physical description, *13*, 1985

survival, *13*, 1998–9

territory, *13*, 1995

elephant shrews

described, *1*, xx

elk

antlers, *4*, 556

food and feeding, *4*, 562

habitats, *2*, 249, *4*, 558

emperor tamarins

social structure, *10*, 1501

survival, *10*, 1507

Endangered Species Act, *13*, 1976

epauletted bats

habitats, *2*, 143

social structure, *2*, 146

equids

evolution, *7*, 1019

family tree, *7*, 1021, *16*, 2450

food and feeding, *7*, 1030

herding, *7*, 1025

life cycle, *7*, 1034

profile, *16*, 2448

social structure, *7*, 1032–3, *16*, 2465

ermines

family tree, *15*, 2216

habitats, *5*, 691

trapping for fur, *15*, 2234, 2237

Erxleben, Johann, *15*, 2247

Eschricht, Daniel, *15*, 2247

Etruscan pygmy shrews

profile, *14*, 2031, 2033

Eurasian hedgehogs

profile, *7*, 966–7

Eurasian lynx

radiotelemetry, *9*, 1275

survival, *9*, 1273

Eurasian mole rats

see blind mole rats

Eurasian otters

behavior, *11*, 1570

calls, *11*, 1571

family tree, *11*, 1566

food and feeding, *11*, 1578–9

habitats, *11*, 1572–3

life cycle, *11*, 1580–1

mating, *11*, 1580

physical description, *11*, 1568–9

profile, *11*, 1564

survival, *11*, 1582–3, 1585–6

territory, *11*, 1576–7

Eurasian weasels

family tree, *15*, 2216

profile, *15*, 2214

Eurasian wildcats

family tree, *9*, 1255

habitats, *9*, 1251, 1260

physical description, *9*, 1256–7

survival, *9*, 1274

European badgers

burrowing, *1*, 114, 124–5

evolution of, *1*, 108–9

family tree, *1*, 110

food and feeding, *1*, 120–1

habitats, *1*, 116–7, *7*, 977, *11*, 1627

life cycle, *1*, 126–7

mating, *1*, 126

physical description, *1*, 112–3

profile, *1*, 107–8

protection of, *1*, 131

social structure, *1*, 122, 124–5

survival, *1*, 128–29, 131

European beavers

description, *3*, 318

evolution, *3*, 316–7

habitats, *3*, 324, 405

reintroduction programs, *3*, 339

size of, *3*, 316

skull, *3*, 321

survival, *3*, 337

European bison

family tree, *3*, 396

food and feeding, *3*, 407

habitats, *3*, 402–3

population, *3*, 417

survival, *3*, 413, 415

European brown hares

profile, *8*, 1150

European common shrews

family tree, *7*, 969

food and feeding, *14*, 2044

habitats, *14*, 2042

life cycle, *14*, 2048–9

social structure, *14*, 2046

European hedgehogs

family tree, *7*, 969

habitats, *7*, 974–5, *11*, 1626

hibernation, *7*, 980

life cycle, *7*, 982–3

physical description, *7*, 970–1

profile, *7*, 966

European minks

family tree, *9*, 1306

habitats, *9*, 1312, 1314

population distribution, *9*, 1325, 1327

survival, *9*, 1325–6

European moles

burrowing, *10*, 1394

family tree, *10*, 1385

food and feeding, *10*, 1397, 1399

habitats, *10*, 1391

life cycle, *10*, 1400–1

physical description,
10, 1386–7
profile, *10*, 1382–3
radio tracking, *10*, 1394
survival, *10*, 1402, 1405
European noctules
reproduction, *2*, 229
European polecats
family tree, *15*, 2216
habitats, *15*, 2224
hunting by, *15*, 2227
profile, *15*, 2213–4, 2216
territory, *15*, 2228
European rabbits
behavior, *12*, 1804
burrowing, *12*, 1806, 1812
family tree, *12*, 1801
habitats, *12*, 1806–8
life cycle,
12, 1814–5, 1817
physical description,
12, 1803
profile, *12*, 1798
survival, *12*, 1818, 1820–1
territory, *12*, 1812–3
European red foxes
habitats, *8*, 1133
European stoats
survival, *15*, 2232
European susliks
social structure,
14, 2096
survival, *14*, 2107
European water shrews
food and feeding, *14*, 2045
habitats, *14*, 2041–2
European water voles
habitats, *15*, 2198
stoats, as prey of,
15, 2232
European wildcats
experiments on, *9*, 1275
family tree, *14*, 2009
habitats, *14*, 2015
hunting by, *9*, 1265
life cycle, *9*, 1268–9
survival, *9*, 1270, 1273,
14, 2026
European wolves
survival, *16*, 2417
eusocial behavior, *9*, 1357,

1362, 1370–2
even-toed hoofed mammals
described, *1*, xx
even-toed ungulates
described, *3*, 419
evolution, *6*, 811–2
family tree,
3, 344, *6*, 781, 812, 838,
11, 1618, *12*, 1748
profile, *6*, 810–1
Everglades bears
survival, *2*, 259
Exmoor ponies
behavior, *7*, 1024
habitats, *7*, 1028
Exxon Valdez oil spill,
11, 1587, *13*, 1976
gray whales, effect on,
15, 2263

F

falanouc
habitats, *4*, 507
survival, *4*, 519
fallow deer
behavior, *4*, 556
food and feeding, *4*, 563
habitats, *4*, 550, 558, 560
life cycle, *4*, 565, 567
social structure, *4*, 568–9
false killer whales
family tree, *15*, 2269
habitats, *15*, 2274–6
hunting by, *15*, 2283
reproduction, *15*, 2284
social structure, *15*, 2279
survival, *15*, 2286–7
false vampire bats, *2*, 207
hunting by, *2*, 199
profile, *2*, 188, 191
range of, *2*, 205
fanaloka
described, *4*, 499
habitats, *4*, 507
survival, *4*, 519
farming
American black bears and,
2, 258
beavers and, *3*, 339
capybaras and, *3*, 390

small bats and, *2*, 204–5
small bears and, *3*, 311
vesper bats and,
2, 230–2, 235
fat dormice
behavior, *7*, 921
family tree, *7*, 917
habitats, *7*, 922
leaping, *7*, 923
life cycle,
7, 929, 931
survival, *7*, 932, 935
fat-tailed dunnarts
food and feeding,
14, 2148
habitats, *14*, 2145
fat-tailed dwarf lemurs
food and feeding,
8, 1187
fat-tailed scorpions
habitats, *7*, 925
fawn antechinuses
survival, *14*, 2156
fea's muntjacs
survival, *4*, 571
feathertail gliders
artificial nest boxes,
12, 1743
behavior, *12*, 1726
food and feeding,
12, 1731
fennec foxes
family tree, *5*, 683, 708
habitats,
5, 688, 690, *16*, 2431
profile, *5*, 681, 708
reproduction, *5*, 699
size, *5*, 690
survival, *5*, 701–2, 728
temperature, effect on,
5, 686, 689
feral horses
habitats, *7*, 1027
fer-de-lance
habitats, *3*, 379
Fernandez de Oviedo
y Valdes, Gonzalo, *14*, 2078
ferret badgers
behavior, *1*, 114
habitats, *1*, 116, 118
survival, *1*, 131

ferrets
domestication,
15, 2236
physical description,
15, 2219
field voles
family tree, *15*, 2190
food and feeding,
15, 2200
habitats, *15*, 2197
life cycle, *15*, 2204
fin whales
family tree, *16*, 2320
food and feeding,
16, 2330–1
habitats, *16*, 2327–9
profile, *16*, 2317
survival, *16*, 2338–9
fire-bellied toads
habitats, *4*, 587
fire salamanders
habitats, *2*, 275
fish-eating rats
adaptations, *13*, 1883
family tree, *13*, 1879
food and feeding,
13, 1888
fisher martens
habitats, *12*, 1705, 1715
porcupines, defenses,
12, 1709
fishers
behavior, *9*, 1311
family tree, *9*, 1306
food and feeding, *9*, 1313
habitats, *9*, 1304–5
hunting by,
9, 1314, 1318–9, 1324
territory, *9*, 1321
trapping for fur,
9, 1326–7
fishing
American black bears,
2, 251
brown bears, *2*, 276
fishing cats
habitats, *9*, 1262
hunting by, *9*, 1265
survival, *9*, 1272–4
Fjord ponies
habitats, *7*, 1027

flat-headed cats
  habitats, *9*, 1262
  hunting by, *9*, 1265
  survival, *9*, 1273
Flemish Giants
  survival, *12*, 1820
Florida manatees
  family tree, *9*, 1281
  food and feeding, *9*, 1291
  habitats, *9*, 1286–9
  migration, *9*, 1285
  studies on, *9*, 1301
  survival,
    9, 1296, 1298–9
Florida Manatee Sanctuary Act
  of 1978, *9*, 1298
Florida salt marsh voles
  survival, *15*, 2210–1
flying foxes
  see fruit bats
flying lemurs
  described, *1*, xx
  social structure,
    14, 2127
flying squirrels, *2*, 136
  behavior, *14*, 2116–7
  family tree,
    14, 2086, 2112
  food and feeding,
    14, 2122–3
  habitats, *14*, 2118
  profile, *14*, 2109–10
  social structure,
    14, 2124–5, 2127
  survival, *14*, 2131
Fly River bandicoots
  survival, *16*, 2443
food and feeding
  see specific animal
foraging
  see specific animal
forest bison
  see wood bison
forest hogs
  African swine fever,
    11, 1638
forest rabbits
  habitats, *12*, 1807
  survival, *12*, 1818
fork-crowned dwarf lemurs
  habitats, *8*, 1183–4

fork-marked dwarf lemurs
  food and feeding, *8*, 1186
  survival, *8*, 1195
Formosan clouded leopards
  family tree, *8*, 1202
fossa
  described, *4*, 499
  family tree, *4*, 500
  habitats, *4*, 507, *8*, 1184
  survival, *4*, 519
Fossey, Dian, *6*, 870, 883–5
four-horned antelopes
  family tree,
    1, 58, *3*, 396, 422
  food and feeding, *1*, 68
  habitats, *1*, 64
foxes
  family tree, *5*, 682–3
  jackals, distinguished,
    8, 1072
  marsupials, hunting of,
    16, 2440, 2444
  oak trees and, *5*, 716–7
  profile, *16*, 2398
fox squirrels
  profile, *14*, 2112
  social structure, *14*, 2125
  survival, *14*, 2132
Foyn, Svend, *16*, 2363
free-tailed bats
  family tree, *2*, 189
  giant free-tailed bats, *2*, 193
  habitats, *2*, 194–5
  hunting by, *2*, 197
  Mexican free-tailed bats,
    2, 194
  migration, *2*, 194
  profile, *2*, 139, 214
  reproduction, *2*, 203
  roosting, *2*, 194
frogs
  habitats, *2*, 275, *5*, 716
fruit bats, *2*, 132–57
  behavior, *2*, 140–51
  big-headed flying foxes,
    2, 142
  black flying foxes, *2*, 152
  breeding, *2*, 157
  cave-dwelling, *2*, 147
  conservation measures,
    2, 154

diseases, *2*, 154
Egyptian fruit bats,
  2, 134, 137
epauletted bats,
  2, 143, 146
evolution, *2*, 135–6
family tree, *2*, 136
flying foxes, *2*, 139, 146,
  148, 150, 163
food and feeding, *2*, 144–5
foraging, *2*, 140, 151
free-tailed bats, *2*, 139
gray-headed flying foxes,
  2, 136–9, 150
habitats,
  2, 142–3, 157, 168, *8*, 1185
hammer-headed bats,
  2, 137, 149
Indian flying foxes, *2*, 150–1
Indian short-nosed bats,
  2, 145, 146
life cycle, *2*, 150–1
Marianas flying foxes,
  2, 155
mating, *2*, 148–50
mortlock flying foxes, *2*, 155
nectar-eating bats,
  2, 145, 170–1, 219
Old World bats,
  2, 133–4, 143, 188
Palau flying foxes, *2*, 155
profile, *2*, 138–9, 213
reproduction, *2*, 148–9
Rodrigues flying foxes,
  2, 154, 157
roosting, *2*, 188
rousette bats, *2*, 147, 151
sheath-tailed bats
  see sheath-tailed bats
short-tailed fruit bats
  see short-tailed fruit bats
smell, sense of, *2*, 141, 150
social structure, *2*, 146–7
survival, *2*, 152–6, 205
Tongan bats, *2*, 155
Truk flying foxes, *2*, 155
tube-nosed bats,
  2, 137, 139, 148
funnel-eared bats
  hibernation, *2*, 201
  profile, *2*, 214

fur seals
  behavior, *13*, 1960
  family tree, *13*, 1983
  food and feeding, *13*, 1969
  habitats, *13*, 1962
  life cycle, *13*, 1971
  physical description,
    13, 1958–9
  profile, *13*, 1955
  survival, *13*, 1976

G

galagos, *5*, 730–55
  behavior, *5*, 738–51
  captivity, *5*, 755
  evolution, *5*, 733–4
  family tree, *5*, 734–5
  food and feeding, *5*, 746–7
  foraging, *5*, 738
  habitats, *5*, 740–3
  life cycle, *5*, 750–1
  locomotion, *5*, 744–5
  mating, *5*, 750
  profile, *5*, 731–7
  rain forests, *5*, 742–3, 755
  reproduction, *5*, 750
  scent marking, *5*, 748
  social structure, *5*, 748–9
  survival, *5*, 752–4
  territory, *5*, 749
  urine-washing, *5*, 748
  zoos, *5*, 755
Galápagos fur seals
  food and feeding, *13*, 1969
  habitats, *13*, 1962, 1964
Galápagos sea lions
  food and feeding, *13*, 1969
  habitats,
    13, 1962, 1964
Gandhi, Indira, *15*, 2184
garden dormice
  behavior, *7*, 920
  life cycle, *7*, 929
gaurs
  defenses, *3*, 343
  described, *3*, 422
  food and feeding, *3*, 431
  habitats,
    3, 428–9, *16*, 2459
  survival, *3*, 441

gazelles, *6*, 756–81
  aggression, *6*, 775
  behavior, *6*, 764–77
  cheetahs, prey of, *4*, 459
  cud-chewing, *6*, 759–60
  defenses, *6*, 768–9
  diseases, *6*, 780
  evolution, *6*, 758–60
  family tree,
    6, 760–1, 839
  food and feeding,
    6, 770–3
  habitats, *6*, 766–7
  hunting of, *4*, 466
  life cycle, *6*, 776–7
  mating, *6*, 777
  nomads, *6*, 773
  profile, *6*, 757–63
  rinderpest, *6*, 780
  scent marking, *6*, 775
  survival, *6*, 778–80
  territory, *6*, 774–5
Geelvinck Bay leaf-nosed bats,
  2, 207
gelada baboons
  habitats, *10*, 1468–9
  survival, *10*, 1481
genets
  anal-dragging, *4*, 512
  behavior, *4*, 504–15
  breeding, *4*, 514–5
  camouflage, *4*, 498
  captivity of, *4*, 521
  defenses, *4*, 513
  domestication, *4*, 518–20
  family tree, *9*, 1332
  food and feeding, *4*, 510–1
  habitats, *4*, 506–9
  handstanding, *4*, 512
  hunting by, *5*, 752
  life cycle, *4*, 514–5
  mating, *4*, 514–5
  pets, as, *4*, 520
  scent marking, *4*, 512–4
  solitariness, *4*, 504–5
  sounds, *4*, 505
  survival, *4*, 516–20
  teat-ownership, *4*, 515
  territory, *4*, 512–3
gentle lemurs
  behavior, *8*, 1180

family tree, *8*, 1177
  profile, *8*, 1175
  survival, *8*, 1197
Geoffroy's cats
  family tree, *12*, 1775
  habitats, *12*, 1782
  profile, *12*, 1773
gerbils
  habitats, *9*, 1366
gerenuks
  behavior, *6*, 765
  food and feeding, *6*, 770
  habitats, *6*, 767
  territory, *6*, 775
gestation
  hyraxes, *1*, 22
Ghenghis Khan, *7*, 1025
ghost bats
  see false vampire bats
giant anteaters
  behavior, *1*, 36–9
  captive breeding, *1*, 52
  family tree, *1*, 33
  food and feeding, *1*, 43–5
  foraging, *1*, 38–9
  habitats, *1*, 38
  physical description, *1*, 34
  profile, *1*, 29–31
  reproduction, *1*, 46–7
  scent marking, *1*, 43
  survival, *1*, 48–52
  territory, *1*, 42
giant armadillos
  defenses, *1*, 97
  food and feeding, *1*, 94
  habitats, *6*, 899
  survival, *1*, 101–3, 105
giant bandicoots
  physical description,
    16, 2426
  survival, *16*, 2443
giant flying squirrels
  behavior, *14*, 2117
  family tree, *14*, 2112
  food and feeding, *14*, 2122
  habitats, *14*, 2119–20
  physical description, *14*, 2114
  profile, *14*, 2112
  social structure, *14*, 2124
  survival, *14*, 2130
giant forest hogs

African swine fever,
  11, 1637
  family tree, *11*, 1619
  fighting, *11*, 1632
  habitats, *11*, 1618, 1624
  survival, *11*, 1637
giant free-tailed bats
  teeth of, *2*, 193
giant golden moles
  burrowing, *10*, 1395
  family tree, *7*, 968
  habitats, *10*, 1391
  survival, *10*, 1403
giant grazing wombats
  evolution, *16*, 2424
giant mole rats
  habitats, *8*, 1081
giant otters
  family tree, *11*, 1567
  food and feeding, *11*, 1579
  habitats, *11*, 1572, 1574
  life cycle, *11*, 1580
  physical description,
    11, 1568–9
  survival, *11*, 1585
  territory, *11*, 1577
  trapping of, *11*, 1582
giant otter shrews
  family tree, *7*, 968
giant pandas
  calling, *11*, 1605
  family tree, *2*, 266, *11*,
    1592–3, 1670
  food and feeding,
    11, 1596, 1602–3
  habitats,
    11, 1596, 1598–1600
  life cycle, *11*, 1607
  mating, *11*, 1606
  national treasure, as,
    11, 1611–2
  parasites, *11*, 1607
  physical description,
    11, 1590, 1594–5
  population, *11*, 1613
  profile, *11*, 1589
  resting sites, *11*, 1597
  scent marking, *11*, 1604
  survival,
    11, 1608–9, 1611
  territory, *11*, 1604

zoos, *11*, 1612
giant pangolins
  family tree, *1*, 85
  habitats, *1*, 92
giant pigs
  evolution, *11*, 1616
giant squirrels
  habitats, *14*, 2119
  social structure, *14*, 2124
gibbons, *6*, 782–807
  behavior, *6*, 790–801
  color variations, *6*, 785
  conservation measures,
    6, 804–5
  family tree,
    6, 786–7, 864, *11*, 1541
  food and feeding,
    6, 794–5
  foraging, *6*, 791
  grooming, *6*, 797
  habitats, *6*, 792–3
  hunting of, *6*, 802
  intelligence, *6*, 806
  leaping, *6*, 790
  life cycle, *6*, 800–1
  physical description,
    6, 788–9
  profile, *6*, 783–9
  rain forests,
    6, 792–3, 803–5
  singing, *6*, 786, 798–9
  social structure, *6*, 796–7
  survival, *6*, 802–6
giraffes, *6*, 808–33
  behavior, *6*, 816–29
  coat patterns, *6*, 810
  cud-chewing, *6*, 822
  discovery of, *6*, 811
  diseases, *6*, 831
  drinking, *6*, 823
  evolution, *6*, 811–12
  family tree, *4*, 553, *6*, 761,
    812–3, *7*, 994, *11*, 1619
  farming of, *6*, 833
  fighting, *6*, 824, 828
  food and feeding,
    6, 822–3
  grazing, *6*, 819
  habitats, *6*, 818–21
  height, *6*, 823
  hunting of, *6*, 830–3

Laufschlag, *6*, 826

life cycle, *6*, 828–9

physical description,
6, 814–5

population distribution,
6, 831

profile, *6*, 759, 809–15

rainfall, effect of, *6*, 820

reproduction, *6*, 826–7

rinderpest, *6*, 831

social structure, *6*, 824–5

survival, *6*, 830–2

temperature, effect of,
6, 820

glacier bears

habitats, *2*, 239

gliders

behavior, *12*, 1727

family tree,
8, 1125, 1151, *12*, 1723

food and feeding,
12, 1730, 1732

habitats, *12*, 1729

social structure, *12*, 1734

global warming, *1*, 84, 101

polar bears, effect on,
11, 1688–9

gnus

habitats, *6*, 820

goat antelopes

behavior, *6*, 842

food and feeding,
6, 848

habitats, *6*, 845

hunting of, *6*, 858

physical description,
6, 837, 838

predators, dealing with,
6, 844

survival, *6*, 857–8

goats, *6*, 834–59

behavior, *6*, 842–53

conservation measures,
6, 856–7, 859

diseases, *6*, 856

domestication,
6, 854–5, 858

family tree,
1, 59, *6*, 761, 839

fighting, *6*, 850, 853

food and feeding,

6, 848–9

grasslands, *6*, 837–8, 849

habitats, *6*, 844–7

hoof-and-mouth disease,
6, 856

hunting of, *6*, 857–8

life cycle, *6*, 852–3

profile, *6*, 835–41

rainfall, effect of, *6*, 846

scent marking, *6*, 852

social structure,
6, 850–1

survival, *6*, 842, 854–8

temperature, effect of,
6, 846

Godman's marsupial mice

survival, *14*, 2156

Goeldi's monkeys

family tree, *10*, 1488

food and feeding,
10, 1498–9

habitats, *10*, 1495

life cycle, *10*, 1503

profile, *10*, 1486

survival, *10*, 1507

trapping of, *10*, 1493

goitered gazelles

habitats, *7*, 1029

golden bamboo lemurs

discovery of, *8*, 1196

survival, *8*, 1195

golden bandicoots

life cycle, *16*, 2439

survival, *16*, 2441–3

golden cats

behavior, *14*, 2012

habitats, *6*, 873

hunting by, *14*, 2020

physical description,
14, 2011

golden crowned sifakas

survival, *8*, 1196

golden eagles

habitats,
2, 275, *7*, 950

golden hamsters

domestication, *7*, 914

habitats, *7*, 923–4

life cycle, *7*, 930–1

survival, *7*, 934

golden-headed lion tamarins

food and feeding, *10*, 1499

profile, *10*, 1486

survival,
10, 1505–7, 1509

golden horseshoe bats

survival, *2*, 207

golden jackals

evolution, *8*, 1071

family tree, *8*, 1073

habitats, *8*, 1076, 1078–9

hunting by, *8*, 1083–4

life cycle, *8*, 1089

physical description,
8, 1070, 1074–5

survival, *8*, 1090, 1092

golden leaf monkeys

behavior, *10*, 1440

food and feeding,
10, 1444

physical description,
10, 1438

golden lion tamarins

behavior, *10*, 1493

captive breeding,
10, 1504, 1509

conservation measures,
10, 1506–7

family tree, *10*, 1489

life cycle, *10*, 1502

survival, *10*, 1504–6

golden-mantled ground
squirrels

behavior, *14*, 2090

life cycle, *14*, 2102

golden moles

burrowing,
10, 1388, 1394–5

evolution, *10*, 1381

family tree, *10*, 1384

food and feeding,
10, 1396, 1398

habitats, *9*, 1341, *10*, 1390–1

life cycle, *10*, 1401

physical description,
10, 1382

survival, *10*, 1404–5

golden monkeys

habitats, *11*, 1600

golden pottos

survival, *5*, 754

golden-rumped lion tamarins

survival, *10*, 1505–7

golden snub-nosed monkeys

survival, *10*, 1454–5

Goodfellow's tree kangaroos

habitats, *8*, 1157

survival, *8*, 1169

gophers

burrowing, *14*, 2091

mating, *14*, 2103

social structure,
14, 2098

gorillas, *6*, 860–85

arthritis, *6*, 881

behavior, *6*, 868–79

bulk of, *6*, 862

chest-beating, *6*, 869

conservation measures,
6, 882–3

discovery of, *6*, 880–1

diseases, *6*, 881

family tree, *6*, 864–5

food and feeding,
6, 874–5

habitats, *6*, 870–3

humans, compared to,
6, 864

hunting of, *6*, 881–2, 884

life cycle, *6*, 878–9

male dominance, *6*, 876–7

mating, *6*, 878–9

nesting, *6*, 868

physical description,
6, 866–7

pneumonia, *6*, 881

profile, *6*, 861–7

rainfall, effect of, *6*, 872

respiratory ailments,
6, 881

social structure, *6*, 876–7

survival, *6*, 880–4

temperature, effect of,
6, 872

zoos, *6*, 885

Gorillas in the Mist,
6, 884–5

Gould, John, *8*, 1155

Gould's long-eared bats

reproduction, *2*, 229

Grant's gazelles

behavior, *6*, 765

food and feeding,

6, 771
  habitats, *6*, 767
  territory, *6*, 775
grasshopper mice
  behavior, *13*, 1883
  food and feeding, *13*, 1888
  life cycle, *13*, 1892
  nesting, *13*, 1890
grasslands
  antelopes, *1*, 66
  armadillos, *1*, 90–1
  pangolins, *1*, 92
grass rats
  habitats, *8*, 1081
gray-backed sportive lemurs
  habitats, *8*, 1184
gray bats
  survival, *2*, 207, 233
gray-cheeked manabeys
  calls, *10*, 1471
  food and feeding, *10*, 1475
gray cuscuses
  habitats, *12*, 1729
gray "four-eyed" opossums
  food and feeding,
    10, 1524–7,
gray foxes
  family tree, *5*, 709
  profile, *5*, 706
  survival, *5*, 726
gray-headed flying
  foxes, *2*, 136
    family tree, *2*, 137
    life cycle, *2*, 150
    profile, *2*, 138–9
gray kangaroos
  behavior, *8*, 1128
  family tree, *8*, 1125
  food and feeding, *8*, 1134
  habitats, *8*, 1130–1
  life cycle, *8*, 1137
  physical description,
    8, 1122, 1126
  survival, *8*, 1144
gray lesser mouse lemurs
  habitats, *8*, 1183
gray seals
  habitats, *13*, 1988
  survival, *13*, 2001–2
  territory, *13*, 1994–5
gray squirrels

food and feeding,
  14, 2122–3
habitats, *2*, 221, *7*, 976,
  9, 1319, *14*, 2118–9
hunting of, *14*, 2130
life cycle, *14*, 2129
physical description,
  14, 2114
profile, *14*, 2111–2
social structure,
  14, 2124–5
survival, *14*, 2130–3
gray whales, *15*, 2238–63
  behavior, *15*, 2246–59
  discovery of, *15*, 2247
  diseases, *15*, 2259
  evolution, *15*, 2240–2
  family tree, *15*, 2242–3,
    2294, *16*, 2321
  food and feeding,
    15, 2256–7
  "Gigi," *15*, 2252–3
  habitats, *15*, 2248–51
  mating, *15*, 2258
  migration, *15*, 2254–5
  petroleum industry,
    effect on, *15*, 2261
  physical description,
    15, 2244–5
  profile,
    15, 2239–45, *16*, 2318
  reproduction, *15*, 2258–9
  social structure,
    15, 2252–3
  songs, *15*, 2252–3
  spy-hopping, *15*, 2253
  survival, *15*, 2260–2
  temperature, effect on,
    15, 2250
  whaling, *15*, 2260–2
gray wolves
  family tree,
    8, 1072, *16*, 2399
  habitats,
    4, 534, 584,
      7, 925, *16*, 2403
  life cycle, *16*, 2412
  physical description,
    4, 524, *16*, 2400
  profile, *16*, 2397–8
  survival,

8, 1090, *16*, 2390,
  2415, 2417
  threats to, *4*, 525
grazing antelopes
  behavior, *1*, 62
  family tree, *1*, 59, *6*, 761, 839
  food and feeding, *1*, 68
  habitats, *1*, 64–5
  profile, *1*, 55
  survival, *1*, 79
great apes
  see gorillas
greater bamboo lemurs
  survival, *8*, 1195
greater bilbies
  habitats, *16*, 2430
  survival, *16*, 2443
greater dwarf lemurs
  food and feeding, *8*, 1187
  habitats, *8*, 1184
greater galagos
  captivity, *5*, 755
  family tree, *5*, 734
  locomotion, *5*, 744
  survival, *5*, 752–3
greater horseshoe bats
  hibernation, *2*, 207
  population, *2*, 207
  profile, *2*, 190–1
  reproduction, *2*, 203
  roosting, *2*, 206
  survival, *2*, 206–7
greater Malay chevrotains
  life cycle, *12*, 1763
  profile, *12*, 1748
greater moonrats
  behavior, *7*, 972
  family tree, *7*, 969
greater mouse-eared bats
  survival, *2*, 207, 233
greater mouse-tailed bats
  reproduction, *2*, 203
greater sheath-tailed bats
  survival, *2*, 207
great killer whales
  reproduction, *15*, 2284
great sperm whales
  habitats, *16*, 2352–3
great white sharks
  habitats, *5*, 639, *15*, 2249
green ring–tailed possums

food and feeding,
  12, 1730
reproduction, *12*, 1737
green turtles
  habitats, *5*, 639
Grevy's zebras
  family tree, *16*, 2451
  food and feeding,
    16, 2461
  habitats, *16*, 2457
  physical description,
    16, 2452
  profile, *16*, 2449
  social structure, *16*, 2464–5
  survival, *16*, 2470–1
Grey Seal Protection Act,
  13, 2001
grisons
  profile, *15*, 2214
grizzled tree kangaroos
  survival, *8*, 1169
grizzly bears
  see also brown bears
  aggression, *2*, 271
  conservation measures,
    2, 284, 285
  family tree, *11*, 1670
  food and feeding, *2*, 270
  habitats, *2*, 248, 273, 284–5,
    7, 951, *16*, 2405
  Mexican silver grizzly,
    2, 285
  profile, *2*, 268–9
  survival, *2*, 258
grooming
  badgers, *1*, 126
  coatis, *12*, 1838
  mandrills, *10*, 1470
  marmosets, *10*, 1501
  meerkats, *9*, 1347
  otters, *11*, 1576
  peccaries, *11*, 1630
  rhesus macaques,
    10, 1472
  titi monkeys, *10*, 1423
  uakaris, *10*, 1423
  wild pigs, *11*, 1631
groove-toothed squirrels
  habitats, *14*, 2119
  survival, *14*, 2131
ground cuscuses

social structure, *12*, 1735
ground-dwelling shrews
  physical description,
    14, 2036
ground squirrels,
  14, 2082–2107
  behavior, *14*, 2090–2103
  burrowing,
    14, 2087, 2090, 2093
  family tree, *14*, 2087, 2113
  food and feeding,
    14, 2100–1
  habitats, *14*, 2092–5
  life cycle, *14*, 2102–3
  profile, *14*, 2083–9
  rainfall, effect on, *14*, 2094
  social structure, *14*, 2096–9
  survival, *14*, 2104–6
  temperature, effect on,
    14, 2094
grysboks
  habitats, *6*, 767
guanacos
  breeding, *3*, 358
  descendants, *3*, 342
  domestication, *3*, 360
  family tree, *3*, 345
  food and feeding, *3*, 355
  habitats, *3*, 341, 351–2
  life cycle, *3*, 359
  pelts, *3*, 363
  social structure, *3*, 356–7
  survival, *3*, 360, 363, 365
guenons
  behavior, *10*, 1467
  family tree, *10*, 1437
  habitats, *10*, 1469
  physical description,
    10, 1464
  profile, *10*, 1461
guereza monkeys
  captive breeding,
    10, 1457
  survival, *10*, 1452, 1454
guinea pigs, *6*, 886–911
  behavior, *6*, 894–905
  evolution, *6*, 889
  food and feeding, *6*, 902–3
  habitats, *6*, 896–9
  profile, *6*, 887–93
  rainfall, effect on, *6*, 898

reproduction, *6*, 904–5
social structure, *6*, 900–1
survival, *6*, 906–10
temperature, effect on,
  6, 898
Gulf of California porpoises
  survival, *5*, 649, 651
Gulf Stream beaked whales
  habitats, *16*, 2353
gundis
  behavior, *9*, 1363
  family tree, *9*, 1358–9
  food and feeding, *9*, 1369
  habitats, *9*, 1355, 1365
  hunting of, *9*, 1376
  profile, *9*, 1358
  reproduction, *9*, 1375
  social structure, *9*, 1372–3
  survival, *9*, 1376–7
Gunn's bandicoots
  habitats, *16*, 2430

H

habitats
  see specific animal
hairy armadillos
  behavior, *1*, 89
  food and feeding, *1*, 94
hairy-legged vampire bats,
  2, 172
hairy-nosed wombats
  behavior, *16*, 2428–9
  family tree, *16*, 2424
  habitats, *16*, 2431
  life cycle, *16*, 2439
  profile, *16*, 2424
  survival, *16*, 2442, 2445
hamadryas baboons
  social structure,
    10, 1472–3
  survival, *10*, 1481–2
hammer-headed bats
  family tree, *2*, 137
  habitats, *6*, 873
hammer-headed fruit bats
  reproduction, *2*, 149
hamsters, *7*, 912–37
  acid rain, effect of, *7*, 937
  behavior, *7*, 920–31
  burrowing, *7*, 920, 923–4

captivity, *7*, 921
cheek pouches,
  7, 916, 926–7
conservation measures,
  7, 934–6
evolution, *7*, 914–6
family tree, *7*, 916–7
food and feeding,
  7, 926–7
foraging, *7*, 920
habitats, *7*, 922–5
life cycle, *7*, 928–31
pets, as, *7*, 936
physical description,
  7, 918–9
profile, *7*, 913–9
rainfall, effect on, *7*, 924
survival, *7*, 932–6
temperature, effect on,
  7, 924
woodlands, *7*, 934, 937
hanuman langurs
  captive breeding, *10*, 1457
  family tree, *10*, 1436
  food and feeding, *10*, 1444
  habitats, *10*, 1443
  life cycle, *10*, 1450–1
  physical description,
    10, 1438
  social structure, *10*, 1447
  survival,
    10, 1452, 1455, 1456
  territory, *10*, 1448–9
harbor porpoises
  habitats, *5*, 636
harems
  spear-nosed bats, *2*, 177
  vicuñas, *3*, 357
hares, *7*, 938–63
  behavior, *7*, 946–59
  courtship, *7*, 956–7
  described, *1*, xxi
  double digestion system,
    7, 952
  evolution, *7*, 941–2
  family tree,
    7, 942–3, *12*, 1800–1
  food and feeding, *7*, 952–3
  habitats,
    7, 948–51, *15*, 2225
  hunting of, *7*, 960

leaping, *7*, 957
life cycle, *7*, 958–9
mating, *7*, 958
migration, *7*, 948
population, *7*, 962, 963
profile,
  7, 939–45, *12*, 1798, 1800
rabbits, differences from,
  7, 941
rainfall, effect of, *7*, 950
scent marking, *7*, 956
scientific research, use in,
  7, 962
survival, *7*, 960–2
temperature, effect on,
  7, 950
territory, *7*, 954–5
hare wallabies
  behavior, *8*, 1155
  family tree, *8*, 1151
  food and feeding, *8*, 1161
  habitats, *8*, 1156–8
  profile, *8*, 1150
  social structure, *8*, 1163
harp seals
  habitats, *13*, 1988–9
  hunting of, *13*, 2000
  life cycle, *13*, 1996–7
  survival, *13*, 1998–2000
  territory, *13*, 1994
harpy eagles
  predator, *1*, 41
Harris's olingos
  survival, *12*, 1847
hartebeests
  see also
    Lichenstein's hartebeests
  behavior, *1*, 62
  communication, *1*, 63
  food and feeding, *1*, 69
  habitats, *1*, 66
  lions, as prey of, *9*, 1238
  social structure, *1*, 70–1
  survival, *1*, 76
harvest mice
  food and feeding, *13*, 1914
  habitats, *13*, 1886
  life cycle, *13*, 1918–9
  survival,
    13, 1894, 1923–4
Hawaiian monk seals

evolution, *13*, 1982

habitats, *13*, 1988

life cycle, *13*, 1997

survival, *13*, 2001

hazardous waste production

anteaters and, *1*, 52

heather voles

habitats, *15*, 2196

hedgehogs, *7*, 964–89

behavior, *7*, 972–83

breeding, *7*, 982

conservation measures,

7, 986–7

convergent evolution,

12, 1696

evolution, *7*, 967–8

family tree,

7, 968–9, *14*, 2034

food and feeding, *7*, 978–9

habitats, *7*, 974–7, *14*, 2043

hibernation, *7*, 980–1

life cycle, *7*, 982–3

pesticides and, *7*, 984–5

pets, as, *7*, 989

physical description,

7, 970–1

profile, *7*, 965–71

saliva, *7*, 980

survival, *7*, 984–8

hedgerows

survival, *7*, 986–7

Heider, David, *3*, 416

hesperomids

see New World rats and

mice

hibernation

badgers, *1*, 124–5

dormice, *7*, 923, 928–31

European hedgehogs, *7*, 980

hedgehogs, *7*, 980–1

Old World rats and mice,

13, 1916–7

raccoon dogs, *4*, 583

Tasmanian devils,

14, 2143

tenrecs, *7*, 981

higher primates

family tree, *5*, 735

hill kangaroos

profile, *8*, 1122

Himalayan black bears

see Asian black bears

hippopotamuses, *7*, 990–1015

behavior, *7*, 998–1009

conservation measures,

7, 1012–13

evolution, *7*, 992–4

eye trouble, *7*, 999

family tree,

6, 760, 812, *7*, 994–5,

11, 1618

food and feeding, *7*, 1006–7

habitats, *5*, 742, *7*, 1000–3

hunting of, *7*, 1014

"jawing," *7*, 998

life cycle, *7*, 1008–9

mating, *7*, 1008

physical description,

7, 996–7

profile, *7*, 991–7, *11*, 1615

rainfall, effect on, *7*, 1002

size of, *7*, 993

skin, *7*, 993–4

social structure, *7*, 1004–5

survival, *7*, 1010–14

temperature, effect on,

7, 1002

territory, *7*, 1001–2, 1005

zoos, *7*, 1015

hirolas

survival, *1*, 74–5, 77

Hispaniolan hutias

conservation measures,

6, 908

survival, *6*, 909

Hispaniolan solenodons

habitats, *14*, 2040, 2042

survival, *14*, 2051–3

hispid hares

family tree, *7*, 943

HIV virus

chimpanzees, *4*, 492

hoary-bellied squirrels

behavior, *14*, 2116

hoary foxes

survival, *5*, 702

hoary marmots

food and feeding, *14*, 2100

Hoffman's two-toed sloths

behavior, *14*, 2065

family tree, *14*, 2060

food and feeding,

14, 2072

habitats, *14*, 2066

life cycle, *14*, 2077

profile, *14*, 2058

survival, *14*, 2079–80

hog badgers

food and feeding,

1, 114, 121

habitats, *1*, 116–7

life cycle, *1*, 127

profile, *1*, 110

hog deer

habitats, *4*, 550, 560

hog-nosed bats

see bumblebee bats

hog-nosed skunks

family tree, *16*, 2373

food and feeding, *16*, 2383

habitats, *16*, 2378

physical description,

16, 2375

profile, *16*, 2372

Homo sapiens, *6*, 862

honey badgers

aggression, *1*, 114

family tree,

1, 111, *11*, 1567, *15*, 2217

food and feeding, *1*, 120–1

habitats, *1*, 116, 118

life cycle, *1*, 127

odor, *1*, 116

profile, *1*, 109–10

social structure, *1*, 124

survival, *1*, 128

honey bears

see sun bears

honey possums

behavior, *13*, 1856, 1857

family tree,

8, 1124, *12*, 1723, *13*, 1852,

16, 2424

food and feeding, *13*, 1864–5

habitats, *13*, 1858

life cycle, *13*, 1868

physical description,

13, 1854–5

profile, *13*, 1851

hooded seals

family tree, *13*, 1982

habitats, *13*, 1988–9

life cycle, *13*, 1996

polar bears, prey of, *11*, 1681

profile, *13*, 1986

survival, *13*, 1999

territory, *13*, 1995

hooded skunks

family tree, *16*, 2373

hoof-and-mouth disease

goats and sheep, *6*, 856

Hooker's sea lions

see New Zealand sea lions

hoolock gibbons

habitats, *6*, 793

physical description, *6*, 786

singing, *6*, 799

survival, *6*, 805

horses, *7*, 1016–41

behavior, *7*, 1024–35

conservation measures,

7, 1038–9

evolution, *7*, 1017–20

family tree,

7, 1020–1, *16*, 2450

food and feeding, *7*, 1030–1

grooming, *7*, 1025

habitats, *7*, 1026–9

herding, *7*, 1025, 1032

life cycle, *7*, 1034–5

physical description, *7*, 1020

ponies, distinguished,

7, 1026

profile, *7*, 1017–23, *16*, 2447

rainfall, effect on, *7*, 1028

social structure, *7*, 1032–3

survival, *7*, 1036–40

temperature, effect on,

7, 1028

vocalization, *7*, 1033

horseshoe bats

golden horseshoe bats

see golden horseshoe bats

greater horseshoe bats

see greater horseshoe bats

hunting by, *2*, 192

mating, *2*, 202

migration, *2*, 192

profile, *2*, 186, 189, 214

reproduction, *2*, 202

Hottentot golden moles

burrowing, *10*, 1394–5

food and feeding, *10*, 1398

house mice

behavior, *13*, 1908

family tree, *13*, 1905

habitats, *2*, 222, *13*, 1910

physical description,
13, 1907

profile, *13*, 1901

survival, *13*, 1920, 1924

house spiders

habitats, *2*, 222

howler monkeys

behavior, *10*, 1414

food and feeding, *10*, 1418–9

profile, *10*, 1408

social structure, *10*, 1421–2

survival, *10*, 1429

Hualapai Mexican voles

survival, *15*, 2210

Hudson Bay Company,
3, 336, *6*, 859, *7*, 963

humans

chimpanzees, similarity to,
4, 474, 495

family tree, *4*, 475, *6*, 787,
865, *10*, 1462, 1488,
11, 1540

gorillas, compared to, *6*, 864

hump-backed dolphins

habitats, *5*, 636–7

humpback whales

behavior, *16*, 2324–5

family tree, *16*, 2320

food and feeding,
16, 2330–1

habitats, *16*, 2327–8, 2433

life cycle, *16*, 2334–5

migration, *16*, 2328

physical description,
15, 2245

profile, *16*, 2317–20

social structure,
16, 2332–3

songs of,
15, 2252, *16*, 2333

survival, *16*, 2337–41

humped baleen whales

see gray whales

hunting by animals

see specific animal

hunting of animals

see specific animal

hutias

conservation measures,
6, 908–9

food and feeding, *6*, 903

hyenas, *7*, 1042–67

aardwolves **see** aardwolves

anal pouch, *7*, 1060

behavior, *7*, 1050–64

courtship, *7*, 1063

digestion, *7*, 1045

evolution,
4, 498, *7*, 1045–6

family tree, *2*, 267, *4*, 501,
7, 1046–7

habitats,
7, 1052–5, *8*, 1211

hunting by, *7*, 1058–9,
15, 2177

jackals, predators of,
8, 1090

life cycle, *7*, 1062–3

physical description,
7, 1048–9

profile, *7*, 1043–9

rainfall, effect on, *7*, 1054

scent marking,
7, 1056, 1060–1, 1063

smell, sense of, *7*, 1044

social structure, *7*, 1056–7

survival, *7*, 1064–6

temperature, effect on,
7, 1054

territory, *7*, 1060–1

hyraxes

see also aardvarks; bush
hyraxes; rock hyraxes;
tree hyraxes

adaptability, *1*, 14

body heat, *1*, 10

captivity, in, *1*, 27

coney, as, *1*, 26

deforestation and, *1*, 26

diseases, carriers of, *1*, 27

eastern tree hyraxes,
protection of, *1*, 26

enemies of, *1*, 11, 15

evolution, *1*, 3–6

family tree, *1*, 6–7

food and feeding,
1, 17–9

gestation, *1*, 22

habitats, *1*, 12–4

interbreeding, *1*, 22

life of, *1*, 10–1

longevity, *1*, 23

physical description, *1*, 8–9

profile, *1*, 3–9

relationships of, *1*, 5–6

reproduction, *1*, 22–3

sex ratio, *1*, 23

social structure, *1*, 20–1

sunbathing, *1*, 5

urine, *1*, 13

I

ibexes

behavior, *6*, 845

captive breeding, *6*, 837

habitats, *7*, 925

hunting of, *6*, 859

physical description,
6, 840–1

social structure,
6, 851, 853

survival,
6, 854, 858

Icelandic horses

habitats, *7*, 1027

ice-whales

profile, *15*, 2292

impalas

behavior, *1*, 62

family tree, *1*, 58

habitats, *1*, 66, *6*, 821

life cycle, *1*, 72–3

mating, *1*, 73

profile, *1*, 57

social structure, *1*, 71

survival, *1*, 74

tongue flashing, *1*, 73

Incas

llamas and, *3*, 364

Indiana bats

survival, *2*, 207, 233

Indian bison

see gaurs

Indian chevrotains

survival, *12*, 1767

Indian civets

food and feeding, *4*, 511

hunting of, *4*, 516

Indian desert cats

experiments on, *9*, 1275

Indian flying foxes

life cycle, *2*, 150–1

Indian gray mongooses

family tree, *9*, 1333

profile, *9*, 1332

Indian mongooses

shrews and solenodons,
effect on, *14*, 2052–4

Indian muntjacs

see muntjacs

Indian nilgiri

trapping for fur, *9*, 1326

Indian porcupines

habitats, *12*, 1704

Indian pythons

habitats, *4*, 509

Indian rhinoceroses

defenses, *13*, 1935

family tree, *13*, 1931

food and feeding, *13*, 1941

habitats, *13*, 1936–7

life cycle, *13*, 1944–5

physical description,
13, 1932–3

profile, *13*, 1927, 1929

social structure, *13*, 1942

survival, *13*, 1949

Indians, pre-Inca

vicuñas, hunting of, *3*, 361

Indian sambar

behavior, *4*, 556

habitats, *4*, 550

Indian short-nosed fruit bats

food and feeding, *2*, 145

social structure, *2*, 146

Indians of North America

beavers, relationship with,
3, 336, 338

bison, relationship with,
3, 414–6

brown bears and, *2*, 284

gray whales, relationship
with, *15*, 2262

killer whales,
relationship with, *15*, 2287

raccoons and,
12, 1825, 1844

Indian spotted chevrotains

behavior, *12*, 1753, 1763

Indian tigers

see Bengal tigers
Indian wolves
   survival, *16*, 2417
Indochinese tigers
   profile, *15*, 2164
   survival, *15*, 2183
Indonesian babirusas
   habitats, *11*, 1624
   social structure, *11*, 1630
Indonesian mountain weasels
   survival, *15*, 2235
indris
   evolution, *8*, 1175
   family tree, *5*, 734, *8*, 1176
   food and feeding, *8*, 1186
   habitats, *8*, 1183
   life cycle, *8*, 1190–1
   physical description,
      8, 1178–9
   social structure, *8*, 1189
   survival, *8*, 1195
insect-eating bats
   see also leaf-nosed bats;
      small bats; vesper bats
   family tree, *2*, 188–9
insectivores
   described, *1*, xx
   evolution, *10*, 1381–3
   family tree, *14*, 2034–5
   profile, *14*, 2031–2, 2034
interbreeding
   hyraxes, *1*, 22
International Tropical Timber
   Agreement, *8*, 1221
International Zoo Yearbook,
   5, 755
Inuits
   beavers, relationship with,
      3, 336, 338
   musk oxen and, *6*, 858–9
   polar bears and,
      11, 1686, 1689
Iriomote cats
   habitats, *9*, 1262
   profile, *9*, 1253
   survival, *9*, 1273
   territory, *9*, 1266
island coatis
   habitats, *12*, 1833
   profile, *12*, 1825
Island gray foxes

survival, *5*, 728
ivory gulls
   habitats, *5*, 690

J

jackals, *8*, 1068–93
   behavior, *8*, 1076–89
   courtship, *8*, 1088
   evolution, *8*, 1071–2
   family tree, *4*, 527, 578,
      5, 604, 709, *8*, 1072–3,
      16, 2398
   food and feeding,
      8, 1077, 1085
   habitats,
      1, 67, *8*, 1078–81
   hunting by,
      8, 1082–5, *15*, 2177
   leopards, prey of,
      8, 1212
   life cycle, *8*, 1088–9
   mating, *8*, 1089
   profile, *8*, 1069–75
   rainfall, effect on, *8*, 1080
   scent marking, *8*, 1087
   social structure, *8*, 1086–7
   survival, *8*, 1090–2
   temperature, effect on,
      8, 1080
   wolves, distinguished,
      8, 1072
jackdaws
   habitats, *2*, 222
jackrabbits
   family tree, *12*, 1800
   habitats, *12*, 1756
jaguars, *8*, 1094–1119
   behavior, *8*, 1102–13
   camouflage, *8*, 1097, 1100
   conservation measures,
      8, 1116–7
   family tree, *8*, 1098–9, 1202,
      9, 1229, *12*, 1775, *15*, 2164
   habitats, *3*, 379, *8*, 1104–7
   hunting by, *8*, 1108–9
   hunting of,
      8, 1117–8, *12*, 1790
   life cycle, *8*, 1112–3
   mating, *8*, 1112
   physical description,

8, 1096, 1100–1, 1205
   profile, *8*, 1095–1101
   rain forests, *8*, 1107
   survival, *8*, 1114–8
   territory, *8*, 1110–1
   worship of, *8*, 1118
jaguarundi
   family tree, *12*, 1775
   habitats,
      3, 378, *12*, 1780–2, 1786
   life cycle, *12*, 1788
   profile, *12*, 1773–4
   survival, *12*, 1793, 1795
Jamaican flower bats
   survival, *2*, 181, 183
Japanese beaked whales
   habitats, *16*, 2353
Japanese dormice
   population, *7*, 937
Japanese macaques
   behavior, *10*, 1466
   survival, *10*, 1481
Japanese martens
   profile, *9*, 1305
   trapping for fur, *9*, 1326
Jarvis, Jenny, *9*, 1371
Javan leopards
   survival, *8*, 1220
Javan mastiff bats
   survival, *2*, 207
Javan rhinoceroses
   diseases, *13*, 1949
   family tree, *13*, 1931
   food and feeding,
      13, 1940–1
   habitats, *13*, 1936–8
   physical description,
      13, 1933
   profile, *13*, 1927, 1929
   social structure,
      13, 1942
   survival, *13*, 1948–9
Javan thick-thumbed bats
   survival, *2*, 207, 233
Javan tigers
   profile, *15*, 2164
   survival,
      15, 2181, 2183
Javan warty pigs
   habitats, *11*, 1618
   relocation of population,

11, 1639
   survival, *11*, 1636, 1638
jays
   habitats, *5*, 717
Jentink's duikers
   camouflage, *6*, 769
   life cycle, *6*, 777
   survival, *6*, 780
jerboas
   family tree, *7*, 917
   habitats, *7*, 1028
Johnston, Sir. Harry,
   6, 811
Juan Fernandez fur seals
   habitats, *13*, 1962
   survival, *13*, 1976
Julia Creek dunnarts
   survival, *14*, 2157
jumping mice
   family tree,
      7, 917, *13*, 1878, 1905
   life cycle, *13*, 1916
jungle cats
   habitats,
      9, 1260–2, *14*, 2015–6
   hunting by,
      9, 1264–5, *14*, 2018
   profile, *14*, 2006, 2008

K

Kangaroo Island dunnarts
   survival, *14*, 2157
kangaroo mice
   profile, *14*, 2084–5
kangaroo rats
   profile, *14*, 2084–5
   survival, *14*, 2107
kangaroos, *8*, 1120–45
   behavior, *8*, 1128–39
   conservation measures,
      8, 1142–3
   evolution, *8*, 1122–4
   family tree, *8*, 1124–5,
      1151, *16*, 2424
   fighting, *8*, 1136
   food and feeding,
      8, 1134–5
   habitats,
      8, 1130–33, 1142, 1148
   hunting of, *8*, 1140–2

life cycle, *8*, 1136–9
pests, as, *8*, 1144
physical description,
    8, 1126–7
profile, *8*, 1121–7
survival, *8*, 1140–4
Kashmir voles
    habitats, *15*, 2196
Kat, Pieter, *5*, 622
Kermode bears
    habitats, *2*, 239
Key Largo cotton mice
    survival, *13*, 1897
Key Largo wood rats
    survival, *13*, 1897
kiang
    habitats, *7*, 1028
    life cycle, *7*, 1035
    survival, *7*, 1037
killer whales, *15*, 2264–89
    behavior, *15*, 2272–85
    captivity, *15*, 2288
    family tree, *15*, 2268–9
    habitats,
        5, 639, *11*, 1679,
        15, 2274–7
    hunting by, *15*, 2280–3
    mating, *15*, 2284
    oil pollution, effect on,
        15, 2287
    physical description,
        15, 2245, 2270–1
    pods, *15*, 2278–9
    profile, *15*, 2265–71
    reproduction, *15*, 2284–5
    social structure,
        15, 2278–9, *16*, 2332
    songs, *15*, 2278–9
    survival, *15*, 2286–8
King Kong, *6*, 884
kinkajous
    behavior, *12*, 1830
    family tree, *12*, 1827
    food and feeding, *12*, 1836–7
    habitats, *1*, 41, *12*, 1832–4
    life cycle, *12*, 1842–3
    physical description,
        12, 1829
    profile, *12*, 1824
    scent marking, *12*, 1839
Kipling, Rudyard, *9*, 1333

kit foxes
    habitats, *5*, 714
    territory, *5*, 723
Kitti's hog–nosed bats
    discovery of, *2*, 186
    survival, *2*, 207
klipspringer gazelles
    habitats, *6*, 767
    profile, *6*, 758
    survival, *6*, 779
kloss gibbons
    physical description, *6*, 786
    singing, *6*, 798–9
    survival, *6*, 805
koalas, *8*, 1146–71
    behavior, *8*, 1154–65
    Chlamydia psittaci,
        8, 1170
    conservation measures,
        8, 1168–9
    discovery of (as Cullawines),
        8, 1148
    diseases, *8*, 1170
    eucalyptus foliage and,
        8, 1154, 1158, 1161,
        1167–8, 1171
    family tree, *8*, 1124, 1150–1,
        11, 1593, *16*, 2424
    food and feeding,
        8, 1160–1
    habitats, *8*, 1156–9
    hunting of, *8*, 1167–8
    life cycle, *8*, 1164–5
    mating, *8*, 1164
    physical description,
        8, 1152–3
    population, *8*, 1167
    profile,
        8, 1147–53, *16*, 2424
    rainfall, effect on, *8*, 1158
    rain forests, *8*, 1168–9
    social structure, *8*, 1162–3
    survival, *8*, 1166–70
    temperature, effect on,
        8, 1158
kobs
    food and feeding, *1*, 68
    life cycle, *1*, 72
    social structure, *1*, 70
    survival, *1*, 76
Kodiak bears

characteristics, *2*, 265
    family tree, *2*, 266
    territories, *2*, 278
kodkods
    profile, *12*, 1773
kookaburras
    habitats,
        8, 1133, 1159, *11*, 1652
kopjes, *1*, 14–5, 20–1, *4*, 454
Korean gray hamsters
    food and feeding,
        7, 927
Korean gray whales
    habitats, *15*, 2248
    migration, *15*, 2255
    survival, *15*, 2260, 2262
kori bustards
    habitats, *1*, 67
kouprey
    discovery of, *3*, 421
    habitats, *3*, 428–9
    hunting of, *3*, 439
    survival, *3*, 439–41
kowari
    survival, *14*, 2157
kudu
    behavior, *1*, 62–3
    habitats, *1*, 64
    profile, *1*, 57

L

langur monkeys
    physical description,
        10, 1439
    profile, *10*, 1434
large Malay leaf-nosed bats
    hunting by, *2*, 197
large-spotted genets
    habitats, *4*, 506
large toothed whales
    family tree, *15*, 2295
large whales
    family tree, *16*, 2320
lar gibbons
    family tree, *6*, 787
    habitats, *6*, 792–3
    physical description,
        6, 785–6, 789
    singing, *6*, 798–9
Leadbeater's possums

behavior, *12*, 1727
    food and feeding,
        12, 1730–2
    habitats, *12*, 1728
    reproduction, *12*, 1737
    social structure, *12*, 1735
    survival, *12*, 1738–41, 1743
leaf-chinned bats, *2*, 159, 169
    family tree, *2*, 162
leaf monkeys
    family tree, *10*, 1436
    food and feeding, *10*, 1444
leaf-nosed bats, *2*, 158–83, 215
    behavior, *2*, 166–77
    caves, *2*, 168–9
    conservation measures,
        2, 180
    Cuban flower bats, *2*, 181
    diseases, *2*, 180–2
    family tree, *2*, 163
    flight, *2*, 159–61, 187
    food and feeding, *2*, 170–1
    foraging, *2*, 161
    habitats, *2*, 168–9
    hunting by, *2*, 172–5, 197
    Jamaican fig-eating bats,
        2, 183
    Jamaican flower bats,
        2, 181, 183
    large Malay leaf-nosed bats,
        2, 197
    life cycle, *2*, 176–9
    little long-nosed bats,
        2, 181
    malaria, *2*, 181
    Mexican long-nosed bats,
        2, 181–2
    New Zealand
        short-tailed bats, *2*, 181
    nighttime, *2*, 166–8
    night vision, *2*, 161–2
    Old World bats, *2*, 191
    profile, *2*, 159–65, 214
    Puerto Rican flower bats,
        2, 181
    rabies, *2*, 180–1
    survival, *2*, 178–82
    tailless leaf-nosed bats,
        2, 195
    yellow fever, *2*, 182
lechwes

behavior, *1*, 63
food and feeding, *1*, 68
habitats, *1*, 64–5
social structure, *1*, 70
survival, *1*, 77
Leisler's bats
survival, *2*, 231
lemmings, *5*, 693–4
behavior, *15*, 2194–2207
evolution, *15*, 2188
family tree, *15*, 2190–1
food and feeding,
15, 2189, 2200–1
habitats, *15*, 2196–9
life cycle, *15*, 2204–5
migration,
15, 2206–7, 2209
nests, *15*, 2195
physical description,
15, 2192–3
suicide, *15*, 2206–7
survival, *15*, 2208–10
temperature, effect on,
15, 2189
territory, *15*, 2202–3
lemuroid ring-tailed possums
social structure, *12*, 1734
survival, *12*, 1741
lemurs, *8*, 1172–97
behavior, *8*, 1180–91
conservation measures,
8, 1194
courtship, *8*, 1190
evolution, *8*, 1173–5, 1194
family tree, *5*, 734, *8*, 1176–7
food and feeding, *8*, 1186–7
habitats, *8*, 1182–5
life cycle, *8*, 1190–1
lower primates, as, *8*, 1177
mating, *8*, 1191
physical description, *8*, 1178–9
profile, *5*, 733, *8*, 1173–9
rainfall, effect on,
8, 1182, 1184
rain forests, *8*, 1184, 1194
scent marking, *8*, 1179
social structure, *8*, 1188–9
survival, *8*, 1192–6
temperature, effect on,
8, 1184
leopard cats

habitats, *9*, 1262
hunting by, *9*, 1265
life cycle, *9*, 1268
survival, *9*, 1272
territory, *9*, 1266
leopards, *8*, 1198–1223
behavior, *8*, 1206–17
camouflage, *8*, 1200
conservation measures,
8, 1220–1
diseases, *8*, 1217
evolution, *8*, 1199–1200
family tree,
8, 1099, 1202–3, *9*, 1229,
15, 2164
fur farms, *8*, 1223
habitats,
1, 93, *8*, 1208–11, *9*, 1367,
11, 1601, *16*, 2458
hunting by,
8, 1212–5, *9*, 1236
hunting of, *8*, 1218–20
life cycle, *8*, 1216–7
lions, as enemies of, *8*, 1215
man-eating, *8*, 1222
mating, *8*, 1217
physical description,
8, 1204–5
profile, *8*, 1199–1205
rabies, *8*, 1217
rainfall, effect on, *8*, 1210
rain forests,
8, 1209, 1220
savannas, *8*, 1210
survival, *8*, 1218–22
temperature, effect on,
8, 1210
zoos, *8*, 1222
leopard seals
family tree, *13*, 1983
habitats, *13*, 1988
hunting by, *13*, 1991–3
leprosy research
armadillos, *1*, 104
lesser apes
family tree, *6*, 787
lesser galagos
captivity, *5*, 755
life cycle, *5*, 750–1
locomotion, *5*, 744
physical description, *5*, 736–7

survival, *5*, 752–3
territory, *5*, 749
lesser Malay chevrotains
food and feeding,
12, 1761
territory, *12*, 1759
zoos, *12*, 1769
lesser moonrats
behavior, *7*, 972
family tree, *7*, 969
lesser mouse deer
territory, *12*, 1759
lesser mouse-tailed bats
survival, *2*, 208
lesser short-tailed bats
survival, *2*, 207
lesser spectral tarsiers
survival, *5*, 754
L'Hoest's monkeys
survival, *10*, 1480–1
Liberian mongooses
captive breeding, *9*, 1353
survival, *9*, 1352
Lichenstein's hartebeests
profile, *1*, 56–7
life cycle
see specific animal
Linnaeus, Carl, *14*, 2078,
15, 2292
Linne's two-toed sloths
family tree, *14*, 2060
habitats, *14*, 2066
lions, *9*, 1224–49
behavior, *9*, 1232–43
captive breeding, *9*, 1247–8
conservation measures,
9, 1246–7
evolution, *9*, 1225–6, 1228
family tree,
8, 1099, 1202, *9*, 1228–9,
12, 1774, *15*, 2164
habitats,
6, 821, *7*, 1055,
8, 1211, *9*, 1234–7
hunting by,
9, 1235–6, 1238–9
hunting of, *9*, 1244–5
infanticide, *9*, 1241
leopards, as enemies of,
8, 1215
life cycle, *9*, 1242–3

man eating, *9*, 1248
mating, *9*, 1242
nomadic existence,
9, 1234–5
physical description,
9, 1230–1
porcupines, defenses,
12, 1708
prides, *9*, 1232–4
profile, *9*, 1225–31
rainfall, effect on,
9, 1236
roaring, *9*, 1226–7, 1241
scent marking, *9*, 1233
senses, *9*, 1227–8
social structure, *9*, 1240–1
survival, *9*, 1244–8
temperature, effect on,
9, 1236
territory, *9*, 1232–3
zoos, *9*, 1247–9
lion-tailed macaques
survival, *10*, 1481, 1483
lion tamarins
conservation measures,
10, 1506–7
food and feeding,
10, 1499
life cycle, *10*, 1503
new species, *10*, 1509
profile, *10*, 1488
survival, *10*, 1509
little long-nosed bats
survival, *2*, 181
llamas
domestication,
3, 342, 348
family tree,
3, 345, *6*, 813
habitats, *3*, 350–1
life cycle, *3*, 359
mating, *3*, 358
physical characteristics,
3, 346
size of, *3*, 344
spitting by, *3*, 349
survival, *3*, 363–5
weight capable of carrying,
3, 349
llanos, *1*, 38, 42, 48, 50–1
locomotion

galagos, *5*, 744–5
lodge-building
  beavers, *3*, 330–1
long-clawed ground squirrels
  food and feeding, *14*, 2100
  habitats, *14*, 2094
long-eared bats
  see common long-eared bats;
    Gould's long-eared bats
long-eared hedgehogs
  family tree, *7*, 969
  habitats, *7*, 974–5
  profile, *7*, 966–7
longevity
  hyraxes, *1*, 23
long-fingered bats
  survival, *2*, 207, 233
long-finned pilot whales
  family tree, *15*, 2268
  habitats, *15*, 2274, 2276
  physical description,
    15, 2271
  profile, *15*, 2267
  reproduction, *15*, 2285
  social structure, *15*, 2279
  survival, *15*, 2288
long-footed potoroos
  food and feeding,
    13, 1867
  habitats, *13*, 1858
  survival, *13*, 1872
  territory, *13*, 1863
long-haired rats
  diseases, *13*, 1921
  survival, *13*, 1922
long-nosed armadillos
  food and feeding, *1*, 94
  habitats, *1*, 89
  leprosy research, *1*, 104
  survival, *1*, 100–5
long-nosed bandicoots
  behavior, *16*, 2429
  food and feeding, *16*, 2434
  habitats, *16*, 2430
  life cycle, *16*, 2439
  profile, *16*, 2422
long-nosed bats
  food and feeding,
    2, 167, 170–1
  survival, *2*, 181
long-nosed echidnas

behavior, *11*, 1648
family tree, *11*, 1645
food and feeding, *11*,
  1656–7
habitats, *11*, 1651, 1652
hunting of, *11*, 1665
physical description,
  11, 1647
profile, *11*, 1643
survival, *11*, 1662–4
long-nosed potoroos
  behavior, *13*, 1856–7
  food and feeding, *13*, 1867
  habitats, *13*, 1858
  survival, *13*, 1870, 1872
  territory, *13*, 1862–3
long-nosed squirrels
  food and feeding, *14*, 2122
long-tailed bandicoots
  habitats, *16*, 2430
long-tailed dunnarts
  habitats, *14*, 2159
  hunting by, *14*, 2150
long-tailed porcupines
  habitats, *12*, 1704
  profile, *12*, 1696
long-tailed pygmy possums
  behavior, *12*, 1727
  social structure, *12*, 1734
  survival, *12*, 1741
long-tailed tenrecs
  survival, *7*, 988
long-tailed weasels
  habitats, *15*, 2222
  hunting by, *15*, 2226–7
  profile, *15*, 2214
Lorini, Maria Lucia,
  10, 1509
lorises, *5*, 732–3
  behavior, *5*, 738–9
  cryptic locomotion,
    5, 739
  family tree, *8*, 1176
  food and feeding,
    5, 747
  habitats, *5*, 742
  life cycle, *5*, 750
  locomotion,
    5, 744, 745
lorisids
  family tree, *5*, 735

foraging, *5*, 739
habitats, *5*, 740–2
hunting of, *5*, 755
night vision, *5*, 739
physical description,
  5, 733
survival, *5*, 752
lower primates
  family tree, *8*, 1177
lowland anoas
  described, *3*, 421
  survival, *3*, 441
lowland tree kangaroos
  survival, *8*, 1169
Lumholtz's tree kangaroos
  habitats, *8*, 1157–8
lupine canids
  family tree, *4*, 579, *8*, 1073
  habitats, *4*, 584
  pack hunting, *4*, 576
lupine dogs
  family tree, *5*, 682
lupine foxes, *5*, 678–703
  behavior, *5*, 686–99
  diseases, *5*, 703
  family tree, *5*, 682–3
  habitats, *5*, 688–91
  hunting, *5*, 692–5
  insecticides, effect of,
    5, 702
  profile, *5*, 679–85
  rabies, *5*, 703
  reproduction, *5*, 698–9
  survival, *5*, 700–2
  temperature, effect on,
    5, 686, 690
  territory, *5*, 696–7
lupines
  family tree, *5*, 605
Lyme disease
  deer, *4*, 560
lynx
  behavior, *12*, 1778–9
  family tree, *8*, 1202, *9*, 1229,
    1255, *12*, 1775, *15*, 2165
  habitats, *9*, 1260–1, *12*, 1704,
    1780, *16*, 2381
  hunting by, *12*, 1784
  hunting of, *9*, 1270–1
  life cycle, *9*, 1269, *12*, 1788–9
  physical description, *9*, 1259

profile, *9*, 1254
survival, *9*, 1270–3, *12*, 1791
wolverines, as prey of,
  16, 2382

M

macaques
  family tree, *10*, 1437
  physical description,
    10, 1464
  social structure, *10*, 1473
Macarthur, Chris, *3*, 416
Machiguenga Indians
  sloths, legends about,
    14, 2079
Madagascan civets, *4*, 498–9
  habitats, *4*, 508
  survival, *4*, 519
Madagascan primates
  family tree, *5*, 734
Madagascar mongooses
  family tree, *9*, 1333
Maharashtra giant squirrels
  survival, *14*, 2132
mahogany gliders
  survival, *12*, 1741
Malabar civets
  conservation measures,
    4, 518
  survival, *4*, 521
Malabar giant squirrels
  behavior, *14*, 2117
  food and feeding,
    14, 2122
  profile, *14*, 2111
Malagasy civets
  see fanaloka
Malagasy lemurs
  profile, *8*, 1176
Malagasy pachypodia
  habitats, *8*, 1183
malaria
  leaf-nosed bats, *2*, 181
Malayan civets
  habitats, *16*, 2459
Malayan pangolins
  food and feeding, *1*, 94
Malayan porcupines
  adaptations, *12*, 1706
  profile, *12*, 1695

Malayan tapirs
  defenses, *16*, 2462
  habitats, *16*, 2457
  profile, *16*, 2450
  reproduction, *16*, 2467
  survival, *16*, 2469–70
Malayan tigers
  see Indochinese tigers
Malay bears
  naming, *3*, 291
mammals
  behavior, *1*, xxiii
  classification of, *1*, xxi
  Cretaceous period, *1*, xix
  evolution of, *1*, xvii–xix
  general description, *1*, xvi
  groups of, *1*, xvi
  habitats, *1*, xxii
  Jurassic Epoch, *1*, xviii
  profile, *1*, xxiii
  Quaternary period, *1*, xix
  reptiles, evolution from,
    1, xvi, xviii
  survival, *1*, xxiii
  Tertiary period, *1*, xix
  Triassic period, *1*, xviii
  types of, *1*, xx–xxi
  warm-blooded, *1*, xvi
manatees, *9*, 1276–1301
  Adopt-a-Manatee program,
    9, 1301
  behavior, *9*, 1284–95
  communication, *9*, 1292–3
  described, *1*, xxi
  evolution, *9*, 1278
  family tree, *9*, 1281
  food and feeding, *9*, 1290–1
  habitats, *9*, 1286–9
  life cycle, *9*, 1294–5
  mermaids, mistaken as,
    9, 1277–8
  migration, *9*, 1285
  physical description,
    9, 1282–3
  profile, *9*, 1277–83
  rainfall, effect on, *9*, 1288
  scent marking, *9*, 1292
  singing, *9*, 1292–3
  survival, *9*, 1296–1300
  temperature, effect on,
    9, 1288

  territory, *9*, 1292–3
mandrills, *10*, 1458–83
  behavior, *10*, 1466–77
  conservation measures,
    10, 1480–1
  diseases, *10*, 1482
  evolution, *10*, 1459–62
  family tree, *10*, 1463
  food and feeding, *10*,
    1474–5
  green monkey virus,
    10, 1482
  grooming, *10*, 1470
  habitats, *10*, 1468–9
  hunting of, *10*, 1478–80
  life cycle, *10*, 1476–7
  physical description,
    10, 1464–5
  profile, *10*, 1459–65
  research, use in, *10*, 1480–1
  social structure, *10*, 1470–3
  survival, *10*, 1478–82
maned sloths
  family tree, *14*, 2061
  habitats, *14*, 2066, 2081
  survival, *14*, 2080
maned wolves
  captive breeding, *4*, 547
  family tree,
    4, 526–7, 579, *5*, 604, 682
  habitats, *4*, 532–4, 547
  hunting by,
    4, 525, 530, 537
  life cycle, *4*, 543
  physical description,
    4, 528–9, 534
  survival, *4*, 544–6
  territory, *4*, 539
manta ray
  habitats, *5*, 638
mantled howler monkeys
  behavior, *10*, 1414
  survival, *10*, 1427
maras
  see Patagonian hares
marbled cats
  family tree, *9*, 1229
  habitats, *9*, 1262
  profile, *9*, 1252
  scent marking, *9*, 1266
  survival, *9*, 1272–3

  territory, *9*, 1266
marbled polecats
  habitats, *15*, 2224
  profile, *15*, 2214
  survival, *15*, 2236
margays
  habitats, *12*, 1781
  hunting by, *12*, 1785
  hunting of, *12*, 1790
  survival, *12*, 1793
Margueritte, General, *14*, 2007
Marianas flying foxes
  survival, *2*, 155
Marine Mammal
    Protection Act,
    5, 650, *15*, 2312
marmoset rats
  habitats, *13*, 1912
marmosets, *10*, 1484–1509
  behavior, *10*, 1492–1503
  captive breeding, *10*, 1503
  family tree,
    10, 1411, 1488–9
  food and feeding,
    10, 1498–9
  grooming, *10*, 1501
  habitats, *10*, 1494–7
  life cycle, *10*, 1502–3
  physical description,
    10, 1490–1
  profile, *10*, 1409, 1485–91
  rainfall, effect on, *10*, 1496
  rain forests, *10*, 1495–7
  social structure,
    10, 1500–1
  survival, *10*, 1457, 1504–8
  temperature, effect on,
    10, 1496
  territory, *10*, 1500
marmots
  family tree, *14*, 2086
  food and feeding,
    14, 2100
  habitats, *14*, 2092
  life cycle, *14*, 2102–3
  social structure, *14*, 2099
  survival, *14*, 2106–7
marsh mongooses
  habitats, *9*, 1338
  profile, *9*, 1331–2
marsh rabbits

  habitats, *12*, 1806–7
marsh rice rats
  nesting, *13*, 1890–1
marsupial carnivores
  profile, *14*, 2136–8
  survival,
    14, 2154, 2157
marsupial lions
  survival, *14*, 2154
marsupial moles
  burrowing, *14*, 2144
  family tree,
    14, 2138–9, *16*, 2425
  survival, *14*, 2158
marsupials
  behavior,
    8, 1129, *12*, 1726
  defined, *8*, 1123
  described, *1*, xvii, xx
  evolution,
    1, xix, *8*, 1122, 1147–8,
    1150, *10*, 1513–4
  family tree, *8*, 1124–5, 1151,
    10, 1514, *12*, 1722,
    13, 1853, *16*, 2424–5
  food and feeding, *16*, 2435
  life cycle, *16*, 2438
  profile,
    8, 1124, *12*, 1719, *13*, 1851
  reproduction, *12*, 1736–7
  survival,
    8, 1166, *12*, 1738, *16*, 2440
  tree-dwelling, *12*, 1721
martens, *9*, 1302–27
  behavior, *9*, 1310–23
  evolution, *9*, 1303–4
  family tree,
    9, 1306–7, *15*, 2217,
    16, 2372
  habitats, *9*, 1312–5
  hunting by, *9*, 1316–9
  life cycle, *9*, 1322–3
  mating, *9*, 1322
  physical description,
    9, 1304
  profile, *9*, 1303–9
  rainfall, effect on,
    9, 1312, 1314
  survival, *9*, 1324–6
  temperature, effect on,
    9, 1312, 1314

territory, *9*, 1320–1

Martin, Dr. Esmond Bradley,
13, 1951

masai lions
profile, *9*, 1228

mating
see specific animal

Matschie's tree kangaroos
survival, *8*, 1169

Maya Indians
jaguars, worship of, *8*, 1118

meadow voles
profile, *15*, 2190

medicine and medical
research, use in,
armadillos, *1*, 100, 104
pangolins, *1*, 102–4
small bears, *3*, 311, 313

Medill, William, *3*, 414

Mediterranean monk seals
behavior, *13*, 1987
survival, *13*, 2000–1

meerkats, *9*, 1328–53
aggression, *9*, 1345–6
behavior, *9*, 1336–49
burrowing, *9*, 1339
evolution, *9*, 1329–30
family tree, *9*, 1333
food and feeding,
9, 1342–3
grooming, *9*, 1347
habitats, *1*, 92, *9*, 1338–41
life cycle, *9*, 1348–9
physical description,
9, 1334–5
profile, *9*, 1329–35
rainfall, effect on, *9*, 1340
rain forests, *9*, 1350–1
scent marking, *9*, 1345
social structure, *9*, 1344–7
survival, *9*, 1350–2
temperature, effect on,
9, 1340

melon-headed whales
family tree, *15*, 2268
habitats, *15*, 2276
physical description,
15, 2270–1
profile, *15*, 2265, 2267
reproduction, *15*, 2285
social structure, *15*, 2278

Melville, Herman, *16*, 2345

Melville, Jack and Betty
Leslie, *6*, 832

Mentawai Islands sureli
food and feeding, *10*, 1444
profile, *10*, 1435
social structure, *10*, 1446

Mentawai langurs
survival, *10*, 1455
territory, *10*, 1448

Menzbier's marmots
habitats, *14*, 2092
survival, *14*, 2106–7

mergansers
habitats, *4*, 587

Mexican cottontails
life cycle, *12*, 1817

Mexican free-tailed bats
food and feeding, *2*, 198
habitats, *2*, 194

Mexican prairie dogs
survival, *14*, 2106–7

Mexican pronghorns
survival, *12*, 1767–8

Mexican silver grizzly,
2, 285

Mexican wolves
survival, *16*, 2417

mice **see also**
New World rats and mice;
Old World rats and mice
family tree,
7, 916, *13*, 1878–9, 1905

Michoacan pocket gophers
survival, *14*, 2106

migration
gray whales, *15*, 2254–5
hares, *7*, 948
humpback whales,
16, 2328
lemmings,
15, 2206–7, 2209
manatees, *9*, 1285
right whales, *15*, 2302
sperm whales, *16*, 2354–5
voles, *15*, 2206–7

migratory hamsters
burrowing, *7*, 923

Mindanao moonrats
survival, *7*, 987

Mindoro buffalo **see** tamaraus

Minimum Viable Population
(MVP), *8*, 1092

minke whales
family tree, *16*, 2320
food and feeding, *16*,
2330–1
profile, *16*, 2317, 2319
social structure, *16*, 2332
survival, *16*, 2339

minks, *9*, 1302–27
behavior, *9*, 1310–23
captive breeding,
9, 1324, 1326
evolution, *9*, 1303–4, 1306
family tree, *15*, 2217
fur farms, *9*, 1325
habitats, *9*, 1312–5
hunting by, *9*, 1316–9
hunting of, *9*, 1305–6
life cycle, *9*, 1322–3
mating, *9*, 1322
physical description,
9, 1304
profile, *9*, 1303–9
rainfall, effect on, *9*, 1314
survival, *9*, 1324–6
temperature, effect on,
9, 1314
territory, *9*, 1320–1
trapping for fur, *9*, 1326

miombo
cheetahs and, *4*, 454

Moby Dick (Melville),
16, 2345

mocos **see** rock cavies

Moi, Daniel T., *5*, 674

mole rats, *9*, 1354–79
behavior, *9*, 1362–75
burrowing, *9*, 1364–6, 1371
evolution, *9*, 1358
family tree, *9*, 1358–9
food and feeding,
9, 1368–9
habitats, *9*, 1364–7
profile, *9*, 1355–61
rainfall, effect on, *9*, 1366
reproduction, *9*, 1374–5
social structure,
9, 1370–3
survival, *9*, 1376–8
temperature, effect on,
9, 1366, 1371, 1373

moles, *10*, 1380–1405
behavior, *10*, 1388–1401
burrowing,
10, 1391, 1394–5
convergent evolution,
10, 1384
evolution, *10*, 1381–3
family tree, *10*, 1384–5
food and feeding,
10, 1390–2, 1396–9
habitats, *10*, 1390–3
life cycle, *10*, 1400–1
profile, *10*, 1381–7
rainfall, effect on, *10*, 1392
survival, *10*, 1402–4
temperature, effect on,
10, 1392
territory, *10*, 1390–1
trapping for fur, *10*, 1402

mole-voles
family tree, *15*, 2191
food and feeding,
15, 2200
habitats, *15*, 2196
profile, *15*, 2190

moloch gibbons
habitats, *6*, 793
physical description, *6*, 786
singing, *6*, 798–9
survival, *6*, 805–6

Monbodo, Lord, *11*, 1538

Mongolian beavers
survival, *3*, 338

Mongolian wild horses
habitat, *3*, 352

mongoose lemurs
behavior, *8*, 1180
physical description,
8, 1178
survival, *8*, 1192

mongooses
Egyptian worship of,
9, 1336
family tree, *9*, 1332–3
food and feeding,
9, 1342–3
habitats, *7*, 925
life cycle, *9*, 1348–9
profile, *9*, 1329–35
social structure, *9*, 1344–7

survival, *9*, 1350–3

monkeys

see also capuchins; cebid
monkeys; colobines;
marmosets

family tree,
4, 475, *6*, 787, *11*, 1541

monk seals

family tree, *13*, 1983

habitats, *13*, 1988

survival, *13*, 2001

monogamy

African yellow-winged bats,
2, 202

monotremes

see also
echidnas; platypuses

behavior, *11*, 1648

defined, *11*, 1643

described, *1*, xvii, xx

evolution, *1*, xix, *11*, 1644

family tree, *11*, 1645

profile, *11*, 1641–2

survival, *11*, 1665

moonrats

behavior, *7*, 972

profile, *7*, 966–7

moose

behavior, *4*, 556–7

evolution, *4*, 551

family tree, *4*, 552

habitats, *4*, 558–9,
16, 2381

life cycle, *4*, 565

survival, *4*, 572

wolves, as prey of,
16, 2408

moray eels

habitats, *5*, 639

morrillos

capybaras and,
3, 384–5

mortlock flying foxes

survival, *2*, 155

mouflons

food and feeding, *6*, 848

survival, *6*, 856–7, 858

mountain anoas

described, *3*, 421

survival, *3*, 441

mountain beavers

burrowing, *3*, 331

description, *3*, 318

habitats, *3*, 325–6

life cycle, *3*, 335

lodge-building, *3*, 331

Point Arena mountain
beavers, *3*, 338

Point Reyes mountain
beavers, *3*, 338

skull, *3*, 321

territory, *3*, 329

mountain brush-tailed
possums

artificial nest boxes,
12, 1743

survival, *12*, 1742

mountain cats

profile, *12*, 1773

mountain cavies

habitats, *6*, 896

social structure, *6*, 900

mountain coatis

habitats, *12*, 1833

profile, *12*, 1825

survival, *12*, 1846

mountain goats

behavior, *6*, 842

conservation measures,
6, 859

food and feeding, *6*, 848

habitats, *6*, 844–5

social structure, *6*, 853

mountain gorillas

family tree, *6*, 865

habitats, *6*, 870–1

physical description, *6*, 867

survival, *6*, 882–3

mountain nyalas

habitats, *8*, 1080

mountain pygmy possums

food and feeding, *12*, 1733

reproduction, *12*, 1736

social structure, *12*, 1734

survival, *12*, 1741–3

mountain tapirs

food and feeding,
16, 2460

habitats, *16*, 2458

mountain viscachas

food and feeding, *6*, 903

habitats, *6*, 898

survival, *6*, 906, 908

mountain voles

habitats, *15*, 2196

mountain zebras

family tree, *16*, 2450

food and feeding, *16*, 2461

habitats, *16*, 2456–7

physical description, *16*, 2452

profile, *16*, 2449–50

reproduction, *16*, 2466–7

survival, *16*, 2468–70

Mount Graham red squirrels

survival, *14*, 2132

mouse bandicoots

survival, *16*, 2444

mouse deer

see chevrotains

mouse–eared bats

flight, *2*, 212

greater mouse-eared bats
see greater mouse-
eared bats

profile, *2*, 139

mouse lemurs

behavior, *8*, 1181

family tree, *8*, 1177

food and feeding, *8*, 1186

life cycle, *8*, 1190

profile, *8*, 1175

mouselike rodents

family tree,
3, 371, *6*, 890, *7*, 917,
15, 2191

profile, *3*, 318

mouse opossums

behavior, *10*, 1518

food and feeding,
10, 1524, 1527

habitats, *10*, 1522

mouse-tailed bats

greater mouse-tailed bats
see greater mouse-
tailed bats

lesser mouse-tailed bats
see lesser mouse-tailed
bats

profile, *2*, 139, 188, 191

mule deer

antlers, *4*, 550

coyotes, prey for, *4*, 537

habitats, *4*, 558–9, *7*, 951

survival, *4*, 570, 571

mulgaras

habitats, *14*, 2144

survival, *14*, 2157

Müller, Fritz, *15*, 2292

Müller's gibbons

habitats, *6*, 792–3

physical description,
6, 785

singing, *6*, 799

multimammate rats

life cycle, *13*, 1918

multituberculates

evolution, *1*, xix

Mundurucu Indians

sloths, legends about,
14, 2079

muntjacs

behavior, *4*, 556

family tree, *4*, 553

social structure, *4*, 568

tusks, *4*, 550

muriqui

see woolly spider monkeys

musk deer

family tree, *11*, 1619

hunting of, *11*, 1611

life cycle, *4*, 566

survival, *4*, 571, 572

musk oxen

behavior, *6*, 842

family tree, *6*, 838

food and feeding, *6*, 849

grazing, *6*, 843

habitats, *6*, 846

predators, dealing with,
6, 844

size, *3*, 396

social structure, *6*, 853

survival, *6*, 858–9

musk rat kangaroos

behavior, *13*, 1856

food and feeding,
13, 1866–7

habitats, *13*, 1858–9, 1861

life cycle, *13*, 1868–9

profile, *13*, 1850

survival, *13*, 1870, 1872

territory, *13*, 1862

muskrats

food and feeding, *15*, 2201

habitats, *4*, 535, *15*, 2198
profile, *15*, 2190
survival, *15*, 2208, 2210
swimming, *15*, 2194
mustached bats
family tree, *2*, 162
hunting by, *2*, 175
life cycle, *2*, 177
mustangs
survival, *7*, 1038–9
mustelids
family tree,
11, 1567, *15*, 2217,
16, 2373
habitats, *16*, 2378
profile, *16*, 2370
trapping for fur, *15*, 2234–5
myxomatosis
rabbits, *12*, 1810, 1818–20
Mzab gundis
food and feeding, *9*, 1369
survival, *9*, 1377–8

N

naked-back bats
family tree, *2*, 162
naked mole rats
eusocial behavior,
9, 1362, 1370–2
family tree, *9*, 1359
food and feeding, *9*, 1368
habitats, *9*, 1364–6
physical description,
9, 1360–1
profile, *9*, 1356–7
reproduction, *9*, 1375
temperature, effect on,
9, 1373
Namib golden moles
burrowing, *10*, 1388
food and feeding,
10, 1398
habitats, *10*, 1390
Nancite coatis
survival, *12*, 1847
narrow-striped mongooses
life cycle, *9*, 1349
survival, *9*, 1352
narwhals
food and feeding,

16, 2356–7
habitats, *16*, 2352–3
migration, *16*, 2354–5
Native Americans see
Indians of North America
native cats
survival, *14*, 2157
nectar-eating fruit bats
food and feeding,
2, 145, 170–1, 219
needle-clawed galagos
captivity, *5*, 755
habitats, *5*, 742
locomotion, *5*, 744
social structure, *5*, 748
survival, *5*, 754
Newcastle virus
fruit bats, *2*, 154
New Forest ponies
food and feeding, *7*, 1031
habitats, *7*, 1026
New Guinea bandicoots
food and feeding,
16, 2436
New Guinea cuscuses
reproduction, *12*, 1736
New Guinea wallabies
family tree, *8*, 1125
New World bats
disc-winged bats, *2*, 206
family tree, *2*, 162
fear of, *2*, 178
food and feeding, *2*, 170
free-tailed bats, *2*, 203
reproduction, *2*, 203
New World bears
spectacled bears, *3*, 298
New World big cats
family tree, *12*, 1775
New World cats
family tree, *9*, 1254
physical description,
12, 1776
New World cavylike rodents
family tree, *9*, 1359
New World monkeys
evolution, *10*, 1487
family tree, *4*, 474, *5*, 735,
6, 786, 865, *10*, 1411, 1462,
1489, *11*, 1540
profile,

10, 1409, 1433, 1459
New World porcupines
behavior, *12*, 1700
defenses, *12*, 1708
habitats, *12*, 1695, 1702
profile, *12*, 1694
survival, *12*, 1716
New World rats and mice,
13, 1874–99
behavior, *13*, 1882–93
conservation measures,
13, 1896–7
evolution,
13, 1876–8, 1894
family tree,
13, 1878–9, 1905
food and feeding,
13, 1888–9
habitats, *13*, 1884–7
life cycle, *13*, 1892–3
mating, *13*, 1892
nesting, *13*, 1890–1
physical description,
13, 1880–1
profile, *13*, 1875–81
rainfall, effect on, *13*, 1886
survival, *13*, 1894–8
temperature, effect on,
13, 1886
tunnels, *13*, 1885
New World small cats
behavior, *12*, 1778–9
family tree,
4, 449, *8*, 1098,
12, 1775, *15*, 2165
profile, *12*, 1774
New World wild dogs
physical description, *4*, 524
survival, *4*, 547
New Zealand fur seals
habitats, *13*, 1963
New Zealand sea lions
habitats, *13*, 1962–3
Nigerian pygmy
hippopotamuses
survival, *7*, 1013
night monkeys
behavior, *10*, 1414
family tree, *10*, 1410
food and feeding,
10, 1418–9

habitats, *10*, 1417
medical research, use in,
10, 1428
social structure, *10*, 1422–3
survival, *10*, 1428–9
Nile crocodiles
habitats, *4*, 457
nilgai
profile, *1*, 58
survival, *1*, 77
Nilgiri langurs
behavior, *10*, 1440
survival, *10*, 1454–5
Nilgiri martens
habitats, *9*, 1305
survival, *9*, 1326
Noack, Theodore, *5*, 655
North African banded weasels
habitats, *15*, 2224
North African leopards
family tree, *8*, 1203
North American beavers
evolution, *3*, 316–7
North American Indians
see Indians of
North America
North American porcupines
adaptations, *12*, 1706–7
behavior, *12*, 1700–1
defenses, *12*, 1708–9
evolution, *12*, 1694
family tree, *12*, 1696
food and feeding,
12, 1710–1
habitats, *12*, 1702–5
life cycle, *12*, 1712–3
physical description,
12, 1698–9
profile, *12*, 1693, 1695
survival, *12*, 1714–7
North American red bats,
2, 226
North American red foxes
habitats, *4*, 561
northern bettongs
habitats, *13*, 1858
survival, *13*, 1871–2
northern bottlenose whales
habitats, *16*, 2353
northern brown bandicoots
life cycle, *16*, 2439

survival, *16*, 2445

northern elephant seals
family tree, *13*, 1983
habitats, *13*, 2003
territory, *13*, 1995

northern fur seals
culling of, *13*, 1974
family tree, *13*, 1956
food and feeding, *13*, 1969
habitats, *13*, 1961
life cycle, *13*, 1970–1
physical description,
13, 1959
survival, *13*, 1974–5, 1977

Northern gliders
survival, *12*, 1741

northern hairy-nosed wombats
survival, *16*, 2442–3

northern pikas
family tree, *7*, 942
territory, *7*, 955

northern right whales
habitats, *15*, 2300–2
profile, *15*, 2293
survival, *15*, 2313

northern seals
family tree, *13*, 1982–3

northern tamanduas
classification, 29, 32
family tree, *1*, 32

Northern white rhinoceroses
survival, *13*, 1949

Norway lemmings
family tree, *15*, 2191
food and feeding, *15*, 2200
habitats,
5, 691, *15*, 2190,
2198–9, 2225
life cycle, *15*, 2204–5
migration, *15*, 2206
physical description,
15, 2193

Norwegian rats
see brown rats

numbats
conservation measures,
14, 2159
family tree, *14*, 2138–9
food and feeding,
14, 2149
survival, *14*, 2157

nutria
coypus, *3*, 369, 377, 389

nyala
behavior, *1*, 63
food and feeding, *1*, 69
habitats, *1*, 64
life cycle, *1*, 72
profile, *1*, 58

O

obi cuscuses
survival, *12*, 1741

oceanic dolphins
family tree, *5*, 631, *16*, 2346

ocelots
evolution, *9*, 1229
family tree,
4, 449, *8*, 1098, 1203,
9, 1229, *15*, 2165
habitats, *12*, 1780
hunting of, *12*, 1790
profile, *12*, 1772, 1774
survival, *12*, 1790, 1792–3
territory, *12*, 1787

odd-toed hoofed mammals
described, *1*, xx

odd-toed ungulates
family tree,
7, 995, 1021, *16*, 2450

okapis
behavior, *6*, 816–7
discovery of, *6*, 811
family tree, *6*, 813
food and feeding, *6*, 823
habitats, *6*, 809, 818–21
life cycle, *6*, 829
physical description, *6*, 810
reproduction, *6*, 826
social structure, *6*, 825
survival, *6*, 832–3

Old World bats
flight, *2*, 187
food and feeding, *2*, 170
fruit bats,
2, 133–4, 143, 188
habitats, *2*, 143
leaf-nosed bats,
2, 187, 191

Old World big cats
family tree, *12*, 1775

Old World camels
food and feeding, *3*, 355
habitats, *3*, 341
humps, *3*, 342
life cycle, *3*, 359

Old World crested porcupines
adaptations, *12*, 1706
behavior, *12*, 1700–1
defenses, *12*, 1708–9
food and feeding, *12*, 1711
habitats, *12*, 1703–4
life cycle, *12*, 1712–3
profile, *12*, 1695–6
survival, *12*, 1717

Old World monkeys
behavior, *10*, 1466–7
family tree,
4, 474, *5*, 735, *6*, 786,
862, 865, *10*, 1411, 1436,
1462–3, 1488, *11*, 1540
habitats, *10*, 1468
life cycle, *10*, 1476–7
profile,
10, 1409, 1433–5,
1459–60, 1462
social structure, *10*, 1470
survival,
10, 1452, 1456–7, 1478

Old World porcupines
behavior, *12*, 1700–1
family tree, *9*, 1358
food and feeding, *12*, 1711
habitats, *12*, 1702–4
life cycle, *12*, 1713
profile, *12*, 1694–6
survival, *12*, 1716

Old World rabbits
habitats, *12*, 1807

Old World rats and mice,
13, 1900–25
behavior, *13*, 1908–19
captive breeding, *13*, 1925
conservation measures,
13, 1922–3
diseases, *13*, 1925
evolution, *13*, 1903–4
family tree, *13*, 1904–5
food and feeding,
13, 1914–5
habitats, *13*, 1910–3
hibernation, *13*, 1916–7

life cycle, *13*, 1916–9
mating, *13*, 1918
profile, *13*, 1901–7
scientific research, use in,
13, 1924
survival, *13*, 1920–4
temperature, effect on,
13, 1912
Weil's disease, *13*, 1925

Old World small cats
family tree,
4, 448, *8*, 1098, *15*, 2165

Old World wildcats
family tree, *9*, 1228

olingos
behavior, *12*, 1830
family tree, *12*, 1827
habitats, *12*, 1833–4
life cycle, *12*, 1842–3
profile, *12*, 1824
scent marking, *12*, 1839
survival, *12*, 1846

olive colobus monkeys
habitats, *10*, 1443
life cycle, *10*, 1451
profile, *10*, 1436
survival, *10*, 1454–5

Onco mice
survival, *13*, 1924

Operation Rhino, *13*, 1950

Operation Stronghold,
13, 1948

opossums, *10*, 1510–35
behavior, *10*, 1518–31
breeding, *10*, 1530
defenses,
10, 1518–9, 1528, 1534
dormant period, *10*, 1527
evolution, *10*, 1512–4
family tree,
10, 1514–5, *16*, 2424
food and feeding, *10*, 1524–7
habitats, *10*, 1520–3
hunting of, *10*, 1534
life cycle, *10*, 1530–1
physical description,
10, 1516–7
"playing possum,"
10, 1519, 1528, 1534
profile, *10*, 1511–7
rainfall, effect on, *10*, 1522

rain forests, *10*, 1535
survival, *8*, 1166, *10*, 1532–4
temperature, effect on,
    10, 1522
territory, *10*, 1528–9
orange-bellied bandicoots
    habitats, *16*, 2430
orange leaf-nosed bats
    survival, *2*, 207
orangutans, *11*, 1536–61
    aggressiveness,
        11, 1547, 1555
    behavior, *11*, 1544–55
    calls, *11*, 1550–1
    captivity, *11*, 1556
    conservation measures,
        11, 1558
    diseases, *11*, 1554
    evolution, *11*, 1538–40
    family tree,
        4, 475, *6*, 864, *11*, 1540–1
    food and feeding,
        11, 1544, 1552–3
    habitats, *11*, 1546–9
    life cycle, *11*, 1554–5
    nest building, *11*, 1550
    pet trade, *11*, 1558–9
    physical description,
        11, 1542–3
    profile, *11*, 1537–43
    rainfall, effect on, *11*, 1548
    sign language, *11*, 1545
    social structure, *11*, 1550–1
    survival, *11*, 1556–60
    temperature, effect on,
        11, 1548
    zoos,
        11, 1538, 1553–4, 1558
oribi
    behavior, *6*, 765
    defenses, *6*, 768
    habitats, *6*, 767
    survival, *6*, 779
    territory, *6*, 774
oryxes
    family tree, *1*, 59
    food and feeding, *1*, 69
    habitats, *1*, 57, 66
    life cycle, *1*, 73
    spotted hyenas, prey of,
        7, 1059

ostriches
    habitats, *1*, 93, *4*, 456
otter cats
    see jaguarundi
otter civets
    habitats, *4*, 508
    survival, *4*, 519, 521
otters, *11*, 1562–87
    behavior, *11*, 1570–81
    calls, *11*, 1571
    conservation measures,
        11, 1584–5
    evolution, *11*, 1564
    family tree,
        9, 1306, *11*, 1566–7,
        15, 2216, *16*, 2372
    food and feeding,
        11, 1578–9
    grooming, *11*, 1576
    habitats,
        9, 1263, *11*, 1572–5
    hunting of, *11*, 1582
    life cycle, *11*, 1580–1
    oil pollution, effect on,
        11, 1584–5, 1587
    pesticides, effect on,
        11, 1583–5
    physical description,
        11, 1568–9
    playfulness of,
        11, 1570
    profile, *11*, 1563–9
    spraints, *11*, 1577
    survival, *11*, 1582–6
    territory, *11*, 1576–7
    trapping of, *11*, 1586
    webbed feet, *11*, 1564
Out of Africa (Blixen),
    5, 620
owl-faced monkeys
    survival, *10*, 1480
Owston's palm civets
    survival, *4*, 519–21
oxen
    banteng
        see banteng
    described, *3*, 421–2
    family tree, *3*, 423
    gaurs
        see gaurs
    survival, *3*, 438–9

P

pacaranas
    habitats, *6*, 898
    profile, *6*, 890
    survival, *6*, 906, 909
pacas
    behavior, *6*, 888
    habitats, *6*, 897
    survival, *6*, 909–10
Pacific white-sided dolphins
    habitats, *15*, 2274
pack hunting
    see specific animal
pack-ice seals
    territory, *13*, 1994
pack mongooses
    behavior, *9*, 1336
    habitats, *9*, 1339
    social structure,
        9, 1344–5
pack rats
    behavior, *13*, 1882
    habitats, *13*, 1885
    nesting, *13*, 1890–1
    profile, *13*, 1875
pademelon wallabies
    family tree, *8*, 1125
Palau flying foxes
    survival, *2*, 155
Palawan stink badgers
    habitats, *1*, 116, 118
    profile, *1*, 110
pale-coated beach mice
    survival, *13*, 1896
pale foxes
    profile, *5*, 708
    survival, *5*, 728
pale-throated sloths
    family tree, *14*, 2061
    habitats, *14*, 2066
    physical description,
        14, 2063
Pallas's cats
    family tree,
        9, 1228, 1254
    habitats, *9*, 1260–1
    survival, *9*, 1272–4
Pallas's fishing eagles
    habitats, *4*, 509
Pallas's pikas
    habitats, *7*, 950

palm civets
    family tree, *9*, 1332
    food and feeding, *4*, 511
    habitats, *4*, 498, 507
    physical description, *4*, 503
pampas
    habitats, *6*, 898–9
pampas cats
    habitats, *12*, 1780
    profile, *12*, 1773
pampas deer
    social structure, *4*, 569
    survival, *4*, 571
pandas, *11*, 1588–1613
    see also giant pandas;
        red pandas
    behavior, *11*, 1596–1607
    captive breeding, *11*, 1610
    Chinese legend, *11*, 1591
    coat, *11*, 1590–1
    conservation measures,
        11, 1610–1
    evolution,
        11, 1591–2, 1608
    family tree, *11*, 1592–3
    food and feeding,
        11, 1600, 1602–3
    habitats, *11*, 1598–1601
    human interference,
        11, 1608
    life cycle, *11*, 1606–7
    male dominance, *11*, 1604
    profile, *11*, 1589–95
    scent marking, *11*, 1605
    survival, *11*, 1608–12
    territory, *11*, 1604–5
    translocation, *11*, 1613
    zoos, *11*, 1610
pangolins, *1*, 80–105
    see also armadillos
    ant baths, *1*, 96
    behavior, *1*, 88–99
    burrowing, *1*, 92, 99
    classification, *1*, 83, 85
    described, *1*, xx
    evolutionary history, *1*, 85
    family tree, *14*, 2061
    food and feeding,
        1, 83, 91, 94–5
    grasslands, *1*, 92
    habitats, *1*, 82, 90–3

hunting of, *1*, 101, 103–4
life cycle, *1*, 98–9
medicine and medical
  research, use in, *1*, 102–4
physical description, *1*, 86–7
profile, *1*, 33, 81–7
rainfall, effect on, *1*, 92
rain forests, *1*, 90
range of species, *1*, 84
scent marking, *1*, 96–7
social structure, *1*, 96–7
survival, *1*, 100–4
temperature, effect on,
  1, 92
termites, feeding habits,
  1, 91–2, 95
parana jaguars
  survival, *8*, 1117
parasitic nematodes, *1*, 46
Parnell's mustached bats
  hunting by, *2*, 175
  life cycle, *2*, 177
pastel minks
  survival, *9*, 1326
Patagonian hares
  behavior, *6*, 888
  family tree, *6*, 890
  food and feeding, *6*, 902
  habitats, *6*, 894, 896–7
  locomotion, *6*, 894–5
  physical description,
    6, 888–9
  social structure, *6*, 901
  survival, *6*, 910
patas monkeys
  food and feeding,
    10, 1474
  habitats, *10*, 1461, 1469
Payne, Katherine, *5*, 668
PCP
  small bats and, *2*, 207
peccaries
  behavior, *11*, 1622
  evolution, *11*, 1616–7
  family tree,
    6, 812, *7*, 994, *11*, 1618–9
  food and feeding, *11*, 1628–9
  grooming, *11*, 1630
  habitats, *11*, 1624–5
  hunting of, *11*, 1638
  profile, *7*, 992, *11*, 1615–7

smell-sharing behavior,
  11, 1630
social structure,
  11, 1630–2
Pel's fishing owls
  habitats, *1*, 93, *4*, 457
pencil-tailed tree mice
  habitats, *13*, 1912
Pennant's red colobus
  monkeys
    social structure,
      10, 1446
    territory, *10*, 1448
Perdido Key beach mice
  survival, *13*, 1897
Père David's deer
  antlers, *4*, 551
  habitats, *4*, 558
  survival, *4*, 573
Persson, Vanessa, *10*, 1509
Peruvian huemuls
  survival, *4*, 571, 573
pesticides
  small bats and,
    2, 204–5, 207
  vampire bats and,
    2, 180–1
Peter's arboreal forest rats
  habitats, *13*, 1911–2
Peter's duikers
  habitats, *6*, 766
Peter's ghost-faced bats
  family tree, *2*, 162
Peter's squirrels
  survival, *14*, 2132
Peter's striped mice
  habitats, *13*, 1912
pets
  binturongs as, *4*, 520
  chimpanzees as, *4*, 493
  genets as, *4*, 520
  sun bears as, *3*, 308
phascogales
  life cycle, *14*, 2152–3
Phayre's langurs
  behavior, *10*, 1441
pichi ciego
  survival, *1*, 103
pied bare-faced tamarins
  survival, *10*, 1507
pied colobus monkeys

habitats, *10*, 1443
life cycle, *10*, 1450
pied tamarins
  survival, *10*, 1506
pigs, *11*, 1614–39
  behavior, *11*, 1622–35
  evolution, *11*, 1616–7
  family tree,
    6, 760, 812, *7*, 995,
    11, 1618
  food and feeding, *11*, 1628–9
  habitats, *11*, 1624–7
  life cycle, *11*, 1634–5
  profile, *7*, 992, *11*, 1615–21
  rainfall, effect on, *11*, 1626
  social structure, *11*, 1630–3
  survival, *11*, 1636–8
  temperature, effect on,
    11, 1626
  truffles, hunting for,
    11, 1628
  vampire bats, as prey of,
    2, 172
pig-tailed macaques
  physical description,
    10, 1465
pig-tailed snub-nosed leaf
  monkeys
    survival, *10*, 1454
pig-tailed snub-nosed
  monkeys
    social structure, *10*, 1446
    survival, *10*, 1455
pikas
  behavior, *7*, 946–7
  breeding, *7*, 957
  calls, *7*, 955
  courtship, *7*, 956
  described, *1*, xxi
  double digestion system,
    7, 952
  family tree,
    7, 942–3, *12*, 1801
  food and feeding, *7*, 952–3
  habitats, *7*, 941, 949, 1029
  life cycle, *7*, 959
  profile, *12*, 1798
  scent marking, *7*, 955–6
  survival, *7*, 960, 962
  territory, *7*, 954–5
Pilbara ningauis

hunting by, *14*, 2150
pileated gibbons
  habitats, *6*, 793
  physical description, *6*, 786
  singing, *6*, 799
  survival, *6*, 802, 805
pilot whales
  behavior, *15*, 2272–3
  habitats, *15*, 2274
  physical description,
    15, 2270–1
  reproduction, *15*, 2284
  social structure, *15*, 2279
  survival, *15*, 2286–8
pine martens
  family tree, *9*, 1307
  habitats, *9*, 1263, 1313–4,
    1319, 1327
  hunting by, *9*, 1316–7
  life cycle, *9*, 1323
  physical description,
    9, 1308–9
  profile, *9*, 1305
  scent marking, *9*, 1321
  survival, *9*, 1326
  trapping for fur, *9*, 1326
  weasels, compared, *9*, 1303
pine voles
  profile, *15*, 2190
Pinzón, Vincente, *10*, 1511
pipistrelle bats
  flight, *2*, 217
  food and feeding, *2*, 225
  habitats, *2*, 219
  hibernation, *2*, 226
  profile, *2*, 213, 215–6
  reproduction, *2*, 229
placentals
  described, *1*, xvii
  evolution, *1*, xix
plague rats
  see long–haired rats
Plains Indians
  bison and, *3*, 414–6
plains viscachas
  behavior, *6*, 895
  habitats, *6*, 897
  social structure,
    6, 901
  survival, *6*, 908
plains zebras

behavior, *16*, 2455

defenses, *16*, 2462–3

family tree, *16*, 2450

food and feeding, *16*, 2461

habitats, *7*, 1054, *16*, 2456–7

physical description,
    16, 2452–3

profile, *16*, 2448–9

reproduction, *16*, 2466–7

social structure, *16*, 2464–5

survival, *16*, 2468–9, 2471

platypuses, *11*, 1640–65

behavior, *11*, 1648–61

family tree, *11*, 1645

food and feeding,
    11, 1654–5

habitats, *11*, 1650–3

hunting of, *11*, 1664

life cycle, *11*, 1660–1

physical description,
    11, 1646–7

profile, *11*, 1641–7

protective measures,
    11, 1665

reproduction, *11*, 1658–9

survival, *11*, 1662–4

temperature, effect on,
    11, 1649–50

platyrrhine (flat–nosed)
    monkeys
        habitats, *10*, 1495
        survival, *10*, 1506

pocket gophers

burrowing, *14*, 2099

family tree,
    14, 2087, 2113

food and feeding, *14*, 2101

profile, *14*, 2083–4

social structure, *14*, 2098

tunnels, *14*, 2090–1

pocket mice

family tree, *14*, 2087, 2112

profile, *14*, 2083–5

social structure, *14*, 2099

Point Arena mountain beavers

survival, *3*, 338

Point Reyes mountain beavers

survival, *3*, 338

polar bears, *11*, 1666–91

aggressiveness of, *11*, 1683

behavior, *11*, 1674–85

conservation measures,
    11, 1688–9

curiosity, *11*, 1675

evolution, *11*, 1669–71

family tree,
    2, 241, 267, *3*, 293,
        11, 1592, 1670–1

global warming, effect on,
    11, 1688–9

habitats, *2*, 272–3, *5*, 690,
    11, 1676–9

hunting by,
    11, 1669, 1680–3

hunting of, *11*, 1686–8

life cycle, *11*, 1684–5

physical description,
    11,1672–3

pollutants and, *11*, 1691

profile, *11*, 1667–73

satellite tracking, *11*, 1690

smell, sense of, *11*, 1683

survival,
    2, 258, *11*, 1686–90

temperature, effect on,
    11, 1667, 1669, 1677–8

polar seals

behavior, *13*, 1987

polecats, *15*, 2212–37

behavior, *15*, 2220–31

evolution, *15*, 2214

family tree,
    9, 1306, *15*, 2216–7

habitats,
    9, 1327, *15*, 2222–5

hunting by, *15*, 2226–7

mating, *15*, 2231

physical description,
    15, 2219

profile, *15*, 2213–9

reproduction, *15*, 2230–1

scent marking, *15*, 2229

survival, *15*, 2232–6

territory, *15*, 2228–9

pollution, effect of
    see specific animal

polyprotodonts

family tree,
    8, 1124, *12*, 1722

pond bats

survival, *2*, 207, 233

ponies

horses, distinguished,
    7, 1026

porcupines, *12*, 1692–1717

adaptations, *12*, 1706–7

behavior, *12*, 1700–13

convergent evolution,
    12, 1696

defenses, *12*, 1708–9

evolution, *12*, 1694–5

family tree, *12*, 1696–7

fishers, as prey of,
    9, 1313, 1318–9, 1324

food and feeding,
    12, 1710–11

habitats,
    1, 41, *12*, 1702–5, *16*, 2405

life cycle, *12*, 1712–3

lions, as prey of, *9*, 1239

mating, *12*, 1712

physical description,
    12,1698–9

profile, *12*, 1693–9

quills, *12*, 1708–9, 1716

rainfall, effect on, *12*, 1704

survival, *12*, 1714–6

temperature, effect on,
    12, 1704

vocalization, *12*, 1704

porpoises

family tree,
    5, 628, 631, *15*, 2243, 2295,
        16, 2320, 2347

food and feeding, *5*, 640

habitats, *5*, 627, 636–8

survival, *5*, 646–7, 650

Portuguese man-of-war

habitats, *5*, 639

possums, *12*, 1718–43

artificial nest boxes,
    12, 1743

behavior, *12*, 1726–37

conservation measures,
    12, 1740–1

evolution, *12*, 1719–21

family tree, *12*, 1722–3

food and feeding,
    12, 1730–3

gliding, *12*, 1721–2

habitats, *12*, 1728–9

hunting of, *12*, 1742

logging, as threat to,

12, 1740–1, 1743

profile, *12*, 1719–25

reproduction, *12*, 1736–7

scent marking, *12*, 1735

social structure, *12*, 1734–5

survival, *12*, 1738–42

potoroos

behavior, *13*, 1856–7

food and feeding, *13*, 1866–7

habitats, *13*, 1858–60

pottos

behavior, *5*, 738–9

captivity, *5*, 755

cryptic locomotion, *5*, 739

family tree, *5*, 735

food and feeding, *5*, 747

habitats, *5*, 740, 742

locomotion, *5*, 744–5

physical description,
    5, 732–3

social structure, *5*, 748

survival, *5*, 752, 754

Pougsargues' mongoose

survival, *9*, 1352

prairie bison
    see American bison

prairie dogs

behavior, *14*, 2090–1

family tree, *14*, 2087

food and feeding, *14*, 2101

habitats,
    14, 2092, *15*, 2223, 2236

life cycle, *14*, 2102–3

physical description,
    14, 2088–9

profile, *14*, 2083, 2086

social structure, *14*, 2096–8

survival, *14*, 2104, 2106

prairie voles

behavior, *15*, 2194

habitats, *15*, 2196

life cycle, *15*, 2205

praying mantises

habitats, *1*, 41

prehensile-tailed porcupines

adaptations, *12*, 1706–7

behavior, *12*, 1701

defenses, *12*, 1709

food and feeding, *12*, 1711

life cycle, *12*, 1713

Preservation of Grayne Act,

7, 986
Price, John, *8*, 1148
primates
    defined, *4*, 473
    described, *1*, xxi
    family tree, *5*, 734, *6*, 787, 865, *11*, 1541
primitive ungulates
    family tree, *7*, 995
proboscis bats
    roosting, *2*, 195
proboscis monkeys
    captive breeding, *10*, 1457
    family tree, *10*, 1437
    food and feeding, *10*, 1445
    physical description, *10*, 1438
    profile, *10*, 1434, 1436
    social structure, *10*, 1446
    survival, *10*, 1454–5
procolobus monkeys
    habitats, *10*, 1442
    physical description, *10*, 1438
    profile, *10*, 1433, 1436
proconsuls
    evolution, *1*, xix
pronghorns, *12*, 1744–69
    behavior, *12*, 1752–63
    conservation measures, *12*, 1766–8
    coyotes, prey for, *4*, 537
    evolution, *12*, 1754–6
    family tree, *4*, 553, *12*, 1748–9
    food and feeding, *12*, 1760–1
    habitats, *12*, 1754–7
    hunting of, *12*, 1764, 1767–8
    life cycle, *12*, 1762–3
    physical description, *12*, 1750–1
    profile, *12*, 1745–51
    rainfall, effect on, *12*, 1756
    scent marking, *12*, 1759
    sheep, compared to, *12*, 1755
    survival, *12*, 1764–8
    temperature, effect on,

12, 1756
    territory, *12*, 1758–9
    zoos, *12*, 1769
prosimians
    family tree, *4*, 475, *6*, 787, 865, *11*, 1541
prosperine rock wallabies
    survival, *8*, 1145
Przewalski, Colonel, *7*, 1036
Przewalski's horses
    discovery of, *7*, 1036
    family tree, *7*, 1020
    food and feeding, *7*, 1031
    habitats, *7*, 1018–20, 1026, 1028–9
    life cycle, *7*, 1034–5
    physical description, *7*, 1022–3
    social structure, *7*, 1033
    survival, *7*, 1036–7, 1039, 1041
    zoos, *7*, 1041
Puerto Rican flower bats
    survival, *2*, 181
pumas, *12*, 1770–95
    behavior, *12*, 1778–89
    conservation measures, *12*, 1792–3
    danger, as, *12*, 1790
    evolution, *12*, 1772
    family tree, *4*, 449, *8*, 1098, 1203, *9*, 1228, *12*, 1774–5
    habitats, *6*, 899, *8*, 1106, *12*, 1705, 1780–3
    hunting by, *12*, 1779, 1784–5
    hunting of, *12*, 1790, 1792
    life cycle, *12*, 1788–9
    pets, as, *12*, 1794
    physical description, *12*, 1776–7
    profile, *8*, 1201, *12*, 1771–7
    rainfall, effect on, *12*, 1782
    survival, *12*, 1790–4
    temperature, effect on, *12*, 1782
    territory, *12*, 1786–7

vocalizations, *12*, 1779
puna mice
    profile, *13*, 1878
punctuated grass mice
    habitats, *13*, 1912
Punjab voles
    behavior, *15*, 2194
    habitats, *15*, 2196
purple-faced monkeys
    territory, *10*, 1448
Pygathrix monkeys
    habitats, *10*, 1442–3
pygmy antelopes
    food and feeding, *6*, 771
    territory, *6*, 774
pygmy chimpanzees
    described, *4*, 472
    family tree, *4*, 475
    habitats, *4*, 480–1
    life cycle, *4*, 489
    social structure, *4*, 485
pygmy dormice
    physical description, *7*, 914
pygmy elephants
    physical description, *5*, 655
pygmy field mice
    habitats, *13*, 1910
pygmy flying squirrels
    profile, *14*, 2112
pygmy hippopotamuses
    behavior, *7*, 998–9
    family tree, *7*, 994
    food and feeding, *7*, 1007
    habitats, *7*, 1000–2
    life cycle, *7*, 1009
    physical description, *7*, 996–7
    profile, *7*, 992
    size of, *7*, 993
    skin, *7*, 993–4
    survival, *7*, 1012–3, 1015
    zoos, *7*, 1015
pygmy hogs
    anatomy, *11*, 1620
    social structure, *11*, 1630
    survival, *11*, 1636–8
pygmy killer whales
    family tree, *15*, 2269
    habitats, *15*, 2274, 2276

hunting by, *15*, 2283
    physical description, *15*, 2270–1
    profile, *15*, 2266
    social structure, *15*, 2279
    survival, *15*, 2287
pygmy marmosets
    behavior, *10*, 1492
    family tree, *10*, 1489
    food and feeding, *10*, 1499
    habitats, *10*, 1495
    profile, *10*, 1486
pygmy mice
    family tree, *13*, 1878
    life cycle, *13*, 1892–3
pygmy opossums
    family tree, *8*, 1124, 1151, *12*, 1723
    food and feeding, *12*, 1732–3
    habitats, *12*, 1729
    profile, *12*, 1722
    reproduction, *12*, 1736
    survival, *12*, 1740
pygmy rabbits
    habitats, *12*, 1807
pygmy right whales
    behavior, *15*, 2299
    family tree, *15*, 2294
    food and feeding, *15*, 2305
    habitats, *15*, 2302
    physical description, *15*, 2297
    profile, *15*, 2294
    reproduction, *15*, 2309
    survival, *15*, 2310, 2313, 2315
pygmy shrews
    behavior, *14*, 2038
    family tree, *14*, 2035
    food and feeding, *14*, 2044
    habitats, *14*, 2041
pygmy slow lorises
    habitats, *5*, 741
    survival, *5*, 754
pygmy sperm whales
    food and feeding, *16*, 2356–7

habitats, *16*, 2352
life cycle, *16*, 2361
profile, *16*, 2344
survival, *16*, 2365, 2367
pygmy spotted skunks
habitats, *16*, 2378
Pyrenean desmans
food and feeding,
10, 1398
habitats, *10*, 1391–2
life cycle, *10*, 1401
profile, *10*, 1383
ranges of, *10*, 1405
survival, *10*, 1404
pythons
habitats, *4*, 457

Q

quaggas
profile, *16*, 2450
survival, *16*, 2468
quokkas
family tree, *8*, 1125
quolls
family tree, *14*, 2139
habitats, *11*, 1653
life cycle, *14*, 2153
survival, *14*, 2156

R

rabbit-eared bilbies
survival, *16*, 2440
rabbits, *12*, 1796–1821
behavior, *12*, 1804–17
described, *1*, xxi
dingoes, hunted by,
4, 588, 599
diseases,
12, 1808, 1810, 1818–20
double digestion system,
7, 952
evolution, *12*, 1799–1800
family tree,
7, 942, *12*, 1800–1
food and feeding,
12, 1810–1
habitats, *4*, 586, 599,
7, 949, 977, *12*, 1806–9
hares, differences from,

7, 941
life cycle,
7, 958, *12*, 1814–7
mating, *12*, 1814
myxomatosis,
12, 1808, 1810, 1818–20
physical description,
12, 1802–3
platypuses, threat to,
11, 1664
population, *15*, 2237
profile, *12*, 1797–1803
scent marking, *12*, 1813
scientific research, use in,
7, 962
stoats, as prey of,
15, 2227, 2232
survival,
8, 1142, *12*, 1818–20
territory, *12*, 1812–3
vulpine foxes, prey of,
5, 718
rabies
African wildcats, *14*, 2028
African wild dogs,
5, 621, 623, 625
coyotes, *4*, 542
leaf-nosed bats, *2*, 180–1
leopards, *8*, 1217
lupine foxes, *5*, 703
mongooses, *14*, 2053
raccoon dogs, *4*, 598
red foxes, *5*, 728
skunks, *16*, 2390, 2392
Small Indian mongooses,
9, 1353
vulpine foxes,
5, 726, 728
raccoon dogs
diseases, *4*, 598
facial markings, *4*, 576
family tree, *4*, 579
fur, breeding for,
4, 597–8
habitats, *4*, 585
hibernation, *4*, 583
hunting by, *4*, 589
life cycle, *4*, 592
physical characteristics,
4, 577, 581
rabies, *4*, 598

social structure, *4*, 591
survival, *4*, 594, 597–9
raccoons, *12*, 1822–47
behavior, *12*, 1830–43
evolution, *12*, 1824
family tree,
4, 500, *11*, 1593,
12, 1826–7
food and feeding, *12*, 1836–7
habitats, *4*, 561, *12*, 1832–5
hunting of, *12*, 1844–5
life cycle, *12*, 1842–3
mating, *12*, 1842–3
pets, as, *12*, 1846
physical description,
12, 1828–9
profile, *12*, 1823–9
pumas, as prey of, *12*, 1785
red pandas, similarity to,
11, 1590–1
social structure, *12*, 1838–9
survival, *12*, 1844–6
swimming, *12*, 1831
urban dwellers, as,
12, 1840–1
vocalizations, *12*, 1831
radiotelemetry
Eurasian lynx, *9*, 1275
radio tracking
African wild dogs, *5*, 625
European moles, *10*, 1394
Raffray's sheath-tailed bats
survival, *2*, 207
rainfall, effect of
see specific animal
rain forests
anteaters, habitats,
1, 40, 50
chimpanzees, habitats,
4, 480
civets, habitats, *4*, 498
destruction of, *1*, 50–1
galagos, *5*, 742–3, 755
gibbons, *6*, 792–3, 803–5
jaguars, *8*, 1107
koalas, *8*, 1168–9
lemurs, *8*, 1184, 1194
leopards, *8*, 1209, 1220
marmosets, *10*, 1495–7
meerkats, *9*, 1350–1
opossums, *10*, 1535

pangolins, habitats, *1*, 90
rodents, *6*, 903
timber,
exploitation for, *1*, 27
ratels
food and feeding, *1*, 121
habitats, *1*, 117
profile, *1*, 108
rat kangaroos, *13*, 1848–73
behavior, *13*, 1856–69
defenses, *13*, 1857
evolution, *13*, 1849–52
family tree,
8, 1124, *13*, 1852–3
food and feeding, *13*,
1864–7
habitats, *13*, 1858–61
life cycle, *13*, 1868–9
mating, *13*, 1868–9
physical description,
13,1854–5
profile, *13*, 1849–55
rainfall, effect on, *13*, 1860
rain forests, *13*, 1860–1
survival, *13*, 1870–2
temperature, effect on,
13, 1860
territory, *13*, 1862–3
ratlike hamsters
burrowing, *7*, 923
survival, *7*, 932
rats
see also New World rats
and mice; Old World rats
and mice
family tree,
7, 916, *13*, 1878–9, 1905
rat-sized mulgaras
habitats, *14*, 2146
hunting by, *14*, 2151
rat-tailed trioks
survival, *12*, 1741
razorbacks
profile, *11*, 1616
red-backed voles
profile, *15*, 2190
red-bellied lemurs
behavior, *8*, 1180
habitats, *8*, 1182
red-chested tamarins
profile, *10*, 1488

red colobus monkeys
  behavior, *10*, 1440
  habitats, *6*, 873, *10*, 1443
  profile, *10*, 1436
  social structure, *10*, 1447
red deer
  antlers, *4*, 550
  behavior, *4*, 556–7
  family tree, *4*, 553
  fighting, *4*, 565–6
  habitats,
    1, 119, *4*, 558–9, 561,
    9, 1263, 1315,
    11, 1626
  life cycle, *4*, 565
  physical description,
    4, 554–5
  roaring, *4*, 566
reddish spiny bandicoots
  habitats, *16*, 2430
red foxes
  behavior, *5*, 712–3
  family tree, *5*, 709
  food and feeding, *5*, 712
  habitats,
    1, 119, *5*, 690, 715–6
    7, 977
  hunting by, *5*, 718–9, 728
  physical description,
    5, 710–1
  profile, *5*, 681, 707, 708
  rabies, *5*, 728
  reproduction, *5*, 724–5
  social structure, *5*, 720
  survival, *5*, 726–8, *8*, 1090
  territory, *5*, 722–3
red-fronted gazelles
  food and feeding, *6*, 771
  survival, *6*, 780
red-fronted lemurs
  food and feeding, *8*, 1186
  habitats, *8*, 1184
  survival, *8*, 1197
red howler monkeys
  food and feeding,
    10, 1419
  habitats, *10*, 1417, 1496
  physical description,
    10, 1412
  social structure,
    10, 1420

survival, *10*, 1430
red jungle fowl
  habitats, *4*, 509
red kangaroos
  behavior, *8*, 1128
  family tree, *8*, 1125
  food and feeding, *8*, 1134
  habitats, *8*, 1130–1
  life cycle, *8*, 1136–9
  physical description,
    8, 1126–7
  speed, *8*, 1129–30
red-necked pademelons
  behavior, *8*, 1128
red-necked wallabies
  habitats, *8*, 1130
  life cycle, *8*, 1137
  physical description,
    8, 1122
red pandas
  behavior, *11*, 1596
  evolution, *11*, 1613
  family tree,
    11, 1593, *12*, 1826
  food and feeding,
    11, 1597, 1602–3
  habitats, *11*, 1598, 1600
  life cycle, *11*, 1607
  physical description,
    11,1594–5
  profile, *11*, 1589
  raccoons, related to,
    11, 1590–1, *12*, 1823
  survival, *11*, 1611
  zoos, *11*, 1612
red river hogs
  see bushpigs
red-ruffed lemurs
  survival, *8*, 1195
red squirrels
  family tree, *14*, 2113
  food and feeding, *14*, 2122
  habitats, *1*, 119, *14*, 2120–1
  hunting of, *14*, 2130
  life cycle, *14*, 2128–9
  physical description,
    14, 2114–5
  profile, *14*, 2112
  survival, *14*, 2130–3
red-tailed sportive lemurs
  survival, *8*, 1195

redtail guenons
  life cycle, *10*, 1476
red-tree voles
  habitats, *15*, 2197–8
red uakaris
  behavior, *10*, 1415
  family tree, *10*, 1410
red wolves
  family tree, *16*, 2399
  habitats, *4*, 525
  life cycle, *16*, 2412
  profile, *16*, 2396
  survival, *16*, 2416–8
reedbucks
  family tree, *1*, 59
  life cycle, *1*, 73
  noises of, *1*, 63
  profile, *1*, 55–56
reindeer
  habitats, *4*, 559
  social structure, *4*, 568
  species, *4*, 550
reproduction
  see specific animal
rhesus macaques
  family tree, *10*, 1462
  grooming, *10*, 1472
  habitats, *10*, 1468
  life cycle, *10*, 1477
  physical description,
    10, 1465
  research, use in,
    10, 1480–1
  survival, *10*, 1480
rhinoceroses, *13*, 1926–51
  behavior, *13*, 1934–45
  Chinese medicine,
    use of horns
    in, *13*, 1946
  conservation measures,
    13, 1948–9
  defenses, *13*, 1934
  evolution, *13*, 1928–9
  family tree,
    7, 1020,
    13,1930–1, *16*, 2451
  food and feeding,
    13, 1940–1
  habitats, *13*, 1936–9
  horns,
    13, 1927–8, 1946,

1948, 1950–1
  life cycle, *13*, 1944–5
  mating, *13*, 1944
  mud baths, *13*, 1934–5
  physical description,
    13, 1932–3
  poaching, *13*, 1946, 1948
  profile, *13*, 1927–33
  social structure,
    13, 1942–3
  spotted hyenas, prey of,
    7, 1059
  survival, *13*, 1946–50
  tigers, prey of,
    15, 2175
  vocalizations,
    13, 1943
  zoos, *13*, 1950
rice rats
  family tree, *13*, 1878
  habitats, *13*, 1885
  survival,
    13, 1895–6, 1898
Ridley's leaf-nosed bats
  survival, *2*, 207
right whales, *15*, 2290–2315
  behavior,
    15, 2298–2309
  conservation measures,
    15, 2312–3
  family tree,
    15, 2294–5, *16*, 2321
  food and feeding,
    15, 2304–5
  habitats, *15*, 2300–3
  lob-tailing, *15*, 2307
  mating, *15*, 2308
  migration, *15*, 2302
  physical description,
    15, 2296–7
  profile, *15*, 2291–7
  reproduction, *15*, 2308–9
  social structure, *15*, 2306–7
  songs, *15*, 2306–7
  sounds, *15*, 2299
  survival, *15*, 2310–4
  temperature, effect on,
    15, 2301–2
  whaling, *15*, 2312–3
Rijksen, Herman,
    11, 1560

rinderpest
African buffalo, *3*, 442
African wild dogs, *5*, 622
gazelles, *6*, 780
giraffes, *6*, 831
sheep, *3*, 442
ringed seals
behavior, *13*, 1987
habitats, *13*, 1988
polar bears, prey of,
11, 1680
ring-tailed coatis
habitats, *12*, 1833
profile, *12*, 1825
ring-tailed cuscuses
habitats, *12*, 1729
ring-tailed lemurs
behavior, *8*, 1180–1
family tree, *8*, 1176
food and feeding,
8, 1186–7
habitats, *8*, 1182–3
life cycle, *8*, 1191
physical description,
8, 1179
profile, *8*, 1175
scent marking, *8*, 1189
social structure,
8, 1188–9
survival, *8*, 1195
ring-tailed mongooses
habitats, *9*, 1338
life cycle, *9*, 1349
survival, *8*, 1195
ring-tailed possums
family tree, *12*, 1722
food and feeding,
12, 1730
habitats, *12*, 1729
social structure,
12, 1734
ringtail opossums
family tree, *8*, 1124
ringtails
climbing, *12*, 1830
family tree, *12*, 1826
food and feeding,
12, 1836
habitats, *12*, 1833
life cycle, *12*, 1842
profile, *12*, 1824–6

social structure,
12, 1839
Rio Grande beavers
survival, *3*, 338
Risso's dolphins
habitats, *15*, 2276
river dolphins
eyesight, *5*, 629
family tree,
5, 630, *16*, 2346
social structure,
5, 642
survival, *5*, 651
river otters
food and feeding,
11, 1579
habitats,
6, 898, *11*, 1573
physical description,
11, 1568–9
profile, *11*, 1564
roan antelopes
habitats, *1*, 66
profile, *1*, 57
survival, *1*, 78
rock cavies
habitats, *6*, 896
vocalization, *6*, 900
rock hyraxes
activeness, *1*, 10
climate changes and, *1*, 26
communication, *1*, 10
family tree, *1*, 7
food and feeding, *1*, 18
habitats, *1*, 13–4
kopjes, *1*, 14
reproduction, *1*, 22–3
rock mice
habitats, *13*, 1910
rock ring-tailed possums
habitats, *12*, 1729
survival, *12*, 1740
rock squirrels
habitats, *14*, 2093
social structure,
14, 2099
survival, *14*, 2104
rock wallabies
habitats, *8*, 1132
rodents
see also beavers; capybaras

cavylike rodents, *3*, 371
described, *1*, xxi
evolution, *14*, 2093
family tree, *3*, 319, 371,
6, 891, *7*, 917, *14*, 2086,
15, 2191
mouselike rodents, *3*, 371
squirrellike rodents
see squirrellike rodents
squirrels
see squirrels
Rodrigues flying foxes
captivity, *2*, 157
conservation measures,
2, 154
roe deer
behavior, *4*, 556–7
food and feeding, *4*, 562–3
habitats, *4*, 559–60
life cycle, *4*, 565
social structure, *4*, 569
roll-tailed lemurs
habitats, *8*, 1185
Roosevelt, Franklin D.,
10, 1534
rorquals, *16*, 2316–41
behavior, *16*, 2324–35
blow, *16*, 2324–5
blubber, *16*, 2340
body temperature,
16, 2319
conservation measures,
16, 2338–9
evolution, *16*, 2320
family tree, *16*, 2320–1
food and feeding,
16, 2330–1
habitats, *16*, 2326–9
life cycle, *16*, 2334–5
mating, *16*, 2334
navigation by, *16*, 2326
profile, *15*, 2241, *16*, 2317–23
satellite tracking, *16*, 2341
social structure, *16*, 2332–3
survival, *16*, 2336–40
temperature, effect on,
16, 2319
whaling,
16, 2336–7, 2339
Ross seals
behavior, *13*, 1987

family tree, *13*, 1983
habitats, *13*, 1988
hunting by, *13*, 1992
rousette fruit bats
life cycle, *2*, 151
social structure, *2*, 147
rufescent bandicoots
habitats, *16*, 2430
ruffed lemurs
behavior, *8*, 1180
habitats, *8*, 1182
life cycle, *8*, 1190–1
rufous hare wallabies
behavior, *8*, 1154
survival, *8*, 1166, 1169
rufous-nosed rats
habitats, *13*, 1910
rufous rat kangaroos
behavior, *13*, 1856
classification, *13*, 1856
food and feeding,
13, 1866
habitats, *13*, 1858–9
life cycle, *13*, 1869
survival, *13*, 1872
territory, *13*, 1863
ruminants
deer, *4*, 562–3
gazelles, *6*, 759–60
giraffes, *6*, 822
goat antelopes, *6*, 848
goats, *6*, 849
okapis, *6*, 823
Rupicaprini
habitats, *6*, 844
rusa deer
habitats, *4*, 550
Russian desmans
conservation measures,
10, 1405
food and feeding,
10, 1397–9
habitats,
10, 1390, 1392
hunting of,
10, 1403–4
life cycle,
10, 1401
profile, *10*, 1383
scent marking,
10, 1401

survival, *10*, 1404

Russian flying squirrels
  habitats, *14*, 2118
  profile, *14*, 2112
  survival, *14*, 2130

Russian raccoon dogs
  habitats, *4*, 585–6

rusty-spotted cats
  behavior, *9*, 1258
  habitats, *9*, 1262
  survival, *9*, 1270, 1273

Ryukyu Island's wild pigs
  survival, *11*, 1638

S

saber-toothed tigers
  family tree, *15*, 2164

saber-tooths
  family tree, *9*, 1228

sable antelopes
  behavior, *1*, 66
  food and feeding, *1*, 69
  physical description, *1*, 61
  profile, *1*, 57
  survival, *1*, 78

sables
  habitats, *9*, 1305
  survival, *9*, 1324–5, 1327
  trapping for fur, *9*, 1326

sac-winged bats
  reproduction, *2*, 202

saddle-back tamarins
  social structure,
    10, 1501

sado moles
  survival, *10*, 1404

sagebrush voles
  behavior, *15*, 2194
  habitats, *15*, 2196

saigas
  family tree, *6*, 838
  food and feeding, *6*, 848
  habitats, *6*, 846
  physical description,
    6, 836
  social structure,
    6, 851, 853
  survival, *6*, 857–8

sailfish
  habitats, *5*, 639

sakis
  food and feeding, *10*, 1418
  social structure, *10*, 1423

salt marsh harvest mice
  survival, *13*, 1895, 1897

sand cats
  habitats, *14*, 2015–6
  hunting by, *14*, 2021
  life cycle, *14*, 2025
  profile, *14*, 2007–8
  rainfall, effect on, *14*, 2016
  survival, *14*, 2027–8
  temperature, effect on,
    14, 2016

sand foxes
  habitats, *5*, 714
  survival, *5*, 728

sandhill dunnarts
  survival, *14*, 2157

sand puppies
  see naked mole rats

Sanford's lemurs
  habitats, *8*, 1184

San Joaquin Valley wood rats
  survival, *13*, 1897

San Martin Island wood rats
  survival, *13*, 1897

satanic black colobus
  monkeys
    profile, *10*, 1436
    survival, *10*, 1455

satellite tracking
  African wild dogs, *5*, 625
  American black bears,
    2, 261
  brown bears, *2*, 287
  polar bears, *11*, 1690
  rorquals, *16*, 2341

savanna grasslands
  armadillos, *1*, 90–1

Savi's pygmy shrews
  physical description,
    14, 2036
  profile, *14*, 2033

scaly-tailed possums
  food and feeding,
    12, 1731
  habitats, *12*, 1729
  survival, *12*, 1740

scaly-tailed squirrels
  family tree, *14*, 2112

physical description,
  14, 2115
profile, *3*, 318
social structure, *14*, 2127

Scammon, Charles, *15*, 2261

scent marking
  armadillos, *1*, 97
  badgers, *1*, 122
  civets, *4*, 512–4
  coyotes, *4*, 538–9
  galagos, *5*, 748
  gazelles, *6*, 775
  genets, *4*, 512–4
  giant anteaters, *1*, 43
  giant pandas, *11*, 1604
  goats, *6*, 852
  hares, *7*, 956
  hyenas, *7*, 1056, 1060–1
  jackals, *8*, 1087
  kinkajous, *12*, 1839
  lemurs, *8*, 1179
  lions, *9*, 1233
  manatees, *9*, 1292
  marbled cats, *9*, 1266
  meerkats, *9*, 1345
  olingos, *12*, 1839
  pandas, *11*, 1605
  pikas, *7*, 955–6
  pine martens, *9*, 1321
  polecats, *15*, 2229
  possums, *12*, 1735
  pronghorns, *12*, 1759
  rabbits, *12*, 1813
  ring-tailed lemurs,
    8, 1189
  Russian desmans,
    10, 1401
  servals, *14*, 2022–3
  shrews, *14*, 2047
  small cats,
    9, 1258, 1266–7
  tamanduas, *1*, 43
  vulpine foxes, *5*, 723
  weasels, *15*, 2228–9

Schaller, George and Kay,
  5, 609, *6*, 881

scientific research
  hares and rabbits, use in,
    7, 962

scimitar oryx
  habitats, *1*, 66

profile, *1*, 57
survival, *1*, 77

Sclater's guenons
  survival, *10*, 1482

Scott, Sir. Peter, *13*, 1950

Scott's tree kangaroos
  habitats, *8*, 1157
  survival, *8*, 1169

Sea Birds and Seal Protection
  Act of 1973, *13*, 1976

sea cats
  family tree, *11*, 1566
  physical description,
    11, 1568
  profile, *11*, 1564–5
  survival, *11*, 1582

sea cows
  described, *1*, xxi
  family tree, *9*, 1280

sea lions
  behavior, *13*, 1960
  described, *1*, xxi
  family tree, *13*, 1983
  food and feeding,
    13, 1966, 1969
  habitats, *13*, 1962
  life cycle, *13*, 1971
  profile, *13*, 1955, 1980

seals **see also**
  eared seals; true seals
    blubber, *13*, 1954, 1983
    described, *1*, xxi
    family tree, *13*, 1956–7

sea minks
  family tree, *9*, 1307

sea otters
  behavior, *11*, 1571
  family tree, *11*, 1567
  food and feeding, *11*, 1579
  habitats,
    11, 1572–4, *15*, 2251
  life cycle, *11*, 1581
  physical description,
    11, 1568–9
  profile, *11*, 1564–6
  survival, *11*, 1582, 1584–5
  territory, *11*, 1577

sea sirens
  see manatees; sirenians

sechuran foxes
  survival, *5*, 702

sei whales
  family tree, *16*, 2321
  food and feeding,
    16, 2330–1
  habitats, *16*, 2329
  profile, *16*, 2317
  social structure, *16*, 2332
  survival, *16*, 2338–9
semiaquatic shrews
  physical description,
    14, 2036
semnopithecus monkeys
  habitats, *10*, 1442
Senegalese lions
  profile, *9*, 1228
Seram Island long–nosed
    mouse bandicoots
      survival,
        16, 2440, 2443
Serengeti, *1*, 74
Serengeti kopjes, *1*, 14–5
serows
  food and feeding,
    6, 848, 849
  habitats,
    6, 837, 844, *11*, 1601
  social structure, *6*, 851
servaline genets
  habitats, *4*, 506
  survival, *4*, 519
servals, *14*, 2004–29
  behavior, *14*, 2012–25
  captivity, *14*, 2029
  evolution, *14*, 2005–6
  family tree,
    4, 449, *14*, 2008–9
  habitats, *14*, 2014–7
  hearing, *14*, 2013
  hunting by, *14*, 2018–21
  hunting of, *14*, 2026
  life cycle, *14*, 2024–5
  physical description,
    14, 2010–1
  profile, *14*, 2005–11
  scent marking,
    14, 2022–3
  survival, *14*, 2026–8
  territory, *14*, 2022–3
  zoos, *14*, 2029
sex ratio
  hyraxes, *1*, 23

Seychelles sheath-tailed bats
  survival, *2*, 207
sheath-tailed bats
  family tree, *2*, 188
  profile,
    2, 139, 163, 213
  scent, *2*, 192
  survival, *2*, 207
sheep
  captive breeding, *6*, 858
  conservation measures,
    6, 856–7
  diseases, *3*, 442, *6*, 856
  domestication,
    6, 854–5, 858
  family tree,
    1, 59, *3*, 396, 422,
      6, 761, 839
  hoof-and-mouth disease,
    6, 856
  hunting of,
    6, 857–8
  predators, dealing with,
    6, 844
  survival, *6*, 842, 854–8
Shetland ponies
  food and feeding,
    7, 1031
  habitats, *7*, 1027
  size, *7*, 1026
short-beaked echidnas
  habitats,
    8, 1159, *16*, 2432
short-faced bears
  evolution, *2*, 240
short-finned pilot whales
  family tree,
    15, 2268
  habitats,
    15, 2274, 2276
  physical description,
    15, 2271
  profile, *15*, 2267
  reproduction, *15*, 2285
  social structure,
    15, 2279
  survival, *15*, 2287
short-nosed bandicoots
  habitats, *16*, 2430–1
short-nosed echidnas
  behavior, *11*, 1648

family tree, *11*, 1645
  food and feeding,
    11, 1656–7
  habitats,
    11, 1650–1, 1652
  profile, *11*, 1643–4
  survival, *11*, 1662–3
short-tailed bats
  habitats, *2*, 168
  survival, *2*, 181
short-tailed chinchillas
  survival, *6*, 907, 909
short-tailed fruit bats
  family tree, *2*, 162
  flight, *2*, 160
short-tailed opossums
  food and feeding,
    10, 1525
  territory, *10*, 1528–9
short-tailed shrews
  habitats, *13*, 1885
short-tailed spear-nosed bats
  foraging, *2*, 166
short-tailed weasels
  see stoats
shrew hedgehogs
  habitats, *7*, 975
shrew-moles
  food and feeding,
    10, 1399
  habitats, *10*, 1390
shrew opossums
  habitats,
    10, 1520, 1522
  territory, *10*, 1529
shrews, *14*, 2030–55
  behavior,
    14, 2038–49
  cold starvation,
    14, 2054
  conservation measures,
    14, 2052–3
  evolution,
    14, 2032, 2035
  food and feeding,
    14, 2044–5
  habitats, *14*, 2040–3
  life cycle, *14*, 2048–9
  nesting, *14*, 2046
  physical description,
    14, 2036–7

profile, *14*, 2031–7
  rainfall, effect on,
    14, 2042
  scent marking,
    14, 2047
  social structure,
    14, 2046–7
  survival, *14*, 2050–4
  temperature, effect on,
    14, 2041–2
  tunnels, *14*, 2046
siamang gibbons
  family tree, *6*, 786
  habitats, *6*, 792–3
  physical description,
    6, 785
  singing, *6*, 799
  social structure, *6*, 796
  survival, *6*, 804, 806
siamangs
  habitats, *16*, 2459
Sibbald's rorquals
  profile, *16*, 2317
Siberian chipmunks
  food and feeding,
    14, 2100
  survival, *14*, 2106
Siberian lemmings
  habitats, *15*, 2197
Siberian tigers
  habitats, *15*, 2170–1
  hunting by, *15*, 2175
  life cycle, *15*, 2178–9
  physical description,
    15, 2166–7
  profile, *15*, 2163–4
  survival,
    15, 2181, 2183
side-striped jackals
  evolution, *8*, 1071
  family tree, *8*, 1073
  habitats, *8*, 1070, 1078–9
  hunting by, *8*, 1082–3
  physical description,
    8, 1070, 1074–5
sifakas
  evolution, *8*, 1175
  family tree, *5*, 734
  habitats, *8*, 1183
  social structure,
    8, 1188–9

sika deer
    survival, *4*, 572–3
silky anteaters
    behavior, *1*, 36–7
    enemies of, *1*, 40
    family tree, *1*, 33
    food and feeding, *1*, 44
    habitats, *1*, 38, 40
    physical description,
        1, 34–5
    profile, *1*, 29–30
    reproduction, *1*, 46–7
    survival, *1*, 51
    territory, *1*, 43
silky two-toed anteaters
    habitats, *1*, 38
silver-backed jackals
    see side-striped jackals
silverbacks
    life cycle, *6*, 879
    social structure, *6*, 876
    survival, *6*, 883
silvered leaf monkeys
    survival, *10*, 1454
silver-haired bats
    migration, *2*, 226
silver rice rats
    survival,
        13, 1897, 1898
silvery-brown bare-faced
tamarins
    survival, *10*, 1507
silvery gibbons
    see moloch gibbons
silvery marmosets
    profile, *10*, 1487
silvery mole rats
    behavior, *9*, 1363
    food and feeding,
        9, 1368
    habitats, *9*, 1364
    reproduction,
        9, 1374
Simien jackals
    behavior, *8*, 1071
    evolution, *8*, 1072
    family tree, *8*, 1072
    habitats,
        8, 1078–81, 1093,
        9, 1366–7
    hunting by, *8*, 1082–3

life cycle, *8*, 1088
    physical description,
        8, 1070, 1075
    social structure, *8*, 1086
    survival, *8*, 1090–1
Sinai leopards
    family tree, *8*, 1203
    habitats, *8*, 1209
    survival, *8*, 1221
Siona Indians
    Amazonian manatees,
        hunting of, *9*, 1300
Sioux Indians
    bison and, *3*, 414
sirenians
    evolution, *9*, 1280
    family tree, *9*, 1280–1
    food and feeding,
        9, 1290
    hunting of, *9*, 1300
    life cycle, *9*, 1294
    profile, *9*, 1278–80
sitatungas
    habitats, *1*, 65
    life cycle, *1*, 72
    social structure, *1*, 70
skunks
    defenses, *16*, 2384–5
    diseases, *16*, 2390
    family tree, *9*, 1307,
        11, 1566, *15*, 2216
    food and feeding, *16*, 2383
    habitats, *4*, 560, *16*, 2378–81
    physical description,
        16, 2374
    profile, *16*, 2369–72
    rabies, *16*, 2390, 2392
    reproduction,
        16, 2388–9
    survival,
        16, 2390
sleeping sickness
    bushpigs and warthogs,
        11, 1638
slender-horned gazelles
    food and feeding, *6*, 771
    survival, *6*, 780
slender lorises
    habitats,
        5, 740, 741
    survival,

5, 752, 753
slender mongooses
    profile, *9*, 1330
Slevin's deer mice
    survival, *13*, 1898
slit-faced bats
    habitats, *2*, 195
    hunting by, *2*, 199
sloth bears
    description,
        3, 292, 294–5
    evolution, *3*, 291
    family tree, *2*, 241, 266,
        11, 1592, 1670–1
    food and feeding,
        3, 290–1, 304–5
    habitats, *3*, 290, 298–9
    life cycle, *3*, 306–7
    sociability, *3*, 297
    survival, *3*, 311–3
    termites, feeding on,
        3, 290–1, 304–5
sloths, *14*, 2056–81
    behavior, *14*, 2064–77
    body temperature,
        14, 2067
    enemies of, *14*, 2067–8
    evolution, *14*, 2060
    family tree,
        1, 85, *14*, 2060–1
    food and feeding,
        14, 2070–3
    habitats, *14*, 2066–9
    life cycle, *14*, 2076–7
    mating, *14*, 2076
    profile,
        1, 30–3, 81, *14*, 2057–63
    rainfall, effect on,
        14, 2068
    smell, sense of,
        14, 2065
    survival, *14*, 2078–80
    swimming, *14*, 2064
    temperature, effect on,
        14, 2068
    territory,
        14, 2074–5
slow lorises
    behavior, *5*, 738–9
    captivity, *5*, 755
    family tree, *5*, 735

food and feeding, *5*, 746
    habitats, *5*, 741, *16*, 2459
small bats, *2*, 160, 184–209
    agriculture and, *2*, 204–5
    behavior, *2*, 192–203
    body temperature,
        2, 192–3, 203
    caves, *2*, 194–5, 200
    climate and, *2*, 192
    conservation measures,
        2, 206
    Doppler method of location,
        2, 196
    echolocation,
        2, 193, 196–8
    evolution, *2*, 186
    family tree, *2*, 188–9
    fear of, *2*, 204
    habitats, *2*, 194–5
    hibernation,
        2, 192, 194, 200–2
    hunting by,
        2, 192–3, 196–9
    profile, *2*, 185–91
    reproduction,
        2, 202–3
    roosting, *2*, 200–1
    survival, *2*, 204–8
small bears, *3*, 288–313
    aggression, *3*, 297
    agriculture and, *3*, 311
    behavior, *3*, 296–307
    cubs, *3*, 306–7
    destruction of habitat,
        3, 308–9
    entertainers, as,
        3, 312
    evolution,
        3, 290–1
    family tree, *3*, 293
    food and feeding,
        3, 302–5
    habitats, *3*, 298–301
    hunting of,
        3, 308–11
    life cycle, *3*, 306–7
    medical research, use in,
        3, 311, 313
    profile, *3*, 289–95
    rainfall, effect of, *3*, 300
    sloth bears

see sloth bears
spectacled bears
    see spectacled bears
sun bears
    see sun bears
survival, *3*, 308–12
temperature, effect of,
    3, 300
trade in bear parts,
    3, 310–1
small cats, *9*, 1250–75
    behavior,
        9, 1258–69, *14*, 2013
    calling, *9*, 1258
    conservation measures,
        9, 1272–3
    diseases, *9*, 1274
    domestication, *9*, 1274
    evolution, *9*, 1252–4
    family tree,
        9, 1254–5, *14*, 2008–9,
        15, 2165
    habitats,
        9, 1260–3
    hunting by,
        9, 1264–5, *12*, 1785,
        14, 2018
    hunting of,
        9, 1270–2, *12*, 1795
    life cycle, *9*, 1268–9
    profile,
        9, 1251–7,
        12, 1771, *14*, 2005
    rainfall, effect on,
        9, 1262
    scent marking,
        9, 1258, 1266–7
    survival,
        9, 1270–4,
        12, 1790, *14*, 2026
    temperature, effect on,
        9, 1262
    territory,
        9, 1266–7, *12*, 1786–7
small-clawed otters
    survival, *11*, 1586
small-eared dogs
    survival, *5*, 702–3
Small Indian mongooses
    rabies, *9*, 1353
smokey woolly monkeys

survival, *10*, 1426
smooth-coated otters
    family tree, *11*, 1567
    habitats, *11*, 1574
    survival, *11*, 1585–6
snow geese
    habitats, *7*, 951
snow leopards
    behavior, *8*, 1206–7
    camouflage, *8*, 1201
    evolution, *8*, 1200
    family tree,
        8, 1099, 1203, *9*, 1229
    habitats, *8*, 1208–10
    hunting by, *8*, 1214
    hunting of, *8*, 1220
    life cycle, *8*, 1217
    physical description,
        8, 1204–5
    profile,
        8, 1199, 1200–2
    survival, *8*, 1220
snowshoe hares
    coat of, *7*, 947
    habitats, *7*, 950
    physical description,
        7, 945
    survival, *7*, 961
snow voles
    habitats, *15*, 2196
snub-nosed monkeys
    family tree,
        10, 1437
    profile, *10*, 1436
    social structure,
        10, 1447
social mongooses
    behavior, *9*, 1336
    profile, *9*, 1332
    vocalization, *9*, 1347
social structure
    see specific animal
Soemmerring's gazelles
    survival, *6*, 778, 780
solenodons
    behavior, *14*, 2038–9
    conservation measures,
        14, 2052–3
    echolocation, *14*, 2044
    family tree,
        7, 969, *14*, 2034–5

food and feeding,
    14, 2044–5
habitats,
    14, 2034, 2042
life cycle, *14*, 2049
physical description,
    14, 2036
profile, *14*, 2031–2
social structure,
    14, 2046–7
survival, *14*, 2050–5
Somali leopards
    survival, *8*, 1223
Somali wild asses
    habitats, *7*, 1018
sonar hunting
    vesper bats, *2*, 217–8
Sonoran pronghorns
    survival,
        12, 1767, 1769
sousliks
    habitats, *7*, 925
South African hedgehogs
    survival, *7*, 987
South American cats
    profile, *9*, 1253
South American climbing rats
    food and feeding,
        13, 1888
South American field mice
    habitats, *13*, 1885
    nesting, *13*, 1891
    physical description,
        13, 1881
South American foxes
    behavior, *5*, 687
    family tree,
        4, 526, 579, *5*, 604, 709
    habitats,
        5, 688, 690, 714
    profile, *5*, 681–2
    reproduction, *5*, 698
    wolves, comparison to,
        5, 686
South American monkeys
    behavior, *12*, 1726
South American sea lions
    behavior, *13*, 1960
South American
    tree porcupines
        adaptations, *12*, 1707

defenses, *12*, 1709
family tree, *12*, 1696
food and feeding,
    12, 1711
life cycle, *12*, 1713
survival, *12*, 1716, 1717
South American yapoks
    life cycle, *16*, 2438
South Arabian leopards
    family tree, *8*, 1203
    survival, *8*, 1221, 1223
South China tigers
    survival, *15*, 2183
Southeastern beach mice
    survival, *13*, 1897
Southern Asian cats
    habitats, *9*, 1261–2
southern bog lemmings
    survival, *15*, 2210
southern brown bandicoots
    survival, *16*, 2441
southern elephant seals
    behavior, *13*, 1987
    family tree, *13*, 1983
    habitats, *13*, 1988
    physical description,
        13, 1984
    survival, *13*, 1998
southern flying squirrels
    behavior, *14*, 2117
    life cycle, *14*, 2129
Southern marsh harvest mice
    survival, *13*, 1897
southern opossums
    behavior, *10*, 1519
    food and feeding,
        10, 1524–5, 1527
    profile, *10*, 1512
    territory, *10*, 1528
Southern pied colobus
    monkeys
        life cycle, *10*, 1451
Southern pocket gophers
    survival, *14*, 2106
Southern reedbucks
    habitats, *7*, 1055
southern right whales
    behavior, *15*, 2298–9
    habitats, *15*, 2300–2
    profile, *15*, 2293
    survival, *15*, 2313

southern sea lions
    habitats, *13*, 1964
    survival, *13*, 1976
southern seals
    family tree,
        13, 1982–3
southern spotted skunks
    habitats, *16*, 2378
southern tamanduas
    family tree, *1*, 32
    survival, *1*, 51
southern water shrews
    profile, *14*, 2033
Spanish lynx
    survival, *9*, 1272–3
spear-nosed bats
    flight, *2*, 160
    harems, *2*, 177
Species Survival Plans (SSPs),
    14, 2029
spectacled bears
    captivity, in, *3*, 313
    description,
        3, 292, 294–5
    evolution, *3*, 291
    family tree,
        2, 266, *11*, 1593, 1670
    food and feeding,
        3, 302–5
    habitats, *3*, 298, 300
    life cycle, *3*, 306–7
    New World bears,
        3, 298
    profile, *2*, 240
    survival,
        3, 308, 311, 313
spectacled hare wallabies
    habitats, *8*, 1156–7
spectral tarsiers
    survival, *5*, 754
Speke's gazelles
    food and feeding,
        6, 771
    survival, *6*, 778, 780
Speke's gundis
    habitats, *9*, 1366
sperm whales, *16*, 2342–67
    behavior, *16*, 2350–61
    blows, *16*, 2350–1
    blubber, *16*, 2364
    breaching, *16*, 2358–9

conservation measures,
    16, 2364–5
diving, *16*, 2358–9
evolution, *16*, 2344, 2346
family tree, *5*, 630, *15*, 2242,
    16, 2347
food and feeding, *16*, 2356–7
habitats,
    15, 2277, *16*, 2352–3
life cycle, *16*, 2360–1
male aggression, *16*, 2361
mating, *16*, 2361
migration, *16*, 2354–5
physical description,
    16, 2348–9
profile, *16*, 2343–9
social structure, *16*, 2359
survival, *16*, 2362–6
whaling, *16*, 2362–4
spider monkeys
    behavior, *10*, 1415
    habitats, *10*, 1417
    hunting of, *10*, 1426
    profile, *10*, 1408
    social structure,
        10, 1420–1
    survival,
        10, 1426, 1429
spinner dolphins
    habitats, *5*, 636
spiny anteaters
    profile, *1*, 31
spiny bandicoots
    habitats, *16*, 2430
    survival, *16*, 2444
spiny mice
    behavior, *13*, 1908
spiny rats
    profile, *13*, 1877
spiny rice rats
    physical description,
        13, 1881
spiral-horned antelopes
    family tree, *3*, 397, 423
    food and feeding, *1*, 68
    habitats, *1*, 64–5
    life cycle, *1*, 72
    profile, *1*, 58
    survival, *1*, 78–9
spitting cobras
    habitats, *1*, 67

sportive lemurs
    family tree, *8*, 1177
    food and feeding,
        8, 1186
    habitats, *8*, 1183
    life cycle, *8*, 1191
    profile, *8*, 1175
spotted cats
    profile, *12*, 1773
spotted cuscuses
    behavior, *12*, 1726
    food and feeding,
        12, 1731, 1733
    habitats,
        12, 1720, 1729
    reproduction,
        12, 1736
spotted hyenas
    family tree, *7*, 1047
    fighting, *8*, 1084–5
    habitats,
        4, 457, *6*, 821,
        7, 1044, 1052–3
    hunting by,
        7, 1050, 1058–9
    hunting of,
        7, 1067
    jackals, threat to,
        8, 1088
    life cycle,
        7, 1062–3
    pack hunting,
        9, 1236
    physical description,
        7, 1048–9
    social structure,
        7, 1056–7
    survival,
        7, 1064, 1066
    territory, *7*, 1060
spotted-necked otters
    family tree, *11*, 1567
    habitats,
        11, 1572, 1574
spotted skunks
    defenses, *16*, 2385
    family tree, *16*, 2373
    food and feeding,
        16, 2383
    habitats, *16*, 2378
    physical description,

        16, 2375
    profile, *16*, 2372
spotted-tail quolls
    hunting by,
        14, 2151
springbok
    behavior, *6*, 764
    defenses, *6*, 769
    family tree, *6*, 760–1
    food and feeding,
        6, 772–3
    physical description,
        6, 762–3
    populations, *6*, 781
    profile, *6*, 759
    survival, *6*, 778–80
springhares
    family tree,
        14, 2087, 2112
    social structure,
        14, 2098
squirrel-like rodents
    behavior, *14*, 2090
    family tree,
        3, 319, 371, *6*, 890, *7*, 916,
        12, 1696, *14*, 2112–3,
        15, 2190
    habitats, *14*, 2093
    profile, *14*, 2083
    survival, *14*, 2107
squirrel monkeys
    behavior, *10*, 1414–5
    family tree, *10*, 1410
    food and feeding, *10*, 1418
    physical description,
        10, 1412
    social structure, *10*, 1420–2
    survival, *10*, 1426–9
squirrels
    see also
        ground squirrels;
            tree squirrels
    family tree,
        3, 319, *14*, 2112–3
    habitats, *14*, 2118
squirrel-sized numbats
    food and feeding,
        14, 2149
star-nosed moles
    burrowing, *10*, 1383
    food and feeding,

10, 1396
hunting by,
10, 1388
water-dwellers,
10, 1389
steenboks
behavior, *6*, 765
defenses, *6*, 768
habitats, *6*, 767
Stein's cuscuses
habitats, *12*, 1729
Steller, Georg, *9*, 1298
Steller's sea cows
discovery of, *9*, 1298–9
family tree, *9*, 1280
Steller sea lions
food and feeding,
13, 1966
habitats, *15*, 2251
survival,
13, 1975–6
steppe lemmings
profile, *15*, 2190
survival, *15*, 2211
steppe pikas
habitats, *7*, 949–50
life cycle, *7*, 959
steppe polecats
survival, *15*, 2236
steppe zebras
profile, *16*, 2449
stink badgers
profile, *1*, 110
stoats
behavior,
15, 2220
family tree, *15*, 2216
habitats,
15, 2199, 2222, 2224
hunting by, *15*, 2226
physical description,
15, 2219
profile, *15*, 2214–5
reproduction,
15, 2230
survival, *15*, 2232–3
temperature, effect on,
15, 2222
stone martens
habitats, *9*, 1305
rubber chewing,

9, 1310
streaked tenrecs
habitats, *8*, 1185
striped civets
survival, *8*, 1195
striped field mice
habitats,
13, 1910
striped grass mice
habitats,
13, 1910
striped hamsters
burrowing, *7*, 923
striped hyenas
behavior, *7*, 1050
family tree, *7*, 1047
habitats,
7, 925, 1051, 1052–4
physical description,
7, 1048–9
social structure,
7, 1056–7
survival, *7*, 1065–6
striped possums
food and feeding,
12, 1732–3
physical description,
12, 1724
reproduction,
12, 1736
striped skunks
behavior, *16*, 2376
defenses, *16*, 2385
family tree, *16*, 2373
habitats, *16*, 2378–9
physical description,
16, 2374–5
profile, *16*, 2371–2
reproduction,
16, 2389
territory,
16, 2387
sucker–footed bats
profile, *2*, 215
survival, *2*, 207
sugar gliders
artificial nest boxes,
12, 1743
food and feeding,
12, 1732
habitats, *8*, 1159

physical description,
12, 1724–5
social structure,
12, 1734–5
Sumatran collared mongooses
survival, *9*, 1352
Sumatran hares
habitats, *12*, 1821
Sumatran rabbits
family tree,
7, 943
Sumatran rhinoceroses
evolution, *13*, 1928
family tree, *13*, 1930
food and feeding, *13*, 1941
habitats, *13*, 1936, 1938
physical description,
13, 1932
profile, *13*, 1927
survival, *13*, 1949
Sumatran tigers
physical description,
15, 2167
profile, *15*, 2164
survival, *15*, 2181, 2183
sun bears
description, *3*, 292,
294–5
family tree,
2, 241, 266,
11, 1592, 1670–1
food and feeding,
3, 302–3
habitats, *3*, 290, 298–9
life cycle, *3*, 306–7
naming, *3*, 291
pets, as, *3*, 308
survival, *3*, 308, 311–3
termites, feeding on,
3, 303
Sunda tree squirrels
food and feeding,
14, 2122
sun–tailed guenons
survival,
10, 1481
survival
see specific animal
susliks
burrowing, *14*, 2093
food and feeding,

14, 2100
swamp antechinuses
survival, *14*, 2156–7
swamp beavers
see capybaras
swamp rabbits
habitats, *12*, 1806–7
swamp wallabies
family tree, *8*, 1125
swift foxes
habitats, *5*, 714
survival, *5*, 729
Syrian hamsters
see golden hamsters

T

taiga voles
territory, *15*, 2203
takins
habitats, *11*, 1601
talpid moles
burrowing, *10*, 1388
evolution, *10*, 1383
profile, *10*, 1382–3
taltuzas
habitats, *14*, 2094
survival, *14*, 2106
talus–dwelling pikas
life cycle, *7*, 959
tamandua mexicana
see northern tamanduas
tamanduas
behavior, *1*, 36–7
borderline species,
1, 38
diseases, *1*, 46
food and feeding,
1, 40, 45
habitats, *1*, 38–40
parasitic nematodes,
1, 46
physical description,
1, 35
profile, *1*, 30
reproduction, *1*, 46–7
scent marking, *1*, 43
survival, *1*, 50
territory, *1*, 42
tamaraus
breeding programs,

3, 440–1

described, *3*, 421

habitats, *3*, 428

physical characteristics,
3, 425

survival, *3*, 438, 440–1

tamarins

behavior,
10, 1492–1503

family tree,
10, 1411, 1489

food and feeding,
10, 1498–9

habitats, *10*, 1494–7

life cycle, *10*, 1502–3

profile, *10*, 1409,
1485–8

social structure,
10, 1500–1

survival, *10*, 1457

tammar wallabies

survival, *8*, 1145

Tana River mangabeys

survival, *10*, 1480

tapirs .

behavior, *16*, 2454–5

family tree,
7, 1020, *16*, 2450–1

food and feeding,
16, 2454, 2460

physical description,
16, 2453

profile, *16*, 2447, 2450

reproduction, *16*, 2467

social structure,
16, 2464

survival, *16*, 2468–71

vampire bats, as prey of,
2, 172

tarsiers

behavior, *5*, 738–9

calling, *5*, 748

captivity, *5*, 755

evolution, *5*, 734

family tree,
5, 734–5, *8*, 1177

food and feeding,
5, 746–7

foraging, *5*, 739

habitats, *5*, 740–2

locomotion, *5*, 744–5

night vision, *5*, 739

social structure, *5*, 748

survival, *5*, 752–4

Tasmanian bettongs

behavior, *13*, 1856

food and feeding,
13, 1867

habitats, *13*, 1858–9

life cycle, *13*, 1868–9

survival, *13*, 1871–2

territory, *13*, 1863

Tasmanian devils,
14, 2134–59

behavior,
14, 2142–53

captive breeding,
14, 2157, 2159

conservation measures,
14, 2156–7

diseases, *14*, 2155

evolution, *14*, 2138

family tree,
14, 2138–9, *16*, 2425

food and feeding,
14, 2148–9

habitats,
11, 1652, *14*, 2144–7

hibernation,
14, 2143

hunting by,
14, 2150–1

life cycle, *14*, 2152–3

pets, as, *14*, 2158

physical description,
14, 2140–1

profile,
12, 1722, *14*, 2135, 2141

rainfall, effect on,
14, 2146

survival, *14*, 2154–8

temperature, effect on,
14, 2146

Tasmanian pademelons

habitats, *16*, 2432

Tasmanian wolves

habitats, *4*, 584

tassel-eared marmosets

behavior, *10*, 1492

survival, *10*, 1507

Tate's trioks

survival, *12*, 1741

Tatra pine voles

survival, *15*, 2210

tawny owls

habitats,
1, 118, *5*, 716, *7*, 977

telefomin cuscuses

survival, *12*, 1741

temperature, effect of

see specific animal

tenrecs

behavior, *7*, 972

food and feeding,
7, 978–9

habitats, *7*, 974–5

hibernation, *7*, 981

profile, *7*, 965, 968

survival, *7*, 987–8

termites

aardvarks, feeding habits,
1, 4, 12, 16–7, 23, 24

aardwolves, feeding on,
3, 291

antelopes and, *1*, 67

armadillos, feeding habits,
1, 91–2

bat-eared foxes, feeding on,
3, 291

pangolins, feeding habits,
1, 91–2, 95

sloth bears, feeding on,
3, 290–1, 304–5

sun bears, feeding on,
3, 303

terrestrial squirrels

food and feeding,
14, 2100–1

social structure,
14, 2096

territory

see specific animal

thick-tailed opossums

habitats, *10*, 1522

survival, *10*, 1534

thin–spined porcupines

survival, *12*, 1717

thirteen-lined ground squirrels

physical description,
14, 2089

profile, *14*, 2084

Thomas's galagos

survival, *5*, 753–4

Thomson's gazelles

behavior, *6*, 765

defenses, *6*, 768

food and feeding,
6, 772–3

habitats,
6, 821, *7*, 1003,
1055, *9*, 1235

leopards, as prey of,
9, 1236

life cycle, *6*, 777

lions, as prey of, *9*, 1239

profile, *6*, 758

spotted hyenas, prey of,
7, 1058–9

survival, *6*, 778

territory, *6*, 775

Thonglongya, Kitti,
2, 186

Thoroughbreds

survival, *7*, 1040

three-banded armadillos

defenses, *1*, 97

survival, *1*, 101, 105

three–toed sloths

behavior, *14*, 2064

captivity, *14*, 2081

family tree, *14*, 2061

food and feeding,
14, 2070–3

habitats,
14, 2066, 2068

life cycle,
14, 2076–7

physical description,
14, 2062–3

profile, *14*, 2059

survival, *14*, 2079

territory, *14*, 2074–5

thumbless bats

profile, *2*, 214

Tibetan wolves

survival, *16*, 2417

tiger cats

see spotted-tail quolls

tigers, *15*, 2160–85

behavior, *15*, 2168–79

camouflage, *15*, 2176

captive breeding, *15*, 2184

Chinese medicine, use in,
15, 2182–3

communications,
15, 2172
conservation measures,
15, 2182–3
evolution, 15, 2161–3
family tree,
4, 448, 8, 1099, 1202,
9, 1229, 15, 2164–5
flehmen reaction,
15, 2172, 2178
habitats, 15, 2170–3
hunting by,
15, 2169, 2174–7
hunting of, 15, 2180
life cycle, 15, 2178–9
mating, 15, 2178
physical description,
15, 2166–7
profile, 15, 2161–7
rainfall, effect on,
15, 2172
survival, 15, 2180–4
swimming, 15, 2170
temperature, effect on,
15, 2171–2
territory, 15, 2169
tiger sharks
habitats, 5, 639
tiger snakes
habitats, 4, 586
timber trade
American black bears and,
2, 258
titi monkeys
behavior, 10, 1415
family tree, 10, 1410
food and feeding,
10, 1414
grooming, 10, 1423
medical research, use in,
10, 1428
physical description,
10, 1413
social structure,
10, 1423
survival, 10, 1428–9
toads
habitats, 7, 977
tomb bats
hunting by, 2, 197
Tongan fruit bats

survival, 2, 155
Tonkin snub-nosed monkeys
food and feeding,
10, 1444
survival, 10, 1455
toolache wallabies
survival, 8, 1143
toothed whales
behavior, 16, 2350
family tree,
5, 631, 15, 2242,
2268, 2295,
16, 2320, 2346–7
food and feeding,
16, 2356
habitats, 5, 627
profile, 16, 2343–5
social structure,
16, 2332
topis
behavior, 1, 62
food and feeding, 1, 69
social structure, 1, 70
Townsend's big-eared bats
survival, 2, 207, 233
Townsend's moles
survival, 10, 1402
Townsend's voles
habitats, 15, 2196
Transvaal lions
profile, 9, 1228
tree hyraxes
climate changes and,
1, 26
communication, 1, 11
family tree, 1, 6
food and feeding, 1, 18
habitats, 1, 12, 14
nocturnal quality, 1, 10
survival, 1, 25–6
tree kangaroos
behavior,
8, 1155
family tree,
8, 1151
food and feeding,
8, 1160
habitats,
8, 1148–9, 1157–8
life cycle, 8, 1165
newly discovered species,

8, 1171
reverse evolution,
8, 1149–50
survival, 8, 1168
tree pangolins
habitats, 1, 92
tree shrews
described, 1, xxi
profile,
14, 2032, 2034
tree squirrels, 14, 2108–33
behavior,
14, 2116–29
evolution,
14, 2109–10, 2112
food and feeding,
14, 2122–3
habitats,
14, 2118–21
hunting of,
14, 2130
life cycle,
14, 2128–9
mating,
14, 2129
profile,
14, 2109–15
rainfall, effect on,
14, 2120
social structure,
14, 2124–7
survival, 14, 2130–2
temperature, effect on,
14, 2120
vocalizations,
14, 2125–6
Tres Marías raccoons
habitats,
12, 1832
tropical tree squirrels
social structure,
14, 2126
tropical weasels
survival,
15, 2235
true beavers
life cycle, 3, 335
true cattle
family tree,
3, 423
survival,

3, 438
true cavies
behavior, 6, 894
habitats, 6, 896
reproduction,
6, 904
species,
6, 888
true foxes
family tree,
5, 605
true moles
burrowing,
10, 1388
food and feeding,
10, 1396
profile,
10, 1382–3
true seals, 13, 1978–2003
behavior,
13, 1986–97
clubbing,
13, 2003
conservation measures,
13, 2000–1, 13, 2003
culling of,
13, 1998, 2001–2
echolocation,
13, 1990
evolution,
13, 1953–4, 1956,
1980, 1982
family tree,
13, 1957, 1982–3
habitats,
13, 1988–9
hunting by,
13, 1990–3
life cycle,
13, 1996–7
mating, 13, 1996
oil from, hunting for,
13, 1998
oil pollution, effect on,
13, 2002
profile,
13, 1954–5, 1979–85
survival,
13, 1998–2002
territory,
13, 1994–5

true shrews
  profile,
    14, 2032, 2034
Truk flying foxes
  survival,
    2, 155
tube-nosed fruit bats
  family tree,
    2, 137
  profile, *2*, 139
  reproduction,
    2, 148
tuberculosis
  badgers,
    1, 124, 128–30
tuco-tucos
  food and feeding,
    6, 902
  habitats,
    6, 896–8
  survival, *6*, 908
Tucuna Indians
  sloths, legends about,
    14, 2078
tundra voles
  habitats,
    15, 2196
  profile,
    15, 2190
  survival,
    15, 2210
tunnels
  pocket gophers,
    14, 2090–1
  shrews, *14*, 2046
tuzas
  habitats, *14*, 2094
  survival, *14*, 2106
two-toed sloths
  captivity,
    14, 2080–1
  family tree,
    14, 2061
  food and feeding,
    14, 2070–3
  habitats,
    1, 41, *14*, 2066
  hunting of, *14*, 2081
  physical description,
    14, 2062–3
  profile, *14*, 2059

survival, *14*, 2078
territory,
  14, 2074–5

U

uakaris
  grooming, *10*, 1423
  habitats, *10*, 1417
  life cycle, *10*, 1425
  social structure,
    10, 1420
  survival,
    10, 1430
ungulates
  behavior, *13*, 1934
  family tree, *7*, 995
  profile, *13*, 1928
unicorn whales
  family tree, *5*, 631
United Nations Conference
  on the Human Environment,
    16, 2366
Upper Amazon porcupines
  habitats,
    12, 1703
  profile,
    12, 1695
urine-washing
  galagos, *5*, 748
U.S. Wild Free-roaming Horse
  and Burro Act of 1971,
    7, 1038–9
Ussuri raccoons
  habitats,
    4, 586–7
Utah prairie dogs
  survival,
    14, 2106–7

V

vampire bats
  classification of, *1*, xxi
  family tree,
    2, 162–3
  fear of, *2*, 179–80
  hairy-legged,
    2, 172
  hunting by, *2*, 172–4
  life cycle, *2*, 176–7

pesticides and,
  2, 180–1
profile, *2*, 164–5
roosting, *2*, 167
survival, *2*, 205
Vancouver Island marmots
  habitats, *14*, 2092
  survival,
    14, 2106–7
vermilion flycatchers
  habitats, *3*, 379
Verreaux eagle,
  1, 11, 15
Verreaux's sifakas
  behavior, *8*, 1180
  food and feeding,
    8, 1186
  habitats, *8*, 1183
  life cycle, *8*, 1190–1
  physical description,
    8, 1179
  survival, *8*, 1196
vesper bats, *2*, 210–35
  Asian painted bats,
    2, 228
  attics, in, *2*, 221, 234
  bamboo bats, *2*, 229
  behavior, *2*, 217–29
  brown bats,
    2, 233, 235
  caves, *2*, 232–3
  common long-eared bats,
    2, 215, 222
  common pipistrelle bats,
    2, 214, 219, 229
  conservation measures,
    2, 232, 235
  Daubenton's bats,
    2, 221, 224
  disc-winged bats,
    2, 215
  echolocation, *2*, 224
  energy, saving of, *2*, 212
  European noctule,
    2, 226, 229
  evolution, *2*, 212
  family tree, *2*, 213
  fear of bats, *2*, 233–4
  flight, *2*, 212–3, 217–20
  food and feeding,
    2, 224

free-tailed bats,
  2, 215
funnel-eared bats,
  2, 215
Gould's long-eared bats,
  2, 229
gray bats, *2*, 233
habitats, *2*, 219–23
hibernation,
  2, 226–7, 233
horseshoe bats, *2*, 214
hunting by,
  2, 217–8, 224–5
Indiana bats, *2*, 233
Javan thick-thumbed bats,
  2, 233
leaf-nosed bats
  see leaf-nosed bats
Leisler's bats, *2*, 231
long-fingered bats, *2*, 233
mating, *2*, 228
migration, *2*, 226
North American red bats,
  2, 226
Oligocene epoch, *2*, 212
pipistrelle bats,
  2, 213, 215–7, 219–20,
    224–6, 229
pond bats, *2*, 233
profile, *2*, 213–6
reproduction, *2*, 228–9
roosting,
  2, 220–1, 232–3, 235
sheath-tailed bats, *2*, 213
silver-haired bats, *2*, 226
sonar hunting by,
  2, 217–8
survival, *2*, 230–4
thumbless bats, *2*, 215
Townsend's big–eared bats,
  2, 233
vesper rats
  family tree, *13*, 1879
  physical description,
    13, 1881
vicuñas
  breeding, *3*, 358
  domestication,
    3, 360
  family tree, *3*, 345
  food and feeding,

3, 354–5
habitats,
   3, 301, 341, 348, 352
harems, *3*, 357
hunting of animals,
   3, 361–2
social structure,
   3, 356–7
speed of, *3*, 349
survival,
   3, 360–3, 365
Virginia flying squirrels
survival,
   14, 2132–3
Virginia opossums
family tree,
   10, 1515
food and feeding,
   10, 1524, 1526
habitats,
   10, 1520–1
life cycle,
   10, 1530–1
physical description,
   10, 1516–7
"playing possum,"
   9, 1373
profile, *10*, 1511–4
survival, *10*, 1532–5
territory,
   10, 1528–9
Virginia polecats
   see fishers
Visayan warty pigs
   survival, *11*, 1638
viscachas
behavior, *6*, 895
food and feeding,
   6, 902
habitats, *6*, 897
reproduction,
   6, 905
size, *6*, 889
social structure,
   6, 900–1
vocalization,
   6, 900
viverrids
   see civets; genets
volcano rabbits
habitats, *12*, 1821

survival,
   12, 1818, 1820
voles, *15*, 2186–2211
behavior,
   15, 2194–2207
burrowing, *15*, 2201
evolution,
   15, 2188
family tree,
   15, 2190–1
food and feeding,
   15, 2189, 2200–1
habitats,
   15, 2196–9
life cycle,
   15, 2204–5
migration,
   15, 2206–7
nests, *15*, 2195
profile,
   15, 2187–93
rainfall, effect on,
   15, 2198
survival,
   15, 2208–10
temperature, effect on,
   15, 2189, 2198
territory,
   15, 2202–3
vulpine foxes, *5*, 704–29
behavior,
   5, 712–25
family tree,
   4, 526, 578,
     5, 605, 683, 708–9
grooming, *5*, 720
habitats, *5*, 714–7
hunting by,
   5, 718–9
hunting of,
   5, 726–7
nomads, as,
   5, 722
physical description,
   4, 524
profile,
   5, 705–11
rabies,
   5, 726, 728
reproduction,
   5, 699, 724–5

scent marking, *5*, 723
social structure,
   5, 720–1
survival, *5*, 726–8
territory, *5*, 722–3
vu quang
discovery of, *3*, 421
survival, *3*, 441

W

wallabies
behavior,
   8, 1128
family tree,
   8, 1125
food and feeding,
   8, 1135
profile,
   8, 1121
survival,
   8, 1140, 1144–5
wallaroos
behavior, *8*, 1128
family tree, *8*, 1125
habitats, *8*, 1132
profile, *8*, 1122
walruses
behavior,
   13, 1972–3
family tree,
   13, 1957, 1983
habitats,
   11, 1679, *13*, 1962
life cycle, *13*, 1971
physical description,
   13,1958–9
polar bears, prey of,
   11, 1681
profile,
   13, 1953, 1979
survival,
   13, 1975
wambengers
   survival, *14*, 2157
wapiti
antlers, *4*, 556
food and feeding,
   4, 562
habitats, *4*, 558
males, *4*, 562

survival, *4*, 570
warthogs, *1*, 13–14
aardvarks, similarity to,
   11, 1633
African swine fever,
   11, 1638
anatomy, *11*, 1621
family tree, *11*, 1618
fighting, *11*, 1622
food and feeding,
   11, 1628–9
habitats,
   11, 1618, 1624
life cycle,
   11, 1634–5
mating, *11*, 1634
mud baths, *11*, 1623
sleeping sickness,
   11, 1638
social structure,
   11, 1632–3
survival, *11*, 1636
water buffalo
bulls, *3*, 435
described, *3*, 420
family tree,
   1, 58, *4*, 553
food and feeding,
   3, 430–1
herds, *3*, 435
life cycle, *3*, 437
physical characteristics,
   3, 425
social structure,
   3, 435
survival,
   3, 440, 441
tigers, prey of,
   15, 2175
water parasites, removal of,
   3, 427
water chevrotains
behavior, *12*, 1753
food and feeding,
   12, 1761
habitats, *12*, 1755–6
life cycle,
   12, 1762–3
survival, *12*, 1766
territory, *12*, 1759
water deer

family tree, *4*, 553

water hogs

  see capybaras

water shrews

  behavior, *14*, 2038–9

  habitats, *14*, 2042

  physical description,

    14, 2037

  territory, *14*, 2047

Waterton, Charles,

  14, 2078

water voles

  food and feeding,

    15, 2201

  habitats,

    15, 2198

  life cycle,

    15, 2205

  survival, *15*, 2208

  territory, *15*, 2202

  tunnels, *15*, 2194

weasels, *15*, 2212–37

  behavior,

    15, 2220–31

  camouflage,

    15, 2216

  conservation measures,

    15, 2234–5

  diseases,

    15, 2233

  evolution,

    15, 2214

  family tree,

    4, 500, *9*, 1306,

      11, 1566, *15*, 2216–7,

      16, 2372

  habitats,

    9, 1263, *15*, 2222–5

  hunting by,

    15, 2226–7

  mating, *15*, 2231

  physical description,

    15, 2218–9

  pine martens, compared,

    9, 1303

  profile,

    15, 2213–9

  rainfall, effect on,

    15, 2224

  reproduction,

    15, 2230–1

scent marking,

  15, 2228–9

survival, *15*, 2232–6

temperature, effect on,

  15, 2224

territory, *15*, 2228–9

weaver birds

  habitats, *1*, 67

Weddell seals

  behavior, *13*, 1987

  family tree, *13*, 1983

  habitats, *13*, 1988–9

  hunting by,

    13, 1990–2

  life cycle, *13*, 1996

  territory, *13*, 1994

Weil's disease

  Old World rats and mice,

    13, 1925

West African manatees

  family tree, *9*, 1281

  food and feeding,

    9, 1290

  habitats, *9*, 1286–8

  life cycle, *9*, 1294–5

  profile, *9*, 1278

  studies on, *9*, 1301

  survival, *9*, 1298–9

western barred bandicoots

  survival,

    16, 2443

Western bearded pigs

  survival,

    11, 1638

western gentle lemurs

  survival,

    8, 1195

western gray kangaroos

  habitats,

    8, 1130

  survival,

    8, 1143

western harvest mice

  survival,

    13, 1894

western lowland gorillas

  family tree, *6*, 864

  habitats, *6*, 870, 871

Western Mexican jaguars

  survival,

    8, 1117

western native cats

  habitats,

    14, 2144, 2146

  profile, *14*, 2137

western pocket gophers

  food and feeding,

    14, 2101

  habitats,

    14, 2094

western quolls

  see western native cats

western ring-tailed possums

  survival,

    12, 1741–2

western spotted skunks

  habitats,

    16, 2378

West Indian giant rice rats

  survival,

    13, 1897

West Indian manatees

  family tree, *9*, 1281

  food and feeding,

    9, 1290–1

  habitats, *9*, 1286–7

  life cycle, *9*, 1294–5

  physical description,

    9, 1279, 1283

  profile, *9*, 1278

  studies on, *9*, 1301

  survival,

    9, 1296–7, 1299

Weyland ring-tailed possums

  population,

    12, 1743

whales

  see also gray whales;

    killer whales; right whales;

    rorquals; sperm whales

  described, *1*, xxi

  family tree,

    5, 631, *15*, 2242, 2269,

      16, 2321, 2347

whale watching,

  16, 2367

white camels

  profile, *3*, 343

white-coated harp seals

  survival, *13*, 2003

white-faced sakis

  behavior,

10, 1414

profile, *10*, 1409

white-footed mice

  see deer mice

white-footed tamarins

  survival,

    10, 1506–7

white-footed voles

  survival,

    15, 2209–10

white foxes

  habitats, *5*, 689

  reproduction,

    5, 698

white-handed gibbons

  see lar gibbons

white-lipped peccaries

  habitats, *11*, 1626

  hunting by,

    11, 1622

  profile, *11*, 1617

white-nosed coatis

  habitats, *12*, 1833

  profile, *12*, 1825

  survival, *12*, 1847

white rhinoceroses

  family tree, *13*, 1930

  food and feeding,

    13, 1940–1

  habitats,

    13, 1936–7, 1951

  life cycle, *13*, 1944–5

  physical description,

    13, 1932

  profile, *13*, 1927–9

  social structure,

    13, 1942–3

  zoos, *13*, 1950

white-tailed deer

  habitats,

    3, 301, *6*, 899

  survival, *4*, 570–1

white-tailed mongooses

  profile,

    9, 1331–2

white-tailed prairie dogs

  behavior,

    14, 2090

  habitats,

    14, 2092

white-throated tree kangaroos

survival, *8*, 1169

white tigers

  physical description,
    15, 2167

  profile,
    15, 2163

white-toothed shrews

  behavior, *14*, 2039

  food and feeding,
    14, 2045

  physical description,
    14, 2037

white whales

  family tree,
    5, 631, *16*, 2346

  food and feeding,
    16, 2356

  profile, *16*, 2343–5

  social structure,
    16, 2359

wild boars

  anatomy, *11*, 1620–1

  family tree, *11*, 1619

  fighting, *11*, 1632

  habitats,
    11, 1618, 1624, 1626–7

  life cycle,
    11, 1634–5

  mating, *11*, 1634

  profile, *11*, 1616

  social structure,
    11, 1630

  survival, *11*, 1636

  territory, *11*, 1631

wildcats

  behavior,
    14, 2012

  family tree,
    8, 1098, 1202, *9*, 1228

  habitats,
    6, 847, *9*, 1260–1,
    1314, *11*, 1627

  survival,
    9, 1270–1, 1275,
    14, 2029

  territory, *9*, 1266

wild cattle, *3*, 418–43

  activities of, *3*, 426–7

  behavior, *3*, 426–37

  black bulls, *3*, 443

  bulls, *3*, 436

  conservation measures,
    3, 440

  defenses, *3*, 432–3

  domestication of,
    3, 440–3

  evolution,
    3, 419–20

  family tree,
    1, 58, *3*, 397,
    422–3, *6*, 761, 838

  food and feeding,
    3, 430–1

  gaurs
    see gaurs

  habitats, *3*, 428–9

  hunting of, *3*, 442

  life cycle, *3*, 436–7

  lowland anoas
    see lowland anoas

  oxen
    see oxen

  profile, *3*, 419–25

  smell, sense of,
    3, 427

  social structure,
    3, 434–5

  survival,
    3, 438–42

  tamaraus
    see tamaraus

  vu quang
    see vu quang

wild cavies

  habitats,
    3, 301, *6*, 897

  physical description,
    6, 892–3

wild dogs

  behavior,
    4, 530–43

  family tree,
    4, 526–7, *16*, 2399

  habitats, *4*, 532–5

  hunting by,
    4, 530–1, 536–7

wildebeests

  behavior,
    1, 62–3

  communication,
    1, 63

  food and feeding,

1, 68–9

  habitats,
    1, 65–6, *7*, 1055

  life cycle, *1*, 72–3

  lions, as prey of,
    9, 1238–9

  mating, *1*, 73

  physical description,
    1, 60–1

  social structure, *1*, 71

  spotted hyenas, prey of,
    7, 1058–9

  survival, *1*, 74, 79

wild horses

  family tree,
    16, 2450

  habitats, *7*, 1026

  profile, *16*, 2448

  survival, *7*, 1038–9

Wildlife and Countryside Act
  of 1981 (Britain),
    7, 986, *14*, 2053

wild pigs

  behavior,
    11, 1622

  defenses,
    11, 1632

  evolution,
    11, 1616

  facial warts,
    11, 1633

  family tree,
    11, 1618–9

  food and feeding,
    11, 1628

  grooming,
    11, 1631

  habitats, *1*
    1, 1617, 1624

  hunting of,
    11, 1638

  mud baths,
    11, 1623

  profile,
    11, 1615–6

  social structure,
    11, 1630

  survival,
    11, 1636

wild quaggas

  profile,

16, 2450

wild sheep

  survival, *6*, 856–8

Wilson and Savage,
    6, 880

wolflike dingoes

  survival, *8*, 1166

wolverines, *16*, 2368–93

  behavior, *1*
    6, 2376–89

  defenses,
    16, 2384–5

  family tree,
    9, 1307, *15*, 2217,
    16, 2372–3

  food and feeding,
    16, 2382–3

  habitats,
    3, 327, *7*, 951, *15*, 2198,
    16, 2378–81

  hunting of,
    16, 2390–2

  mating, *16*, 2388–9

  physical description,
    16, 2374–5

  profile,
    16, 2369–75

  rainfall, effect on,
    16, 2380

  reproduction,
    16, 2388–9

  survival, *16*, 2390–2

  temperature, effect on,
    16, 2380

  territory, *16*, 2386–7

wolves, *16*, 2394–2419

  alpha pairs, *16*, 2418

  behavior,
    16, 2402–13

  beta wolves,
    16, 2406

  conservation measures,
    16, 2416–7

  dens, *16*, 2413

  evolution, *16*, 2396–7

  family tree,
    4, 526, 579,
    5, 604, 709, *16*, 2398–9

  habitats,
    3, 327, 353, *4*, 584,
    7, 951, *15*, 2199, 2225,

16, 2381, 2403–5
howling,
  16, 2408, 2411
hunting by,
  16, 2408–9
jackals, distinguished,
  8, 1072
life cycle,
  16, 2412–3
lone wolves,
  16, 2407, 2411
pack hunting,
  16, 2402, 2408–10
physical description,
  16, 2400–1
profile,
  16, 2395–2401
rainfall, effect on,
  16, 2403
social structure,
  16, 2406–7
survival,
  16, 2414–8
temperature, effect on,
  16, 2403
territory,
  16, 2410–1
wombats, *16*, 2420–45
  behavior,
    16, 2428–39
  burrowing,
    16, 2423–4,
      2428, 2437
  conservation measures,
    16, 2442–3
  diseases,
    16, 2442
  evolution,
    16, 2421, 2424
  family tree,
    8, 1125, 1150
  food and feeding,
    16, 2434–5
  habitats,
    11, 1653, *16*, 2430–3
  inbreeding,
    16, 2442–3
  life cycle,
    16, 2438–9
  mating, *16*, 2438
  physical description,

16, 2426–7
profile,
  16, 2421–7
rainfall, effect on,
  16, 2432
survival,
  16, 2440–4
temperature, effect on,
  16, 2432
territory,
  16, 2436–7
wood bison
  habitats, *3*, 403
  physical characteristics,
    3, 396
  population, *3*, 417
woodlands
  badgers and,
    1, 118
Woodlark Island cuscuses
  survival, *12*, 1741
wood lemmings
  profile, *15*, 2190
wood lice
  habitats,
    3, 327, *7*, 977
wood mice
  behavior,
    13, 1908
  food and feeding,
    13, 1914–5
  habitats, *13*, 1910
  life cycle,
    13, 1916–7
  survival, *13*, 1925
woodpeckers
  habitats,
    1, 119, *3*, 405, *5*, 717
wood pigeons
  habitats, *1*, 118
wood rats
  habitats,
    13, 1884, 1886
  nesting,
    13, 1890–1
woolly monkeys
  family tree,
    10, 1410
  hunting of,
    10, 1426
  physical description,

10, 1413
profile, *10*, 1408
social structure,
  10, 1420
survival,
  10, 1426, 1429
woolly opossums
  family tree,
    10, 1515
  food and feeding,
    10, 1525–7
  habitats,
    10, 1520, 1522
  profile,
    10, 1512
  survival,
    10, 1532, 1534
woolly spider monkeys
  food and feeding,
    10, 1418
  habitats,
    10, 1416, 1497
  physical description,
    10, 1412
  profile,
    10, 1408
  survival,
    10, 1426, 1428–9
Wroughton's free–tailed
  bats
    survival, *2*, 207

Y

yaks
  domestication,
    3, 422, 443
  evolution,
    3, 394
  food and feeding,
    3, 430
  habitats,
    3, 428
  physical characteristics,
    3, 425
  size, *3*, 396
  survival,
    3, 438–41
  temperature, effect of,
    3, 421
Yangtze dolphins

survival,
  5, 649, 651
yapoks
  behavior,
    10, 1519
  family tree,
    10, 1515
  food and feeding,
    10, 1526–7
  profile,
    10, 1512–3
  survival,
    10, 1534
yellow armadillos
  family tree, *1*, 84
yellow-bellied gliders
  food and feeding,
    12, 1731
  social structure,
    12, 1734–5
  survival,
    12, 1743
yellow-bellied marmots
  profile,
    14, 2085
  social structure,
    14, 2099
yellow fever
  leaf-nosed bats,
    2, 182
yellow-footed antechinuses
  survival,
    14, 2156–7
yellow-footed rock
  wallabies
    family tree,
      8, 1125
    habitats,
      8, 1132
    survival,
      8, 1145
yellow ladybirds
  habitats, *1*, 119
yellow mongooses
  behavior, *9*, 1336
  habitats,
    9, 1339
  life cycle,
    9, 1349
  physical description,
    9, 1335

profile,
   9, 1331, 1332
social structure,
   9, 1344
yellow-necked mice
   habitats,
      13, 1910
   survival,
      13, 1925
yellow-tailed woolly monkeys
   habitats,
      10, 1417
   survival,
      10, 1429–30
yellow-throated martens
   family tree,
      9, 1307
   markings, *9*, 1305
   trapping for fur,
      9, 1326
yellow-toothed cavies
   habitats,
      6, 894, 896
   reproduction,

6, 904
social structure,
   6, 900–1

Z

Zanzibar galagos
   survival,
      5, 753, 754
Zanzibar leopards
   family tree,
      8, 1203
Zanzibar red colobus monkeys
   profile,
      10, 1435
Zapotecs
   jaguars, worship of,
      8, 1118
zebra duikers
   camouflage, *6*, 769
   habitats,
      6, 766
   survival,
      6, 780

zebras, *16*, 2446–71
   behavior,
      16, 2454–67
   defenses,
      16, 2462–3
   evolution,
      16, 2447–8
   family tree,
      7, 1021, *16*, 2450–1
   food and feeding,
      16, 2454, 2460–1
   habitats,
      4, 456, *16*, 2456–9
   mating, *16*, 2467
   profile,
      16, 2447–53
   rainfall, effect on,
      16, 2458
   reproduction,
      16, 2466–7
   social structure,
      16, 2464–5
   spotted hyenas, prey of,
      7, 1058–9

   survival,
      16, 2468–70
   temperature, effect on,
      16, 2458
Zebroids
   survival, *16*, 2470
zebu cattle
   vampire bats, as prey of,
      2, 172–3
zorillas
   see African polecats
zorros
   behavior, *5*, 686
   hunting by, *5*, 693
   profile, *5*, 682

CLASSIFICATION INDEX

A

aardvarks, *1*, 3, 7–9
African buffalo, *3*, 425
African civets, *4*, 503
alpine ibex, *6*, 841
American bison,
  3, 399
American black bears,
  2, 243
armadillos, *1*, 85

B

bats, *2*, 133–4
Bengal tigers,
  15, 2167
black-tailed prairie dogs,
  14, 2089
blue whales,
  16, 2323
blue wildebeests, *1*, 61
brown hares,
  7, 945
brown rats, *13*, 1907
bush hyraxes, *1*, 6–7

C

Canadian beavers, *3*, 321
capybaras, *3*, 373
cavies, *6*, 888
common armadillos, *1*, 87
common chimpanzees, *4*, 477
common dormice, *7*, 919
common hamsters, *7*, 919
common marmosets, *10*, 1491
common pipistrelle, *2*, 216
common raccoons,
  12, 1829
common seals, *13*, 1985
common shrews, *14*, 2037
common weasels, *15*, 2219
common wombats,
  16, 2427
coyotes, *4*, 529

D

deer mice, *13*, 1881
dholes, *4*, 581
dromedaries, *3*, 347

E

Eurasian otters, *11*, 1569
Eurasian wildcats, *9*, 1257
European hedgehogs, *7*, 971
European moles,
  10, 1387
European rabbits,
  12, 1803

G

giant anteaters, *1*, 35
giant pandas, *11*, 1595
giraffes, *6*, 815
golden jackals, *8*, 1075
gray-headed fruit bats,
  2, 139
gray whales, *15*, 2246
gray wolves, *16*, 2401
greater horshoe bats,
  2, 191

H

hippopotamuses, *7*, 997

J

jaguars, *8*, 1101

K

killer whales, *15*, 2271
koalas, *8*, 1153

L

lar gibbons, *6*, 789
leopards, *8*, 1205

lesser galagos, *5*, 737
lions, *9*, 1231
long-nosed echidnas, *11*, 1647

M

mandrills, *10*, 1465

N

naked mole rats, *9*, 1361
North American porcupines,
  12, 1699
northern fur seals, *13*, 1959
northern tamanduas, *1*, 29, 32
Norway lemmings, *15*, 2193

O

orangutans, *11*, 1543

P

pangolins, *1*, 7–9, 83, 85
pikas, *7*, 942
pine martens, *9*, 1309
plains zebras, *16*, 2453
platypuses, *11*, 1647
polar bears, *11*, 1673
pronghorns, *12*, 1751
Przewalski's horses,
  7, 1022–3
pumas, *12*, 1777

R

red colobus monkeys,
  10, 1439
red kangaroos, *8*, 1127
red squirrels, *14*, 2115
right whales, *15*, 2294, 2297
ring-tailed lemurs,
  8, 1179
rufous rat kangaroos,
  13, 1855, 1856

S

senegalensis (lesser galagos),
  5, 737
servals, *14*, 2011
Siberian tigers,
  15, 2167
silky anteaters,
  1, 29, 35
spectacled bears, *3*, 295
sperm whales, *16*, 2349
spotted hyenas, *7*, 1049
springbok, *6*, 763
sugar gliders, *12*, 1725

T

tamanduas, *1*, 29, 35
Tasmanian devils, *14*, 2141
thirteen-lined ground squirrels,
  14, 2089
tree hyraxes, *1*, 6

V

vampire bats, *1*, xxi
Verreaux's sifakas,
  8, 1179
Virginia opossums,
  10, 1517

W

walruses, *13*, 1959
West Indian manatees,
  9, 1283
white-faced capuchins,
  10, 1413
white rhinoceroses,
  13, 1933
wild boars, *11*, 1621
wild cavies, *6*, 893
wolverines, *16*, 2375

ENDANGERED SPECIES INDEX

A

aardvarks, *1*, 24
Abbot's duikers, *6*, 780
Abyssinian genets, *4*, 519
addaxes, *1*, 77
Ader's duikers, *6*, 780
African elephants,
    5, 673–7
African lions, *9*, 1247
African pygmy squirrels,
    14, 2132
African sand cats,
    14, 2029
African wild dogs, *5*, 623
Alabama beach mice,
    13, 1897
Amami rabbits, *12*, 1820
Amargosa voles, *1*
    5, 2210
Amazon dolphins, *5*, 649
Amazonian manatees,
    9, 1299
American badgers, *1*, 131
American bison, *3*, 415
American black bears,
    2, 258–61
Amur leopards,
    8, 1221
Anastasia Island beach mice,
    13, 1897
Anatolian leopards,
    8, 1221
Angolan mongooses,
    9, 1352
anoas, *3*, 441
anteaters, *1*, 50–2
antelopes, *1*, 74–6
Anthony's wood rats,
    13, 1897
Arabian oryx, *1*, 76–7
Arabian tahrs, *6*, 857
Arabian wolves,
    16, 2417
Argentine gray foxes,
    5, 702

Arizona jaguars, *8*, 1117
armadillos,
    1, 101, 103–5
Asian black bears, *3*, 311
Asian elephants,
    5, 673–7
Asiatic lions, *9*, 1247
Asiatic wild asses,
    7, 1039

B

babirusas, *11*, 1638
back–striped weasels,
    15, 2236
Bactrian camels,
    3, 360, 363
badgers, *1*, 131
Bahamian hutias, *6*, 909
Baird's tapirs, *16*, 2470
bald uakaris, *10*, 1429
Bali tigers,
    15, 2181, 2183
banded hare wallabies,
    8, 1169
banteng, *3*, 441
Barbados raccoons,
    12, 1846–7
Barbary leopards, *8*, 1221
Bavarian pine voles,
    15, 2210
Bawean warty pigs,
    11, 1638
bay cats, *9*, 1273
beach voles, *15*, 2210
bearded sakis, *10*, 1429
bear-ear marmosets,
    10, 1507
beavers, *3*, 338
Bengal foxes, *5*, 728
Bengal tigers, *15*, 2183
big thicket hog-nosed skunks,
    16, 2392
bison, *3*, 415
blackbucks, *6*, 780

black-faced tamarins,
    10, 1506
black-footed ferrets,
    15, 2234–6
black-footed rock wallabies,
    8, 1145
black lemurs, *8*, 1195
black rhinoceroses,
    13, 1949
black-spotted cuscuses,
    12, 1741
black uakaris, *10*, 1429
blue whales, *16*, 2339
bowhead whales, *15*, 2313
Brelich's snub-nosed
    monkeys, *10*, 1455
bridled nail-tailed wallabies,
    8, 1143, 1145
broad-striped mongooses,
    9, 1352
broad-tail beavers, *3*, 338
brown bats, *2*, 233, 235
brown bears, *2*, 284–7
brown hyenas, *7*, 1066
brown mongooses,
    9, 1352
brown-throated three–toed
    sloths,
    14, 2080
brush-tailed bettongs,
    13, 1872
brush-tailed rock wallabies,
    8, 1145
Bryde's whales,
    16, 2339
buffy-headed marmosets,
    10, 1507
buffy-headed tamarins,
    10, 1506
buffy tufted-ear marmosets,
    10, 1507
Bunker's wood rats,
    13, 1897
burrowing bettongs,
    13, 1872

bush dogs, *4*, 546
bush hyraxes, *1*, 56
bushy-tailed hutias,
    6, 909
bushy-tailed mongooses,
    9, 1352

C

Cabrera's hutias, *6*, 909
cacomistles, *12*, 1846
Calamian deer,
    4, 571, 572
Californian pronghorns,
    12, 1767
capuchins, *10*, 1429
capybaras, *3*, 390
Caribbean monk seals,
    13, 2001
Carolina flying squirrels,
    14, 2132
Carruther's mountain
    squirrels, *14*, 2132
Caspian seals, *13*, 2001
Caspian tigers,
    15, 2181, 2183
cervus schombergki,
    4, 570
Chapman's prehensile-tailed
    hutias, *6*, 909
cheetahs, *4*, 468
chimpanzees, *4*, 493
Chinese desert cats,
    9, 1273
Choctawatchee beach mice,
    13, 1897
Clara bandicoots, *16*, 2443
clouded leopards, *8*, 1221
Colombian weasels,
    15, 2236
Colorado River cotton rats,
    13, 1897
common chimpanzees,
    4, 493
common hamsters, *7*, 935

concolor gibbons, *6*, 805

Corsican red deer, *4*, 572

cotton-top tamarins,
10, 1506

coypus, *3*, 390

Cozumel Island coatis,
12, 1846–7

crescent nail-tailed wallabies,
8, 1143

Cuban flower bats,
2, 181

Cuban solenodon,
14, 2053

Cuvier's gazelles, *6*, 780

D

Dama gazelles, *6*, 780

Dangs giant squirrels,
14, 2132

Delmarva fox squirrels,
14, 2132

dholes, *4*, 597

diadem sifakas, *8*, 1195

diana monkeys, *10*, 1481

dibblers, *14*, 2157

dolphins, *5*, 649

dorcas gazelles, *6*, 780

Doria's tree kangaroos,
8, 1169

dormice, *7*, 935

drills, *10*, 1481

dugongs, *9*, 1299

dune mole rats, *9*, 1378

dwarf hutias, *6*, 909

E

East Caucasian tur, *6*, 857

eastern barred bandicoots,
16, 2443

Eastern Mexican jaguars, *8*,
1117

eastern needle-clawed galagos,
5, 754

eastern tree hyraxes,
1, 25, 26

emperor tamarins,
10, 1507

Eurasian otters, *11*, 1585

European badgers, *1*, 131

European bison, *3*, 415

European minks, *9*, 1326

European wolves,
16, 2417

everglades bears, *2*, 259

F

falanouc, *4*, 519

false vampire bats,
2, 207

fanaloka, *4*, 519

fat dormice, *7*, 935

fea's muntjacs, *4*, 571

fennec foxes,
5, 702, 728

fin whales, *16*, 2339

fishing cats, *9*, 1273

flat-headed cats, *9*, 1273

Florida salt marsh voles,
15, 2210

Fly River bandicoots,
16, 2443

fork-marked dwarf lemurs,
8, 1195

Formosan serows, *6*, 857

Formosan sika, *4*, 572

fossa, *4*, 519

Francois' leaf monkeys,
10, 1455

fruit bats, *2*, 154–7

G

Ganges dolphins, *5*, 649

Garrido's hutias, *6*, 909

gaurs, *3*, 441

gazelles, *6*, 780

Geelvinck Bay leaf-nosed bats,
2, 207

Geoffrey's pied colobus
monkeys, *10*, 1455

giant anteaters, *1*, 49

giant armadillos, *1*, 103

giant bandicoots,
16, 2443

giant otters, *11*, 1585

giant pandas, *11*, 1611

giraffes, *6*, 832

Goeldi's monkeys,
10, 1507

golden bamboo lemurs,
8, 1195

golden bandicoots,
16, 2443

golden langurs, *10*, 1455

golden lion tamarins,
10, 1506

golden moles, *10*, 1404

golden pottos, *5*, 754

golden snub-nosed monkeys,
10, 1455

Goodfellow's tree kangaroos,
8, 1169

gorillas, *6*, 883

gray bats, *2*, 207, 233

gray wolves,
16, 2417

greater bilbies,
16, 2443

greater mouse-eared bats,
2, 207, 233

greater sheath–tailed bats,
2, 207

Grevy's zebras, *16*, 2470

grizzled leaf monkeys,
10, 1455

grizzled tree kangaroos,
8, 1169

grizzly bears, *2*, 284–7

Guadalupe fur seals,
13, 1976

Gulf of California porpoises,
5, 649

H

hamsters, *7*, 935

hartebeests, *1*, 76

Hawaiian monk seals,
13, 2001

Himalayan tahrs, *6*, 857

hirola, *1*, 77

Hispaniolan hutias,
6, 909

Hispaniolan solenodons,
14, 2053

hoary foxes, *5*, 702

Hoffman's two-toed sloths,
14, 2080

hoolock gibbons, *6*, 805

Hose's palm civets, *4*, 519

howler monkeys,
10, 1429

Hualapai Mexican voles,
15, 2210

humpback whales,
16, 2339

hutias, *6*, 908

hyraxes, *1*, 25, 26

I

impalas, *1*, 74

Indiana bats,
2, 207, 233

Indian rhinoceroses,
13, 1949

Indian wolves,
16, 2417

Indochinese tigers,
15, 2183

Indonesian mountain weasels,
15, 2236

indris, *8*, 1195

Indus dolphins,
5, 649

Isla de la Juventud hutias,
6, 909

Island gray foxes,
5, 728

J

jaguars, *8*, 1117

jaguarundi,
12, 1793, 1795

Jamaican fig-eating bats,
2, 183

Jamaican flower bats,
2, 181, 183

Jamaican hutias, *6*, 909

Japanese macaques,
10, 1481

Javan mastiff bats, *2*, 207

Javan rhinoceroses,
13, 1949

Javan thick-thumbed bats,
2, 207, 233

Javan tigers,
15, 2181, 2183

Javan warty pigs, *11*, 1638

Jentink's duikers, *6*, 780

Jerdon's palm civets, *4*, 519

Johnston's genets, *4*, 519

Juan Fernandez fur seals, *13*, 1976

Julia Creek dunnarts, *14*, 2157

K

ka'apor capuchins, *10*, 1429

Kangaroo Island dunnarts, *14*, 2157

Kasmir deer, *4*, 572

Key Largo cotton mice, *13*, 1897

Key Largo wood rats, *13*, 1897

Kitti's hog-nosed bats, *2*, 207

kloss gibbons, *6*, 805

kouprey, *3*, 440, 441

kowari, *14*, 2157

L

lapp deer, *4*, 573

large-eared hutias, *6*, 909

Leadbeater's possums, *12*, 1741

lechwe, *1*, 77

leopards, *8*, 1221

lesser short-tailed bats, *2*, 207

lesser spectral tarsiers, *5*, 754

L'Hoest's monkeys, *10*, 1481

Liberian mongooses, *9*, 1352

lion-tailed macaques, *10*, 1481

lion tamarins, *10*, 1507

little earth hutias, *6*, 909

little long-nosed bats, *2*, 181

llamas, *3*, 365

llanos, *1*, 51

long-fingered bats, *2*, 207, 233

long-footed potoroos, *13*, 1872

long-nosed echidnas, *11*, 1662

long-tailed chinchillas, *6*, 909

long-tailed gorals, *6*, 857

lorisids, *5*, 754

Lowe's otter civets, *4*, 521

lowland anoas, *3*, 441

lowland tree kangaroos, *8*, 1169

M

Maharashtra giant squirrels, *14*, 2132

mahogany gliders, *12*, 1741

mainland serows, *6*, 857

Malaysian tapirs, *16*, 2470

mandrills, *10*, 1481

maned sloths, *14*, 2080

maned wolves, *4*, 546

Manipur brow-antlered deer, *4*, 573

marbled cats, *9*, 1273

margays, *12*, 1793

Marianas flying foxes, *2*, 155

markhors, *6*, 857

marsh deer, *4*, 571

Matschie's tree kangaroos, *8*, 1169

Mediterranean monk seals, *13*, 2000–1

Mentawai langurs, *10*, 1455

Menzbier's marmots, *14*, 2106–7

Mexican long-nosed bats, *2*, 181–2

Mexican prairie dogs, *14*, 2106–7

Mexican pronghorns, *12*, 1767

Mexican silver grizzly, *2*, 285

Mexican wolves, *16*, 2417

Michoacan pocket gophers, *14*, 2106

Mindanao moonrats, *7*, 987

minke whales, *16*, 2339

moloch gibbons, *6*, 805

Mongolian beavers, *3*, 338

mongooses, *9*, 1352

mortlock flying foxes, *2*, 155

mountain anoas, *3*, 441

mountain coatis, *12*, 1846

mountain gazelles, *6*, 780

mountain gorillas, *6*, 882

mountain pygmy possums, *12*, 1741

mountain zebras, *16*, 2470

Mount Graham red squirrels, *14*, 2132

mouse-eared bats, *2*, 233

mule deer, *4*, 571

mulgaras, *14*, 2157

N

narrow-striped mongooses, *9*, 1352

native cats, *14*, 2157

needle-clawed galagos, *5*, 754

New Zealand short-tailed bats, *2*, 181

Nigerian pygmy hippopotamuses, *7*, 1013

night monkeys, *10*, 1429

nilgae, *1*, 77

Nilgiri langurs, *10*, 1455

Nilgiri martens, *9*, 1326

Nilgiri tahrs, *6*, 857

northern bettongs, *13*, 1872

northern gliders, *12*, 1741

northern hairy-nosed wombats, *16*, 2443

northern right whales, *15*, 2313

northern white rhinoceroses, *13*, 1949

Nubian ibex, *6*, 857–8

numbats, *14*, 2157

O

Obi cuscuses, *12*, 1741

ocelots, *12*, 1793

Ogilby's duikers, *6*, 780

okapis, *6*, 832

olingos, *12*, 1846

olive colobus monkeys, *10*, 1455

orange leaf-nosed bats, *2*, 207

orangutans, *11*, 1559

otter civets, *4*, 519, 521

otters, *11*, 1585

Owston's palm civets, *4*, 519

P

pacaranas, *6*, 909

Palau flying foxes, *2*, 155

pale foxes, *5*, 728

Pallas's cats, *9*, 1273

pampas deer, *4*, 571

pangolins, *1*, 101–5

parana jaguars, *8*, 1117

Perdido Key beach mice, *13*, 1897

Père David's deer, *4*, 573

Peruvian huemuls, *4*, 571

Philippines tarsiers, *5*, 754

pichi ciego, *1*, 103

pied bare-faced tamarins, *10*, 1507

pied tamarins, *10*, 1506

pig-tailed snub-nosed monkeys, *10*, 1455

pileated gibbons, *6*, 805

Point Arena mountain beavers, *3*, 338

Point Reyes mountain beavers, *3*, 338

polar bears, *11*, 1689

pond bats, *2*, 207, 233

porcupines, *12*, 1716

Pougsargues' mongoose, *9*, 1352

Preuss's guenons, *10*, 1481

proboscis monkeys, *10*, 1455

pronghorns, *12*, 1767

prosperine rock wallabies, *8*, 1145

Przewalski's horses, *7*, 1039

Puerto Rican flower bats, *2*, 181

pumas, *12*, 1793

pygmy chimpanzees, *4*, 493

pygmy hippopotamuses, *7*, 1013

pygmy hogs, *11*, 1638

pygmy right whales, *15*, 2313

pygmy slow lorises, *5*, 754

Pyrenean desmans, *10*, 1404

R

raccoons, *12*, 1846

Raffray's sheath-tailed bats, *2*, 207

rat–tailed trioks, *12*, 1741

red-bellied guenons, *10*, 1481

red-fronted gazelles, *6*, 780

red pandas, *11*, 1611

red-ruffed lemurs, *8*, 1195

red-shanked doucs, *10*, 1455

red-tailed sportive lemurs, *8*, 1195

red viscacha rats, *6*, 909

red wolves, *4*, 525, *16*, 2417

Ridley's leaf-nosed bats, *2*, 207

ring–tailed lemurs, *8*, 1195

Rio Grande beavers, *3*, 338

rock hyraxes, *1*, 56

rufous hare wallabies, *8*, 1169

Russian desmans, *10*, 1404

rusty-spotted cats, *9*, 1273

Ryukyu Island's wild pigs, *11*, 1638

S

sado moles, *10*, 1404

sand foxes, *5*, 728

sandhill dunnarts, *14*, 2157

San Joaquin Valley wood rats, *13*, 1897

San Martin Island wood rats, *13*, 1897

satanic black colobus monkeys, *10*, 1455

scimitar oryx, *1*, 77

Scott's tree kangaroos, *8*, 1169

sea otters, *11*, 1585

sechuran foxes, *5*, 702

sei whales, *16*, 2339

Seram Island long-nosed mouse bandicoots, *16*, 2443

servaline genets, *4*, 519

Seychelles sheath-tailed bats, *2*, 207

short-nosed echidnas, *11*, 1662

short-tailed chinchillas, *6*, 909

Siberian tigers, *15*, 2183

silky anteater, *1*, 51

Silver Rice rats, *13*, 1897

silvery-brown bare-faced tamarins, *10*, 1507

Sinai leopards, *8*, 1221

slender-horned gazelles, *6*, 780

sloth bears, *3*, 311

small bats, *2*, 206–8

small bears, *3*, 310–1

small-eared dogs, *5*, 702

smooth-coated otters, *11*, 1585

snow leopards, *8*, 1221

Soemmerring's gazelles, *6*, 780

Sonoran pronghorns, *12*, 1767

South African hedgehog, *7*, 987

South Arabian leopards, *8*, 1221

South China tigers, *15*, 2183

Southeastern beach mice, *13*, 1897

Southern marsh harvest mice, *13*, 1897

Southern pocket gophers, *14*, 2106

southern right whales, *15*, 2313

Spanish lynx, *9*, 1273

spectacled bears, *3*, 311

spectral tarsiers, *5*, 754

Speke's gazelles, *6*, 780

spider monkeys, *10*, 1429

squirrel monkeys, *10*, 1429

striped hyenas, *7*, 1066

sucker-footed bats, *2*, 207

Sulawesian palm civets, *4*, 519

Sumatran collared mongooses, *9*, 1352

Sumatran orangutans, *11*, 1559

Sumatran rhinoceroses, *13*, 1949

Sumatran tigers, *15*, 2183

sun bears, *3*, 311

sun-tailed guenons, *10*, 1481

swamp deer, *4*, 571

T

tamanduas, *1*, 51

tamaraus, *3*, 440–1

tammar wallabies, *8*, 1145

tarsiers, *5*, 754

tassle-ear marmosets, *10*, 1507

Tate's trioks, *12*, 1741

telefomin cuscuses, *12*, 1741

Thailand brow-antlered deer, *4*, 572

thin-spined porcupines, *6*, 909

Thomas's galagos, *5*, 754

Tibetan wolves, *16*, 2417

titi monkeys, *10*, 1429

Tongan fruit bats, *2*, 155

Tonkin snub-nosed monkeys, *10*, 1455

toolache wallabies, *8*, 1143

Townsend's big-eared bats, *2*, 207, 233

tree hyraxes, *1*, 25

tropical weasels, *15*, 2236

Truk flying foxes, *2*, 155

U

Utah prairie dogs, *14*, 2106–7

V

Vancouver Island marmots,
  14, 2106
vicuñas, *3*, 363
Virginia flying squirrels,
  14, 2132
Visayan warty pigs,
  11, 1638
volcano rabbits,
  12, 1820

W

walia ibex, *6*, 857
wambengers, *14*, 2157
water buffalo,
  3, 440, 441
West African chimpanzees,
  4, 493
West African manatees,
  9, 1299

West Caucasian tur,
  6, 857
western barred bandicoots,
  16, 2443
western bearded pigs,
  11, 1638
western gentle lemurs,
  8, 1195
Western Mexican jaguars,
  8, 1117
western pied colobus
  monkeys,
  10, 1455
western ring-tailed possums,
  12, 1741
West Indian manatees,
  9, 1299
whales,
  16, 2365
white-footed tamarins,
  10, 1506

white-throated guenons,
  10, 1481
white-throated tree kangaroos,
  8, 1169
white tufted-ear marmosets,
  10, 1506
wild cattle, *3*, 441
wildebeests, *1*, 74
wolverines, *16*, 2392
Woodlark Island cuscuses,
  12, 1741
woolly monkeys, *10*, 1429
woolly spider monkeys,
  10, 1429
Wroughton's free-tailed bats,
  2, 207

Y

yaks, *3*, 441
Yangtze dolphins,

  5, 649
yellow-footed rock wallabies,
  8, 1145
yellow-tailed woolly monkeys,
  10, 1429

Z

Zanzibar galagos, *5*, 754
zebra duikers, *6*, 780

GEOGRAPHIC INDEX

A

Afghanistan
  Asian black bears, *3*, 298
Africa
  aardvarks,
    1, 2, 5, 12, 27, 31
  African golden cats, *14*, 2015
  African wildcats,
    14, 2014–5, 2028–9
  angwantibo, *5*, 740
  antelopes, *1*, 55, 57, 64, 66,
    68, 74, 78
  apes, *4*, 473
  black-footed cats,
    14, 2015
  black rhinoceroses,
    13, 1927, 1937
  brown bears, *2*, 264
  brown hyenas, *7*, 1052
  brush-tailed porcupines,
    12, 1704
  buffalo, *3*, 419–20, 423–8,
    431–4, 438, 442
  bushpigs,
    11, 1618, 1625, 1638
  Cape fox, *5*, 706, 721
  Cape fur seals,
    13, 1963, 1976
  Cape ground squirrels,
    14, 2093
  caracals,
    14, 2015, 2027
  cheetahs, *4*, 452, 454
  chevrotains, *12*, 1745
  chimpanzees, *4*, 490
  civets, *4*, 506, 514, 517
  clawless otters,
    11, 1574
  Cyrenaica voles,
    15, 2211
  dormice, *7*, 928
  dromedaries, *3*, 360
  dwarf antelopes,
    6, 766
  elephants, *9*, 1236

  fennec foxes, *16*, 2431
  fruit bats, *2*, 142, 143
  galagos, *5*, 730–55
  gaurs, *3*, 422
  gazelles,
    6, 767, 778, 780, 781
  genets, *4*, 506, 515
  giant forest hogs,
    11, 1618
  giraffes, *6*, 808–33
  golden cats, *9*, 1253–4
  golden moles,
    10, 1390
  gorillas, *6*, 863
  hares, *7*, 949
  hartebeests, *1*, 66
  hedgehogs,
    7, 966–7, 972
  hippopotamuses,
    7, 992, 1002, 1010–3
  house shrews, *14*, 2040
  hunting dogs, *4*, 576–7
  hyenas,
    7, 1044, 1051, 1067
  hyraxes, *1*, 6, 13, 14
  jackals, *8*, 1078, 1088
  jungle cats, *14*, 2008,
    2015, 2016
  lemurs, *8*, 1174
  leopards,
    8, 1208–11, 1219
  linsangs, *4*, 506, 507
  lions, *9*, 1227, 1232,
    1234–5, 1245–9
  lorises, *5*, 732–3
  lorisids, *5*, 741
  mandrills,
    10, 1478, 1480
  mole rats,
    9, 1355–6, 1364
  mongooses, *9*, 1351–2
  multimammate rats,
    13, 1918
  palm civets,
    4, 498, 501–4, 507, 521

  pangolins, *1*, 31, 82, 85,
    90–2, 95, 96, 103, 104
  pikas, *7*, 941
  possums, *12*, 1728
  pottos, *5*, 740
  rhinoceroses,
    13, 1944–5
  rock hyraxes, *1*, 14
  sand cats, *14*, 2015
  Sclater's guenons,
    10, 1482
  servals, *14*, 2005
  shrews, *14*, 2051
  slit-faced bats, *2*, 199
  small cats,
    12, 1775, *14*, 2013
  Somali wild asses,
    7, 1018
  spotted hyenas, *7*, 1052–3
  spotted-necked otters,
    11, 1572, 1574
  springhares, *14*, 2087
  squirrels, *12*, 1721
  tree hyraxes, *1*, 12
  tree squirrels, *14*, 2112
  vesper bats, *2*, 226
  warthogs,
    11, 1618, 1624, 1638
  water chevrotains,
    12, 1753, 1755, 1759, 1761
  white rhinoceroses,
    13, 1927, 1937
  wild asses, *7*, 1021, 1027–8,
    1030, 1033, 1035, 1038
  wild dogs, *4*, 526, 527, 579,
    5, 600–25, 708, *8*, 1072
  wildebeests, *1*, 79
  wild pigs, *11*, 1636
  yellow-winged bats,
    2, 196, 202
  zebras, *16*, 2456, 2462
Africa, Central
  anteaters, *1*, 29
  brush-tailed porcupines,
    12, 1696

  chimpanzees,
    4, 474, 480
  galagos, *5*, 742
  rock hyraxes, *1*, 14
  yellow-winged bats,
    2, 202
Africa, Eastern
  aardvarks, *1*, 24
  bat-eared foxes, *3*, 291
  bush hyraxes, *1*, 12
  cheetahs, *4*, 454, 456–7,
    461–2, 466
  chimpanzees, *4*, 474
  civets, *4*, 518
  gorillas, *6*, 871, 881
  jackals, *8*, 1079
  rock hyraxes, *1*, 14
  silvery mole rats,
    9, 1364
  Simien jackals,
    8, 1071
  spotted hyenas,
    7, 1067
  Thomson's gazelles,
    6, 758
Africa, Northern
  Barbary lions, *9*, 1245
  barbary macaques,
    10, 1468
  brown bears, *2*, 273
  brown hyenas,
    7, 1066
  camels, *3*, 344
  cheetahs,
    4, 447, 466
  dromedaries, *3*, 350
  European rabbits,
    12, 1817
  fennec foxes, *5*, 701
  golden jackals,
    8, 1078
  gundis,
    9, 1355, 1365, 1376–7
  hartebeests, *1*, 76
  leopards, *8*, 1208

red deer, *4*, 559

striped hyenas, *7*, 1053

Africa, Southern

   black-backed jackals,

      8, 1085

   Cape porcupines,

      12, 1716

   cheetahs, *4*, 466

   Hottentot golden moles,

      10,1395

   mole rats, *9*, 1365

   rhinoceroses,

      13, 1938–9

Africa, Western

   cheetahs, *4*, 467

   chevrotains, *12*, 1756

   chimpanzees,

      4, 490, 493

   fruit bats, *2*, 135

   gazelles, *6*, 780

   gorillas, *6*, 864, 881

   guenons, *10*, 1469

   Guinea forest black colobus,

      10, 1444

   Guinea forest red colobus,

      10, 1441

   hippopotamuses,

      7, 1010, 1015

   Liberian mongooses,

      9, 1353

   manatees, *9*, 1278, 1281,

      1286–8, 1290, 1294–5,

      1298–9, 1301

   mandrills,

      10, 1478, 1480

   monkeys, *10*, 1430

   pygmy hippos, *7*, 992

   spotted palm civets,

      4, 517

   sun squirrels, *14*, 2118

Alaska

   American black bears,

      2, 253

   bison, *3*, 395

   blue bears, *2*, 239

   bowhead whales,

      15, 2312

   brown bears, *2*, 264–6, 272,

      276–7, 283

   brown lemmings,

      15, 2230

coyotes, *4*, 532–3

glacier bears, *2*, 239

gray whales, *15*, 2263

grizzly bears, *2*, 286

hoary marmots, *14*, 2100

humpback whales,

   16, 2327

killer whales, *15*, 2273

wolverines, *16*, 2390–1

wolves, *16*, 2403

Algeria

   Barbary ground squirrels,

      14, 2093

   brown bears, *2*, 273

   Mzab gundis,

      9, 1369, 1377–8

   red gazelles, *6*, 778

   rock hyraxes, *1*, 12

Altai Moutains

   leopards, *8*, 1210

   Przewalski's horses,

      7,1018–20, *7*, 1026,

      1028–9, 1036

Amazon

   agoutis, *6*, 897

   anteaters, *1*, 41

   black-shouldered opossums,

      10, 1529

   capuchins, *10*, 1416–7

   dolphins, *5*, 636, 649

   jaguars, *8*, 1105

   manatees,

      9, 1278–81, 1283–4,

      1286–8, 1290–2, 1294–5,

      1297–1300

   marmosets,

      10, 1494, 1496–7

   opossums, *10*, 1535

   small–eared dogs, *5*, 703

   tamanduas, *1*, 38

   tamarins, *10*, 1494

   tassel-eared marmosets,

      10,1492

   uakaris, *10*, 1430

Amazonia

   giant anteaters, *1*, 50

   Hoffman's two-toed sloths,

      14, 2079

   hunting dogs, *4*, 576

   sloths, *14*, 2078

   three-toed sloths, *14*, 2079

America, Central

   anteaters, *1*, 53

   armadillos,

      1, 81, 84, 88, 90

   climbing mice, *13*, 1885

   dawn dogs, *5*, 707

   disc-winged bats, *2*, 188

   dolphins, *5*, 646

   dromedaries, *3*, 350

   free-tailed bats, *2*, 197

   giant anteaters, *1*, 49, 50

   grison, *15*, 2214

   hog-nosed skunks,

      16, 2378

   jaguars,

      8, 1095, 1097,

         1104–5, 1115–7

   leaf-nosed bats, *2*, 180

   peccaries, *11*, 1624

   pocket gophers,

      14, 2084

   silky anteaters, *1*, 40

   sloths,

      1, 32, *14*, 2057,

         2066, 2080

   squirrel monkeys,

      10, 1427, 1429

   vampire bats, *2*, 172

   vesper rats, *13*, 1879

Amsterdam

   aardvarks, *1*, 27

Andes

   alpacas, *3*, 364

   camels, *3*, 362

   capybaras, *3*, 376

   chinchillas, *6*, 898

   llamas, *3*, 364

   pampas cats,

      12, 1780

   spectacled bears,

      3, 298, 300

   tamanduas, *1*, 38

   vicuñas, *3*, 352, 354

Antarctica

   crabeater seals,

      13, 1988

   rorquals,

      16, 2326, 2328–9,

      16, 2339, 2341

   sperm whales,

      16, 2355

true seals,

   13, 1988–92, 2002–3

Arabia

   Arabian oryx,

      1, 57, 65, 69,

         71, 73, 76–7

   Bactrian camels,

      3, 341

   camels, *3*, 356

   gazelles, *4*, 466

   golden jackals,

      8, 1078

   horses, *7*, 1027, 1034

   leopards, *8*, 1208

Arctic

   brown lemmings,

      15, 2190

   collared lemmings,

      15, 2188–90, 2195

   foxes,

      5, 680–90, 693, 696–703,

         708, 714, 716, 722

   leaf-nosed bats, *2*, 159

   narwhals, *16*, 2352

   Norway lemmings,

      15, 2190

   polar bears,

      11, 1667–73

   rorquals, *16*, 2326

   sperm whales, *16*, 2355

   true seals, *13*, 1988

   vesper bats, *2*, 219

   walruses,

      13, 1957, 1972–3

   wolverines, *16*, 2390

   wolves, *16*, 2404, 2405

Argentina

   Chacoan peccaries,

      11, 1638

   coypus, *3*, 388, 390

   giant anteaters, *1*, 49

   gray foxes, *5*, 689–90, 693,

      695–6, 698, 701–2

   guanacos, *3*, 363

   jaguarundi, *12*, 1781

   llamas, *3*, 364

   maned wolves, *4*, 545

   margays, *12*, 1781

   mountain cavies,

      6, 896

   ocelots, *12*, 1780

pampas, *6*, 898–9
Patagonian hares, *6*, 910
peccaries, *11*, 1616
prehensile–tailed
    porcupines, *12*, 1701
Arizona
    jaguars, *8*, 1117
    Mount Graham red
        squirrels, *14*, 2132
    small bats, *2*, 204
Asia
    African small cats,
        14, 2015
    antelopes, *1*, 58
    Asian golden cats,
        14, 2016
    Asian small-clawed otters,
        11, 1574
    babirusas, *11*, 1626
    badgers, *1*, 116
    bears, *2*, 240
    beavers, *3*, 326
    bison, *3*, 394–5, 402
    black bears, *2*, 240, 266
    brown bears,
        2, 264, 278, 283
    brush-tailed porcupines,
        12, 1696, *12*, 1704
    caracals, *14*, 2015, 2027
    Celebes wild pigs,
        11, 1626
    cheetahs, *4*, 447, 466
    chevrotains,
        12, 1746–8, 1756
    Chinese desert cats,
        9, 1261
    chipmunks, *14*, 2087
    civets, *4*, 506
    common raccoons,
        12, 1832
    crested porcupines,
        12, 1703–4
    deer, *4*, 573
    dholes, *4*, 526
    dromedaries,
        3, 350, 360
    fruit bats, *2*, 142
    galagos, *5*, 731, 742–3
    gaurs, *3*, 422
    gazelles,
        6, 775, 780, 781

giant flying squirrels,
    14, 2112
goats, *6*, 854
golden cats,
    9, 1253–4, 1259, 1261,
        1265, 1268, 1272–3
golden jackals, *8*, 1090
gorillas, *6*, 863
hamsters, *7*, 924
hares, *7*, 941
hippopotamuses, *7*, 992
house shrews, *14*, 2040
hunting dogs, *4*, 576
Javan rhinoceroses,
    13, 1938, 1941
jungle cats,
    14, 2008, 2015
lions,
    9, 1234, 1244, 1246–7, 1249
lorises, *5*, 732–3
lorisids, *5*, 741
marbled polecats,
    15, 2214
marmots, *14*, 2086
mongooses, *9*, 1350–2
New World rats and mice,
    13, 1894
orangutans, *11*, 1540
palm civets, *4*, 498
pangolins,
    1, 31, 82–5, 90, 102
pikas, *7*, 941–2, 955
pottos, *5*, 732–3
red-cheeked squirrels,
    14, 2119
red deer, *4*, 559
red squirrels,
    14, 2112
Russian flying squirrels,
    14, 2112
sand cats, *14*, 2015
serows, *6*, 849
servals, *14*, 2005
shrew-moles,
    10, 1389, 1399
shrews, *14*, 2032
small cats, *12*, 1775
smooth-coated otters,
    11, 1574
Southern Asian cats,
    9, 1261–2

Sumatran rhinoceroses,
    13, 1938, 1941
takins, *6*, 843
tigers, *15*, 2162, 2180
tree squirrels,
    14, 2112
vesper bats, *2*, 228
water buffalo, *3*, 428–9
wild asses,
    7, 1019, 1021, 1025–8,
        1031, 1033, 1035,
1037–9
wildcats, *14*, 2029
wild pigs,
    11, 1615, 1618
wolves, *4*, 584
Asia, Central
    gazelles, *6*, 776
    long-clawed ground
        squirrels, *14*, 2094
    mountain voles,
        15, 2196
Asia, Southern
    cheetahs, *4*, 452
    dholes, *4*, 595–6
Assam
    giant forest hogs,
        11, 1637
    pygmy hogs, *11*, 1637
Atlantic Forest
    capuchins, *10*, 1416
Australasia
    deer, *4*, 550
    echidnas, *11*, 1640–65
    marsupials,
        8, 1122, *12*, 1721
    platypuses,
        11, 1640–65
    razorbacks,
        11, 1616
    vesper bats, *2*, 219
Australia
    anteaters, *1*, 31
    Australian hopping mice,
        13, 1916, 1922–3
    bandicoots,
        16, 2430, 2435
    banteng, *3*, 443
    Bennett's tree kangaroos,
        8, 1157–8
    big-headed flying foxes,

2, 142
bilbies, *16*, 2422, 2430
black-footed rock wallabies,
    8, 1131
bottle-nosed dolphins,
    5, 642
brumbies, *7*, 1036, 1039
deer, *4*, 573
dingoes,
    4, 578–9, 582–6, 588, 593–9
dromedaries, *3*, 350–1
eastern hare wallabies,
    8, 1169
echidnas, *12*, 1696
European rabbits,
    12, 1814, 1817
false vampire bats,
    2, 188, 199, 205
foxes,
    5, 715, *16*, 2440, 2444
fruit bats, *2*, 142, 154
golden horseshoe bats,
    2, 207
gray kangaroos, *8*, 1134
hare wallabies, *8*, 1156–8
honey possums, *13*, 1864
kangaroos, *8*, 1120–45
koalas, *8*, 1146–71, *11*, 1593
Leadbeater's possums,
    12, 1728
long-haired rats,
    13, 1921–2
long-tailed dunnarts,
    14, 2159
Lumholtz's tree kangaroos,
    8, 1157–8
marsupial moles,
    10, 1384, *14*, 2144
marsupials,
    8, 1166, *10*, 1514, 1520,
        12, 1719–20, 1726, 1738
merinos, *6*, 858
numbats, *14*, 2149, 2159
possums,
    12, 1729, 1738–43
pygmy possums,
    12, 1740
rabbits, *4*, 586, 588,
    598, *8*, 1142, *12*, 1818–9
rat kangaroos, *13*, 1848–73
rat-sized mulgara, *14*, 2151

red foxes, *5*, 712, 727

red kangaroos,
  8, 1131, 1134

rufous hare wallabies,
  8, 1169

short-nosed echidnas,
  11, 1643

spectacled hare wallabies,
  8, 1156–7

spotted cuscuses,
  12, 1720

Tasmanian devils,
  14, 2134–59

water buffalo, *3*, 420

wombats, *16*, 2420–45

yellow-footed rock
  wallabies,
  8, 1132, 1145

Austria
  polar bears, *11*, 1671

B

Bahamas
  hutias, *6*, 908–9

Bahia
  maned sloths,
  14, 2081

Baja California (Mexico)
  Bryde's whales,
  16, 2326
  gray whales,
  15, 2246, 2249–51,
  2255, 2258, 2263

Balaeric Islands
  cave goats, *6*, 856

Balé Moutains
  Simien jackals,
  8, 1079–81, 1092–3
  Speke's gundis, *9*, 1366

Bali
  banteng, *3*, 443
  fruit bats, *2*, 156

Bangkok
  gibbons, *6*, 807

Bangladesh
  Asian black bear,
  3, 309
  fruit bats, *2*, 152
  otters, *11*, 1586
  sun bears, *3*, 298

Barro Colorado Island sloths,
  14, 2068–9, 2074, 2079

Barrow Island
  spectacled hare wallabies,
  8, 1156

Bay of Plenty
  killer whales, *15*, 2276–7

Belgium
  mountain gorillas, *6*, 882

Belize
  giant anteaters, *1*, 49

Bering Sea
  California gray whales,
  15, 2254
  northern fur seals,
  13, 1961
  Steller's sea lions,
  13, 1976

Bering Strait
  bison, *3*, 395, 403

Bhutan Manas Forest
  tigers, *15*, 2184

Black Forest
  wild boars, *11*, 1626–7

Bolivia
  tamandua, *1*, 38

Borneo
  bay cats,
  9, 1253, 1262, 1267, 1271
  bearded pigs,
  11, 1629, 1631
  colobines, *10*, 1455–6
  groove-toothed squirrels,
  14, 2119, 2131
  long-tailed porcupines,
  12, 1704
  orangutans,
  11, 1536–61

Botswana
  leopards, *8*, 1223
  territory, *7*, 1060

Brazil
  anteaters, *1*, 48
  armadillos, *1*, 101, 105
  black tamarins, *10*, 1488
  buffy-headed marmosets,
  10, 1495
  capybaras, *3*, 379
  cavies, *6*, 896
  common marmosets,
  10, 1486

coyotes, *4*, 547

funnel-eared bats, *2*, 201

Geoffrey's marmosets,
  10, 1492

giant anteaters, *1*, 49, 53

golden lion tamarins,
  10, 1504, 1506

jaguars,
  8, 1105, 1107, 1114

leaf-nosed bats, *2*, 168

lion tamarins,
  10, 1488, 1507

maned sloths, *14*, 2081

marmosets, *10*, 1496

opossums, *10*, 1534–5

pied tamarins, *10*, 1506

short-tailed opossums,
  10, 1529

sloths, *14*, 2079

three-toed sloths,
  14, 2070

Britain
  American minks,
  9, 1313
  badgers, *1*, 124
  beavers, *3*, 338
  chevrotains, *12*, 1756
  common European shrews,
  14, 2033
  deer, *4*, 573
  dolphins, *5*, 647–8
  domestic cats, *9*, 1274
  Exmoor ponies,
  7, 1024, 1028
  gray squirrels, *9*, 1319,
  14, 2119, 2130, 2132–3
  harvest mice, *13*, 1923
  hedgehogs, *7*, 985–7
  hedgerows, *7*, 986
  otters, *11*, 1583–4, 1586
  pine martens, *9*, 1319
  rabbits, *12*, 1808
  red squirrels, *14*, 2132–3
  shrews, *14*, 2050, 2053
  small bats, *2*, 206
  white-toothed shrews,
  14, 2039
  wild cattle, *3*, 443

British Columbia
  American black bears,
  2, 250, 258

brown bears, *2*, 272

creamy white bears,
  2, 239

gray whales, *15*, 2249

Kermode bears, *2*, 239

killer whales, *15*, 2280

British Isles
  Scilly shrews, *14*, 2040

Bulgaria
  golden jackals,
  8, 1090
  wolves, *16*, 2418

Burma
  deer, *4*, 472
  pandas, *11*, 1592
  tigers, *15*, 2171
  zebras, *16*, 2458–9

C

Caledonian Forest
  pine martens, *9*, 1314–5

Calgary
  American black bears,
  2, 249

California
  American black bears,
  2, 250, 257
  beavers, *3*, 324
  common seals,
  13, 1988
  dolphins, *5*, 636
  fruit bats, *2*, 154
  grizzly bears, *2*, 284
  kit foxes, *5*, 723
  northern elephant seals,
  13, 2003
  porpoises,
  5, 649, 651
  salt marsh harvest mice,
  13, 1895
  sea otters,
  11, 1572, 1574
  vesper bats, *2*, 221
  Virginia opossums,
  10, 1521

Camargue delta
  horses,
  7, 1024–6, 1028, 1040

Cameroon
  aardvarks, *1*, 12

Canada
  American black bears,
    2, 248, 253
  beavers,
    3, 319–21, 324–6,
      337, 339
  bison, *3*, 415–6
  brown bears,
    2, 264, 272, 276, 283
  coyotes, *4*, 533, 544
  deer, *4*, 560
  geese, *4*, 535
  ground squirrels,
    14, 2104
  hoary marmots,
    14, 2100
  lynx, *12*, 1775
  musk oxen, *6*, 846
  North American porcupines,
    12, 1693–4, 1702,
      1704–5, 1715
  pocket mice, *14*, 2099
  polar bears,
    11, 1674, 1683, 1690
  raccoons, *12*, 1832
  stoats, *15*, 2226
  striped skunks, *16*, 2387
  taiga voles, *15*, 2203
  true seals,
    13, 1986, 2000
  Vancouver Island marmots,
    14, 2092, 2106–7
  vesper bats, *2*, 226
  Virginia opossums, *10*, 1524
  western pocket gophers,
    14, 2094
  wolverines, *16*, 2392
  wolves, *16*, 2414, 2416
  wood bison, *3*, 403
Canary Island
  short-finned pilot whales,
    15, 2287
Cape Cod
  right whales, *15*, 2302–3
Caribbean
  Antillean manatees,
    9, 1286
  funnel-eared bats, *2*, 201
  leaf-nosed bats, *2*, 168
  raccoons, *12*, 1833
  rice rats, *13*, 1898

solenodons,
    14, 2039, 2045, 2050
Carpathians
  brown bears, *2*, 274–5
Caspian Sea
  true seals, *13*, 1999
Caucasus
  free-tailed bats, *2*, 194
Cedros Island
  mule deer, *4*, 570
Central Asia
  gazelles, *6*, 780
Chad
  antelopes, *1*, 79
Channel Islands
  Scilly shrews, *14*, 2040
  white-toothed shrews,
    14, 2039
Chernobyl
  Lapp deer, *4*, 573
Cheyne Beach
  Tasmanian devils,
    14, 2146–7
Chile
  capybaras, *3*, 376
  chinchilla-rats, *6*, 910
  chinchillas, *6*, 911
  coruros, *6*, 903
  deer, *4*, 573
  guanacos, *3*, 363
  Juan Fernandez fur seals,
    13, 1962
  long-tailed chinchillas,
    6, 907
  sea cats, *11*, 1582
  sloths, *1*, 32
China
  Asian black bears, *3*, 290,
    298, 302
  badgers, *1*, 108
  Biet's snub-nosed monkeys,
    10, 1439, 1455
  Brelich's snub-nosed
    monkeys, *10*, 1455
  Chinese shrew-moles,
    10, 1383, 1389
  complex-toothed flying
    squirrels, *14*, 2119
  deer, *4*, 472
  gibbons,
    6, 784, 804

golden monkeys, *10*, 1446
golden snub-nose monkeys,
    10, 1454
hamsters, *7*, 914
Kansu moles, *10*, 1405
Korean gray hamsters,
    7, 917
large-spotted civets, *4*, 517
otters, *11*, 1586
pandas, *11*, 1591–2, 1596,
    1598–9, 1608–12
porcupines, *12*, 1717
ratlike hamsters,
    7, 923, 932
rock squirrels, *14*, 2093
small bears, *3*, 310, 313
sun bears, *3*, 298
tigers, *15*, 2180–3
Colombia
  anteaters, *1*, 53
  capybaras, *3*, 378
  giant anteaters, *1*, 50
  Goeldi's monkeys,
    10, 1495
  jaguars, *8*, 1097, 1106–7
  Upper Amazon porcupines,
    12, 1703
Colombia, Western
  tamanduas, *1*, 38
Colorado
  bison, *3*, 414
  coyotes, *4*, 539
  gray foxes, *5*, 712
  llamas, *3*, 365
  long-tailed weasels,
    15, 2222
Congo
  galagos, *5*, 742–3, 755
  mandrills, *10*, 1479
Corfu
  slit-faced bats, *2*, 199
Costa Rica
  anteaters, *1*, 53
  coyotes, *4*, 532
  Nancite coatis, *12*, 1847
  two-toed sloths,
    14, 2078
Cozumel Island
  Cozumel Island raccoons,
    12, 1832, 1846–7
  island coatis, *12*, 1825

Crozet Islands
  killer whales, *15*, 2283
Cuba
  Cuban solenodon,
    14, 2040, 2051–3
  flower bats, *2*, 181
  hutias, *6*, 908

D

Denmark
  hedgehogs, *7*, 986
  polar bears, *11*, 1689
Dominican Republic
  Hispaniolan solenodons,
    14, 2051

E

Ecuador
  manatees, *9*, 1300
  small bears, *3*, 312
Egypt
  antelopes, *1*, 75
  cats, *14*, 2028
  fruit bats, *2*, 134, 137
  hyraxes, *1*, 6
England
  badgers, *1*, 129
  foxes, *5*, 719
  gibbons, *6*, 805, 807
  moles, *10*, 1394, 1403
  New Forest ponies, *7*, 1031
  rabbits, *12*, 1808–9, 1815
  red foxes, *5*, 723
  roe deer, *4*, 559
  Thoroughbreds, *7*, 1040
  white rhinoceroses,
    13, 1950
  wild cattle, *3*, 427
Ethiopia
  antelopes, *1*, 64, 78
  civets, *4*, 516, 518
  gelada baboons, *10*, 1468–9
  golden jackals, *8*, 1079
  Simien jackals, *8*, 1079–81,
    1090, 1092–3
  Speke's gundis, *9*, 1366–7
Etosha Pan
  armadillos, *1*, 93
  pangolins, *1*, 93

Eurasia
  beavers, *3*, 339
  bison, *3*, 394, 402–4, 413
  blind mole rats, *9*, 1355,
    1357–8, 1363, 1375
  brown bears, *2*, 273
  camels, *3*, 344
  European beavers, *3*, 318
  lemmings, *15*, 2186–2211
  lynx, *9*, 1260
  raccoons, *12*, 1845
  squirrels, *12*, 1721
  tundra voles, *15*, 2210
  vesper bats, *2*, 219–20
  voles, *15*, 2186–2211
Europe
  African wild dogs, *5*, 623
  American minks, *9*, 1314
  badgers, *1*, 116
  beavers,
    3, 316–9, 321, 324–6
      337, 339, 405
  bison,
    3, 395–6, 404–7, 413, 417
  brown bears, *2*, 264, 265,
    272–5, 278, 283, 287
  brown hares, *7*, 946, 948
  civets, *4*, 506
  common hamsters, *7*, 922
  common raccoons,
    12, 1832
  crested African porcupines,
    12, 1717
  deer, *4*, 549–50
  dholes, *4*, 584
  Eurasian otters,
    11, 1572–3
  European minks, *9*, 1306,
    1312–3, 1325–7
  European moles,
    10, 1385, 1391, 1394, 1397,
      1399–1401, 1402, 1405
  fallow deer, *4*, 560
  fruit bats, *2*, 136
  gaurs, *3*, 422
  giraffes, *6*, 811
  goats, *6*, 849
  hamsters,
    7, 916, 922, 924
  hedgehogs, *7*, 985, 988,
    989, *12*, 1696

house shrews, *14*, 2040
lynx, *12*, 1775
marbled polecats, *15*, 2237
marmots, *14*, 2086
martens, *9*, 1305
New Forest ponies,
  7, 1026
Old World rats and mice,
  13, 1910–1
porcupines, *12*, 1701
pygmy field mice,
  13, 1910
raccoons, *12*, 1845
red deer, *4*, 559
red foxes, *5*, 728, *8*, 1090
red squirrels, *14*, 2112
rock mice, *13*, 1910
Russian flying squirrels,
  14, 2112
small bats, *2*, 204, 206
snow voles, *15*, 2196
steppe polecats, *15*, 2237
striped field mice,
  13, 1910
Tatra pine voles, *15*, 2210
vesper bats,
  2, 226, 229, 231–4
vulpine foxes, *5*, 728
wild boars, *11*, 1618
wild pigs, *11*, 1615, 1624
wild sheep, *6*, 856
wolves, *16*, 2404
wood mice, *13*, 1910
yellow-necked mice,
  13, 1910
Europe, Eastern
  bison, *3*, 402
  Bobak marmots, *14*, 2107
Everglades
  pumas, *12*, 1782–3

F

Faeroe Island
  long-finned pilot whales,
    15, 2288
Falkland Islands
  wolves, *5*, 681
Finland
  beavers, *3*, 338
  wolves, *16*, 2418

Flinders Island
  wombats, *16*, 2432–3
Florida
  aardvarks, *1*, 27
  American black bears,
    2, 247, 253
  armadillos, *1*, 89
  beavers, *3*, 324
  Chadwick Beach cotton
  mice,
    13, 1897
  Florida mice, *13*, 1895–6
  manatees,
    9, 1281, 1285–9, 1291,
      1296, 1298–9, 1301
  pumas, *12*, 1782–3
  red wolves, *4*, 525
  shrews, *14*, 2051
Fontainebleu
  badgers, *1*, 119
Forest hogs
  galagos, *5*, 743
France
  Ariegeois, *7*, 1028
  beavers, *3*, 339
  bison, *3*, 395
  horses,
    7, 1024–6, 1028, 1040

G

Gabon
  chimpanzees, *4*, 490, 495
  linsang, *4*, 506
Galápagos Islands
  black rats, *13*, 1896–7
  California sea lions,
    13, 1962
  Galápagos fur seals,
    13, 1964–5
  giant rats, *13*, 1897
  rice rats, *13*, 1895–7
Ganges
  dolphins, *5*, 649
Germany
  aardvarks, *1*, 27
  common hamsters, *7*, 923
  hedgehogs, *7*, 986
  moles, *10*, 1402
  raccoon dogs, *4*, 598
  small bats, *2*, 186, 209

stone martens, *9*, 1310
titi monkeys, *10*, 1428
vulpine foxes, *5*, 727
wild boars, *11*, 1626–7
wolves, *16*, 2418
Gibraltar
  barbary macaques,
    10, 1468
Gobi Desert
  Asiatic wild asses, *7*, 1038
  Bactrian camels,
    3, 348, 350, 356, 360, 365
  camels, *3*, 353
  Mongolian wild horses,
    3, 352
  Pallas's pikas, *7*, 950
  Przewalski's horses, *7*, 1028
Gough Island
  seals, *13*, 1963
Great Britain
  gray seals, *13*, 2001
  wildcats, *12*, 1795
Great Plains
  ground squirrels,
    14, 2094–5
Greece
  brown bears, *2*, 283, 287
  chamois, *6*, 856
  otters, *11*, 1587
  wolves, *16*, 2418
Greenland
  goats, *6*, 836
  musk oxen, *6*, 846
Grenada
  Small Indian mongooses,
    9, 1353
Guam
  fruit bats, *2*, 154–5
  vesper bats, *2*, 230
Guano
  fruit bats, *2*, 157
Guatemala
  giant anteater, *1*, 38
  giant anteaters, *1*, 49
  Guatemalan howlers,
    10, 1427
  silky anteater, *1*, 38
Guinea
  chimpanzees, *4*, 490
Guyana
  giant otters, *11*, 1580

manatees,
  9, 1290, 1300
sloths, *14*, 2067

H

Hawaii
  Hawaiian monk seals,
    13, 1988, 1997, 2001
Himalayas, *4*, 508
  Bengal foxes, *5*, 714
  goats, *6*, 855–6
  Himalayan rhesus
  macaques, *10*,1468
  musk deer, *4*, 571
  sheep, *6*, 855–6
Hispaniola
  Hispaniolan solenodons,
    14, 2040, 2051–3
Hudson Bay
  polar bears, *11*, 1674,
    1683, 1690
Hungary
  brown bears, *2*, 275
  European susliks,
    14, 2107

I

Iceland
  arctic foxes, *5*, 700
  horses, *7*, 1027
  lupine foxes, *5*, 686
Idaho
  American black bears,
    2, 253
India
  antelopes, *1*, 58
  Asian black bears, *3*, 290
  Asiatic lions,
    9, 1244, 1246
  Asiatic striped palm
  squirrels, *14*, 2118
  Bengal foxes,
    5, 708, 714–5, 719, 728
  Bengal tigers, *15*, 2164
  blackbuck, *4*, 466
  caracals, *14*, 2027
  cattle, *3*, 436
  chital deer, *4*, 560
  civets, *4*, 511, 516, 518

clouded leopards, *8*, 1210
colobines, *10*, 1456
dholes, *4*, 596, 598
elephants, *5*, 674, 676
fruit bats, *2*, 156–7
gibbons, *6*, 784
hanuman monkeys,
  10, 1439, 1452
hog deer, *4*, 560
hyenas, *7*, 1044
leopards, *8*, 1200
lion-tailed macaques,
  10, 1483
Malabar giant squirrels,
  14, 2111, 2117
mandrills, *10*, 1478
nilgiri martens,
  9, 1305, 1326
oriental civets, *4*, 517
pangolins, *1*, 83
pygmy hogs, *11*, 1630
slender loris, *5*, 741
slender lorises, *5*, 740
sloth bears,
  3, 290, 298
sun bears, *3*, 298
tigers,
  15, 2180, 2182
white tigers, *15*, 2163
India, Southern
  cave swiftlet, *2*, 198
Indiana
  coyotes, *4*, 544
Indonesia
  babirusas,
    11, 1624, 1630
  banteng, *3*, 431
  civets, *4*, 518–9
  colobines, *10*, 1455
  crested porcupines,
    12, 1696, 1703–4
  flying lemurs,
    14, 2127
  Javan leopards, *8*, 1220
  Javan rhinoceroses,
    13, 1937
  long-nosed echidnas,
    11, 1662, 1665
  lorisids, *5*, 755
  Old World crested
    porcupines, *12*, 1711

primates, *10*, 1457
tarsiers, *5*, 733–4
tigers, *15*, 2171
tree squirrels, *14*, 2112
wolflike dingoes, *8*, 1166
Indo-Pacific
  hump-backed dolphins,
    5, 636
Iran
  Asian black bears, *3*, 298
  brown bears, *2*, 273
  cheetahs, *4*, 468
Iraq
  dromedaries, *3*, 343
Ireland
  bison, *3*, 394
  dolphins, *5*, 634
  otters, *11*, 1584
  pine martens, *9*, 1313
  weasels, *15*, 2216
  wolves, *16*, 2414
Iriomote
  Iriomote cats,
    9, 1253, 1262, 1266, 1273
Israel
  gazelles, *6*, 781
  Nubian ibex, *6*, 857
  rock hyraxes, *1*, 14
Italy
  brown bears, *2*, 287
  ibex, *6*, 854
  wolves, *16*, 2416, 2417
Ivory Coast
  chimpanzees,
    4, 480, 487, 490

J

Jamaica
  fig-eating bats, *2*, 183
  hutias, *6*, 909
  leaf-nosed bats,
    2, 181, 183
Japan
  Amami rabbits,
    12, 1806, 1820
  Asian black bears,
    3, 297, 312
  brown bears, *2*, 264
  dolphins, *5*, 646
  dormice, *7*, 937

elephants, *5*, 674
Japanese moles, *10*, 1405
pandas, *11*, 1611
pygmy dormice, *7*, 914
raccoon dogs, *4*, 592
rorquals, *16*, 2340–1
shrew-moles, *10*, 1389
wild pigs, *11*, 1615
Jordan
  dromedaries, *3*, 343

K

Kalahari Desert
  brown hyenas, *7*, 1053–4,
    1060, 1064–5, 1067
  marsh mongooses,
    9, 1331
  meerkats, *9*, 1340–1
Kansas
  bison, *3*, 415
Kashmir
  woolly flying squirrels,
    14, 2119
Kentucky
  vesper bats, *2*, 233
Kenya
  aardvarks, *1*, 17
  African wild dogs,
    5, 611, 622
  antelopes, *1*, 74, 75
  black rhinoceroses,
    13, 1950
  busy-tailed mongooses,
    9, 1352
  cheetahs, *4*, 466
  dwarf mongooses,
    9, 1336
  elephants, *5*, 672, 676
  gazelles, *6*, 766
  giraffes,
    6, 816, 828, 832
  impala, *1*, 66
  naked mole rats,
    9, 1365
  rhinoceroses, *13*, 1951
  rock squirrels,
    14, 2099
  silvery mole rats, *9*, 1364
Kilimanjaro
  eastern tree hyraxes, *1*, 25

Korea
  bison, *3*, 394
Krakatoa volcano,
  13, 1948–9

L

Labrador
  beavers, *3*, 326–7
Lake Superior
  coyotes, *4*, 534–5
Lapland
  stoats, *15*, 2224–5
  weasels, *15*, 2224–5
Latin America
  anteaters, *1*, 53
  jaguars, *8*, 1102, 1119
  proboscis bats, *2*, 195
  short-tailed
    spear-nosed bats, *2*, 166
  tree squirrels, *14*, 2112
  vampire bats, *2*, 180, 205
Lebanon
  rock hyraxes, *1*, 12
  wolves, *16*, 2417
Liberia
  chimpanzees, *4*, 480
  hippopotamuses, *7*, 1015
  otters, *11*, 1585
  pygmy hippopotamuses,
    7, 1000, 1012–3
Libya
  gundis, *9*, 1363
  rock hyraxes, *1*, 12
Lithuania
  gaurs, *3*, 422
Los Angeles
  coyotes, *4*, 546
Louisiana
  American black bears,
    2, 259
  coypus, *3*, 388
  red wolves, *4*, 525

M

Madagascar
  bushpigs, *11*, 1625
  civets, *4*, 498–9, 518, 519
  hedgehogs, *7*, 965, 968,
    975, 979, 988–9

lemurs, *5*, 733, *8*, 1172–97
mongooses,
  9, 1333, 1350–3
palm civets, *4*, 498, 508
ring-tailed mongooses,
  9, 1338
Maine
  beavers, *3*, 339
Malay
  pangolins, *1*, 101
Malay Peninsula
  chevrotains, *12*, 1756
Malaysia
  colobines, *10*, 1456
  fruit bats, *2*, 156
  leaf-nosed bats, *2*, 197
  long-tailed porcupines,
    12, 1704
  mandrills, *10*, 1480–1
  tapirs, *16*, 2469–70
Maríamadre Island
  Tres Marías raccoons,
    12, 1832
Marianas
  fruit bats, *2*, 152, 155
Masai Mara
  African wild dogs,
    5, 611, 620, 625
  giraffes, *6*, 828, 832
  spotted hyenas, *7*, 1066
Mayanja Forest
  Old World rats and mice,
    13, 1912–3
McNeil River
  brown bears, *2*, 286
Mediterranean
  blind mole rats, *9*, 1366
  fallow deer, *4*, 560
  goats, *6*, 847
  voles, *15*, 2204
Mednij Island
  lupine foxes, *5*, 703
Mentawai Islands
  Mentawai Islands sureli,
    10, 1444–5, 1446
  Mentawai langurs,
    10, 1448, 1455
  pig-tailed snub-nosed leaf
    monkeys, *10*, 1454
Meru
  eastern tree hyraxes, *1*, 25

Mexico
  American black bears,
    2, 248, 257
  armadillos, *1*, 81
  Barbados raccoons,
    12, 1832
  broad-tail beavers, *3*, 338
  brown bears, *2*, 264
  Bryde's whales, *16*, 2326
  coyotes, *4*, 532
  dolphins, *5*, 651
  Eastern Mexican jaguars,
    8, 1117
  free-tailed bats,
    2, 194, 196
  funnel-eared bats, *2*, 201
  gray whales, *15*, 2246,
    2249–51, 2255, 2258, 2263
  grizzly bears, *2*, 284
  ground squirrels,
    14, 2094, 2104
  island coatis, *12*, 1825
  jaguars, *8*, 1097, 1104–5,
    1112, 1114–5, 1117–8
  long-nosed armadillo, *1*, 101
  long-nosed bats,
    2, 170–1, 181–2
  margays, *12*, 1781
  mouse opossums, *10*, 1524
  New World rats and mice,
    13, 1886–7
  Peter's squirrels, *14*, 2132
  raccoons, *12*, 1824, 1833
  Rio Grande beavers,
    3, 338
  small bats, *2*, 204
  spotted skunks, *16*, 2378
  tamandua, *1*, 38
  vesper bats, *2*, 220, 226, 235
  volcano rabbits, *12*, 1820–1
  voles, *15*, 2188, 2210
  Western Mexican jaguars,
    8, 1117
Michigan
  otters, *11*, 1586
Middle East
  gundis, *9*, 1377
  hyraxes, *1*, 14
  mouse-tailed bats, *2*, 188
Minnesota
  coyotes, *4*, 539

Mississippi
  vesper bats, *2*, 233
Mongolia
  Asian black bears, *3*, 290
  leopards, *8*, 1210
  Przewalski's horses,
    7, 1018–20, 1026,
    1028–9, 1036
Montana
  American black bears, *2*, 258
  coyotes, *4*, 541
Morocco
  Barbary ground squirrels,
    14, 2093
  brown bears, *2*, 273
  gundis, *9*, 1363
Mount Kilimanjaro
  African wild dogs, *5*, 610
Mournpall Paddock,
  8, 1142–3
Mozambique
  dolphins, *5*, 634
Muskeget Island
  beach voles, *15*, 2210

N

Nairobi Desert
  warthogs, *11*, 1628
Namib Desert
  antelopes, *1*, 64
  brown hyenas,
    7, 1064–5, 1067
  Namib golden moles,
    10, 1388, 1390, 1398
Namibia
  African wildcats, *14*, 2020
  armadillos, *1*, 92
  black-footed cats, *14*, 2014
  brown hyenas, *7*, 1053–4
  dune mole rats, *9*, 1365
  Etosha National Park, *1*, 92
  giraffes, *6*, 819
  lions, *9*, 1249
  pangolins, *1*, 92
  rhinoceroses, *13*, 1951
Nepal
  small bears, *3*, 308
  tigers, *15*, 2182, 2184
Netherlands
  greater horseshoe bats,

2, 207

Nevada
  beavers, *3*, 324
  brown bears, *2*, 272
New England
  deer, *4*, 560–1
Newfoundland
  pilot whales, *15*, 2288
New Guinea
  anteaters, *1*, 31
  Arfak ring-tailed possums,
    12, 1743
  Australian dingoes, *4*, 578
  bandicoots, *16*, 2430, 2436
  echidnas, *11*, 1651
  fruit bats,
    2, 141, 155, 156
  kangaroos, *8*, 1130
  koalas, *8*, 1168
  long-nosed echidnas,
    11, 1643, 1648, 1651,
      1662, 1665
  possums, *12*, 1719, 1728
  Seram Island long–nosed
    mouse bandicoots,
      16, 2440
  short-nosed echidnas,
    11, 1643
  spotted cuscuses, *12*, 1726
  tree kangaroos,
    8, 1155, 1171
  Weyland ring–tailed
    possums, *12*, 1743
New Mexico
  free-tailed bats,
    2, 194, 196
New South Wales
  bettongs, *13*, 1872
  rufous rat kangaroos,
    13, 1872
New York
  ermine, *15*, 2234
New Zealand
  brush-tailed possums,
    12, 1729
  common brush-tailed
    possums, *12*, 1740–1
  common weasels, *15*, 2232
  deer, *4*, 472, 573
  dolphins, *5*, 634
  echidnas, *12*, 1696

Himalayan tahrs, *6*, 857
killer whales, *15*, 2276–7
rabbits, *12*, 1805
short-tailed bats,
  2, 162, 168, 181
spotted cuscuses,
  12, 1720
stoats, *15*, 2222, 2232
weasels, *15*, 2222
Ngorongoro Crater
  golden jackals,
    8, 1076, 1084
  hyenas,
    7, 1054–5, 1058, 1060
  lions, *9*, 1234
  spotted hyenas, *7*, 1064
Niah Caves
  orangutans, *11*, 1556
Niger
  addaxes, *1*, 76
  antelopes, *1*, 79
Nilgiri Hills
  tahr, *6*, 856–7
North America
  American black bears,
    2, 236–61
  American coast moles,
    10, 1400–1
  American martens, *9*, 1314
  American river otters,
    11, 1572–3
  anteaters, *1*, 32, 33
  antelopes, *1*, 55
  armadillos, *1*, 84
  beavers, *3*, 324, 339
  bighorn sheep,
    6, 852–3, 855–6, 858–9
  bison, *3*, 395–404, 406,
    410, 412–4, 417
  black-tailed prairie dogs,
    14, 2105
  bobcats,
    12, 1772, 1780, 1789
  brown bears, *2*, 264
  camels, *3*, 344, 350
  chipmunks, *14*, 2087
  coyotes, *8*, 1090
  dawn dogs, *5*, 707
  deer, *4*, 560–1
  deer mice, *13*, 1877, 1884
  eastern pocket gophers,

14, 2094
Eurasian weasels,
  15, 2214
fishers, *9*, 1304–5, 1324
goat antelopes, *6*, 858
goats, *6*, 836
gray foxes,
  5, 709, 712, 726
gray squirrels,
  14, 2118, 2119, 2130
gray whales, *15*, 2240
ground squirrels,
  14, 2087, 2092
hares, *7*, 950
horses, *7*, 1024
jackals, *8*, 1070
jaguars, *8*, 1119
jaguarundi, *12*, 1781
lemmings, *15*, 2186–2211
long-tailed weasels,
  15, 2214
marmots, *14*, 2086
marsupials,
  8, 1122, 1150, 1166
mountain beavers, *3*, 325
mountain goats, *6*, 859
muskrats, *15*, 2210
mustangs, *7*, 1038
New World rats and mice,
  13, 1884, 1894–5
North American porcupines,
  12, 1693–5, 1702,
    1704–5, 1715
opossums, *10*, 1520
peccaries, *11*, 1616
pikas, *7*, 942, 954
pine squirrels, *14*, 2125
pocket gophers,
  14, 2084, 2098
prairie dogs, *14*, 2087, 2104
prairie voles, *15*, 2205
pronghorns, *12*, 1746,
  1754–7, 1764–9
pumas, *12*, 1770–95
rabbits, *12*, 1800
raccoons,
  12, 1823, 1824
right whales, *15*, 2311
short-tailed shrews, *13*, 1885
shrew-moles,
  10, 1389, 1390, 1399

shrews, *14*, 2032
skunks, *16*, 2372
sloths, *14*, 2060
small cats, *12*, 1771
snowshoe hare, *7*, 947
snowshoe hares, *7*, 961
southern flying squirrels,
  14, 2117
squirrels, *12*, 1721
star-nosed moles,
  10, 1383, 1388–9
stoats, *15*, 2214, 2216
swift foxes, *5*, 728
vesper bats, *2*, 220, 226,
  232–3, 235
Virginia opossums,
  10, 1533
voles, *15*, 2186–2211
wild boars, *11*, 1616
wild horses, *7*, 1038
wolves, *4*, 534, *16*, 2404,
  2414, 2416
wood rats, *13*, 1890
North Atlantic
  rorquals, *16*, 2338
  sperm whales, *16*, 2364
Northern Hemisphere
  humpback whales,
    16, 2336
  rorquals, *16*, 2326, 2336
North Pacific
  gray whales, *15*, 2242
North Sea
  dolphins, *5*, 648
  gray seals, *13*, 1994
Norway
  brown bears, *2*, 287
  Fjord ponies, *7*, 1027
  ground squirrels, *14*, 2107
  killer whales, *15*, 2283
  polar bears, *11*, 1688
  rorquals, *16*, 2341

O

Oklahoma
  long-nosed armadillo, *1*, 101
Oregon
  American black bears, *2*, 250
Orinoco River
  capybaras, *3*, 378–9

P

Pacific
  gray whales, *16*, 2318
Pakistan
  African sand cats, *14*, 2029
  Asian black bears,
    3, 290, 298
  gazelles, *6*, 781
Palau
  fruit bats, *2*, 155
Panama
  mantled howler monkeys,
    10, 1414
  prehensile-tailed
    porcupines, *12*, 1701
  sloths, *14*, 2080
  tamanduas, *1*, 39, 42
Papua New Guinea
  Scott's tree kangaroos,
    8, 1157
Paraguay
  Chacoan peccaries, *11*, 1638
  giant anteater, *1*, 38
  vicuñas, *3*, 362
Patagonia
  sloths, *1*, 32
Pemba
  eastern tree hyraxes, *1*, 25
Peru
  dolphins, *5*, 646
  guanacos, *3*, 363
  jaguars, *8*, 1105–6
  llamas, *3*, 351, 364
  ocelots, *12*, 1787
  sea cats, *11*, 1582
  spectacled bears, *3*, 311
  vicuñas, *3*, 362
  viscachas, *6*, 905
  yellow-tailed woolly
    monkeys, *10*, 1430
Peruvian Andes
  chinchillas, *6*, 900
  short-tailed chinchillas,
    6, 907
Philippines
  Calmian deer, *4*, 572
  Cuming's slender-tailed
    cloud rats, *13*, 1902
  flying lemurs,
    14, 2127
  fruit bats, *2*, 152, 155

Old World rats and mice,
    13, 1921–2
  tarsiers, *5*, 733, 739, 754
Poland
  bison,
    3, 402, 404–5, 412, 415
  brown bears, *2*, 275
  gaurs, *3*, 422
  greater horseshoe bats,
    2, 207
  red foxes, *5*, 728
  wolves, *16*, 2416
Portugal
  otters, *11*, 1587
  wolves, *16*, 2416
Pribilof Islands
  eared seals, *13*, 1963–4,
    1969, 1974, 1977
Prussia
  gaurs, *3*, 422
Puerto Rico
  flower bats, *2*, 181
  solenodons,
    14, 2042, 2052
Pyrenees Moutains
  Pyrenean desmans,
    10, 1383, 1391–2, 1398,
    1401, 1404–5

Q

Qionglai Moutains
  golden snub-nosed
    monkeys, *10*, 1454
Queensland
  northern bettongs,
    13, 1871
  rat kangaroos, *13*, 1860–1
  tree kangaroos, *8*, 1155

R

Ranomafana
  golden bamboo lemurs,
    8, 1196
Rio de Janeiro
  golden lion tamarins,
    10, 1504, *10*, 1506
  maned sloths,
    14, 2081
  marmosets, *10*, 1497

River Shannon
  otters, *11*, 1574–5
Rocky Moutains
  American black bears,
    2, 246, 248–9, 261
  mountain goats, *6*, 842, 844
Romania
  brown bears, *2*, 275, 287
Russia
  antelopes, *1*, 79
  beavers, *3*, 339
  brown bears,
    2, 264, 272–3, 285, 287
  foxes, *5*, 691
  free-tailed bats, *2*, 194
  hamsters, *7*, 924
  lupine foxes, *5*, 703
  polecats, *15*, 2228
  raccoon dogs, *4*, 585–6, 598
  Russian desmans, *10*, 1383,
    1390, 1392, 1397–9,
    1401, 1403–5
  water voles, *15*, 2208
Ruwenzori
  hippopotamuses,
    7, 1002–3
Rwanda
  gorillas, *6*, 884–5
  mountain gorillas, *6*, 882

S

Sahara Desert
  antelopes, *1*, 64, 75
  caracals, *14*, 2014
  cheetahs, *4*, 454–5
  foxes, *5*, 693
  golden jackals, *8*, 1078
  gundis, *9*, 1376
  hedgehogs, *7*, 987
  hippopotamuses,
    7, 1001
  lupine foxes, *5*, 679
  mongooses, *9*, 1332
  North African banded
    weasels, *15*, 2224
  scimitar oryx, *1*, 77
  servals, *14*, 2016–7
Saudi Arabia
  dromedaries, *3*, 343
  gazelles, *6*, 781

Savanna Grasslands
  armadillos, *1*, 90–1
Scandinavia
  badgers, *1*, 116
  beavers, *3*, 339
  brown bears, *2*, 272–3
  deer, *4*, 550
  Norway lemming,
    15, 2198–9
  Shetland ponies, *7*, 1027
  wolverines, *16*, 2390
  wolves, *16*, 2415, 2416
Scotland
  badgers, *1*, 130
  Eurasian wildcats,
    9, 1274
  European moles,
    10, 1394
  pine martens, *9*, 1327
  polecats, *9*, 1327
  red deer, *4*, 558
  red squirrels, *14*, 2120–1
  small cats, *9*, 1262–3
  wildcats,
    9, 1260, 1266, 1268
Sea of Okhotsk
  bison, *3*, 413
Senegal
  antelopes, *1*, 64
  gazelles, *6*, 781
  manatees, *9*, 1288
Serengeti
  cheetahs, *4*, 466
  giraffes, *6*, 819–20, 826,
    828, 832
  golden jackals, *8*, 1084
  hyenas, *7*, 1053
  leopards, *8*, 1209
  spotted hyenas,
    7, 1060, 1066
  striped hyenas, *7*, 1050
  zebras, *16*, 2456
Serengeti Plains
  lions,
    9, 1233, 1238, 1247
  Thomson's gazelles,
    6, 773, 778
Siberia
  Baikal seals, *13*, 1987
  bison, *3*, 394–5
  gray wolves, *4*, 584

horses, *7*, 1041

leopard cats, *9*, 1268

martens, *9*, 1304–5, 1312, 1317–8

polar bears, *11*, 1670

raccoon dogs, *4*, 594

Russian flying squirrels, *14*, 2130

sables, *9*, 1324, 1327

tigers, *15*, 2162

voles, *15*, 2210

wolverines, *16*, 2378, 2380–1

wolves, *16*, 2414

Sierra da Canastra

anteaters, *1*, 53

Sierra Leone

chimpanzees, *4*, 480, 490, 492

linsang, *4*, 506

spotted palm civets, *4*, 517

Sinai

rock hyraxes, *1*, 14

Solomon Islands

tube-nosed fruit bats, *2*, 148

Somalia

African wild asses, *7*, 1030

antelopes, *1*, 74

elephants, *5*, 675

Sonoran Desert

New World rats and mice, *13*, 1876

South Africa

aardvarks, *1*, 24

antelopes, *1*, 64, 66, 72, 75, 78, 79

bat-eared foxes, *3*, 291

black-backed jackals, *8*, 1090

black wildebeest, *1*, 66

breeding programs, *4*, 469

brown hyenas, *7*, 1067

Cape mole rats, *9*, 1362

chimpanzees, *4*, 474

dune mole rats, *9*, 1365

giant golden moles, *10*, 1391, 1403

hartebeest, *1*, 76

honey badger, *1*, 128

jackals, *8*, 1093

lions, *9*, 1238

mountain zebras, *16*, 2468–9

rock hyraxes, *1*, 14

spotted hyenas, *7*, 1067

springbok, *6*, 781

South America

anteaters, *1*, 32, 33, 39, 53

armadillos, *1*, 81, 84, 88, 90, 100, 103

Bactrian camels, *3*, 341

Brazilian shrew mice, *13*, 1885

Brazilian tapirs, *16*, 2457–8

camels, *3*, 342, 344, 360

capuchins, *10*, 1430

capybaras, *3*, 367–70, 374–8, 388–9

cebid monkeys, *10*, 1429

Chacoan peccaries, *11*, 1624

climbing mice, *13*, 1885

coypus, *3*, 389–91

disc-winged bats, *2*, 188

doglike bats, *2*, 202

dolphins, *5*, 636–7

forest rabbits, *12*, 1818

foxes, *4*, 526, 579, *5*, 681–2, 686–90, 693, 698, 703, 709, 714

Geoffroy's cats, *12*, 1782

giant anteaters, *1*, 36, 49, 50

giant armadillos, *1*, 97, 102

giant otters, *11*, 1572, 1574, 1580

grison, *15*, 2214

guanacos, *3*, 356, 363

guinea pigs, *6*, 886–911

Hoffman's two-toed sloths, *14*, 2066

hog-nosed skunks, *16*, 2378

jaguars, *8*, 1095, 1098, 1104–6, 1116–7

jaguarundi, *12*, 1781

kinkajous, *12*, 1824

koalas, *8*, 1148

leaf-nosed bats, *2*, 159, 168

Linne's two-toed sloths, *14*, 2066

lion tamarins, *10*, 1505

llamas, *3*, 350, *3*, 364–5

mandrills, *10*, 1459

maned wolves, *4*, 525, 533, 545

marmosets, *10*, 1494

marsupials, *8*, 1166, *10*, 1514

Mexican cottontails, *12*, 1817

mole rats, *9*, 1355

New World porcupines, *12*, 1695

New World rats and mice, *13*, 1877, 1886, 1894

ocelots, *12*, 1790

oilbirds, *2*, 198

Old World camels, *3*, 359

olingos, *12*, 1824

opossums, *10*, 1520–2

peccaries, *11*, 1616, 1617, 1624–5

pocket mice, *14*, 2099

porcupines, *12*, 1717

possums, *12*, 1728

pumas, *12*, 1794

pygmy right whales, *15*, 2310

raccoons, *12*, 1824, 1832

sac-winged bats, *2*, 202

silky anteaters, *1*, 40

skunks, *16*, 2372

sloths, *1*, 32, *14*, 2057, 2060, 2066, 2080

small bears, *3*, 289, 310

small cats, *12*, 1771, 1773, 1787, 1789, 1792–3

spectacled bears, *3*, 292, 308

spiny rats, *13*, 1877

squirrel monkeys, *10*, 1428

thick-tailed opossums, *10*, 1534

vampire bats, *2*, 172

vicuñas, *3*, 348, 356, 361

wild dogs, *4*, 523

yapoks, *10*, 1519

South Atlantic

sperm whales, *16*, 2364

South Carolina

gibbons, *6*, 804

red wolves, *16*, 2418

South Downs

moles, *10*, 1392–3

Southeast Asia

arrow-tailed flying squirrels, *14*, 2119

Asian black bears, *3*, 290

badgers, *1*, 131

Berdmore's palm squirrels, *14*, 2120

cave swiftlet, *2*, 198

crested porcupines, *12*, 1696

European hedgehogs, *7*, 969

flying lemurs, *14*, 2127

fruit bats, *2*, 136, 146

gibbons, *6*, 782–807

hedgehogs, *7*, 966

hyenas, *7*, 1051

Indian short-nosed fruit bats, *2*, 145–6

jackals, *8*, 1078

long-nosed squirrels, *14*, 2122

marmoset rats, *13*, 1912

orangutans, *11*, 1557

otter civets, *4*, 508

pygmy flying squirrels, *14*, 2112

rorquals, *16*, 2340

serows, *6*, 837

squirrels, *12*, 1721

sun bears, *3*, 290, 298

Sunda tree squirrels, *14*, 2122

tailless leaf-nosed bats, *2*, 195

tree shrews, *14*, 2032

vesper bats, *2*, 221

wild pigs, *11*, 1615, 1617

Southern Hemisphere

blue whales, *16*, 2338

South Korea

Bengal tigers, *15*, 2183

South Pacific

rorquals, *16*, 2338

Soviet Union
  polar bears,
    11, 1686, 1691
  saigas, *6*, 857
  wild sheep, *6*, 857
Spain
  American minks,
    10, 1404
  beavers, *3*, 338
  bison, *3*, 413
  brown bears,
    2, 273, 287
  European rabbits,
    12, 1806, 1817
  Pyrenean desmans,
    10, 1405
  wolves,
    16, 2404, 2416
Sri Lanka
  golden palm civets,
    4, 520
  Indian chevrotains,
    12, 1767
  Indian spotted mouse deer,
    12, 1753
  rusty-spotted cats,
    9, 1262
  sloth bears,
    3, 290, 298
St. Francis Island
  rat kangaroos, *13*, 1873
Sudan
  antelopes, *1*, 64, 72, 75
Sulawesi
  dwarf cuscuses,
    12, 1728
Sumatra
  gibbons, *6*, 792
  long-tailed porcupines,
    12, 1704
  Old World crested
    porcupines,
    12, 1711
  orangutans,
    11, 1536–61
Superagui Island
  black-faced lion tamarins,
    10, 1509
Surinam
  giant armadillos,
    1, 102

Sweden
  brown bears, *2*, 287
  dolphins, *5*, 649
  wolverines,
    16, 2392
  wolves, *16*, 2414
Switzerland
  Eurasian lynx, *9*, 1275
  hedgehogs, *7*, 987
  stone martens,
    9, 1310
Syria
  brown bears, *2*, 273
  dromedaries, *3*, 343
  long-eared hedgehogs,
    7, 974
  rock hyraxes, *1*, 14
Syrian Desert
  hamsters, *7*, 924–5
Szechwan
  pandas,
    11, 1598, 1600, 1603, 1611

T

Tai Forest
  chimpanzees, *4*, 487
Taiwan
  small bears, *3*, 309
  tigers, *15*, 2183
Tanzania
  African wild dogs,
    5, 608
  chimpanzees, *4*, 486–7
  elephants, *5*, 675
  giraffes, *6*, 817, 820
  hippopotamuses,
    7, 1014
  hyenas,
    7, 1054–5, 1058
  lions,
    9, 1234, 1236–7, 1247
  shrews, *14*, 2055
  spotted hyenas,
    7, 1064
  zebras, *16*, 2469
Tasmania
  kangaroos, *8*, 1130
  pilot whales,
    15, 2286
  platypuses,

    11, 1652–3
  red foxes, *5*, 727
  short-nosed echidnas,
    11, 1643–4
  Tasmanian bettongs,
    13, 1850, 1856, 1858–9,
      1863, 1867–9, 1871–2
  wolves, *4*, 584
  wombats,
    16, 2432–3
Texas
  free-tailed bats,
    2, 194, 196
  long-nosed armadillo,
    1, 101
  red wolves, *4*, 525
  small bats, *2*, 209
  vesper bats, *2*, 232
Thailand
  Asiatic golden cats,
    9, 1259
  bumblebee bats,
    2, 186
  cervus schombergki,
    4, 570
  deer, *4*, 472
  dholes, *4*, 584
  fruit bats, *2*, 154
  gibbons, *6*, 806–7
  lar gibbons, *6*, 793
  Malay bears, *3*, 291
  pileated gibbons,
    6, 802, 805
  sun bears, *3*, 308
Tibet
  Biet's snub-nosed monkeys,
    10, 1439
  kiang, *7*, 1037
  pandas, *11*, 1608
  yaks, *3*, 428
Tierra del Fuego
  foxes, *5*, 693
Tsavo
  lions, *9*, 1248
Turkestan
  goitered gazelles,
    6, 781
Turkey
  blind mole rats,
    9, 1366
  brown bears, *2*, 283

U

Uganda
  antelopes, *1*, 72
  elephants, *5*, 662
  genets, *4*, 506
  gorillas, *6*, 884
  hippopotamuses,
    7, 1002, 1012
  mongooses,
    9, 1339
  mountain gorillas,
    6, 882
  Old World rats and mice,
    13, 1912–3
  pangolins, *1*, 104
Ukraine
  horses, *7*, 1041
United Kingdom
  badgers, *1*, 131
  common dormice,
    7, 937
  dolphins, *5*, 649
  Eurasian wildcats,
    9, 1251, 1260
  rabbits, *12*, 1820
United States
  American river otters,
    11, 1585–6
  armadillos,
    1, 84, 88, 90, 104
  Barbary sheep,
    6, 855
  black-tailed jackrabbits,
    7, 948
  collared peccaries,
    11, 1638
  cottontails,
    12, 1804, 1806
  coyotes, *4*, 532, 544
  deer, *4*, 559, 568
  domestic dogs,
    16, 2397
  fallow deer, *4*, 560

V

Vietnam
  colobines, *10*, 1442–3, 1456
  doucs, *10*, 1453–4
  Javan rhinoceroses, *13*, 1937
  kouprey, *3*, 421, 429, 440

large-spotted civets, *4*, 517
pandas, *11*, 1592
pygmy slow lorises, *5*, 741
vu quang, *3*, 441
vu quang (wild cattle) *3*, 421
Virginia
American black bears, *2*, 247
oppossum, *8*, 1166
ponies, *7*, 1026
Virungas
gorillas, *6*, 870–3, 880, 884–5

W

Wales
European polecats,
15, 2228
European water shrews,
14, 2042–3
Washington State
American black bears,
2, 246–7, 250, 259
killer whales, *15*, 2280
raccoons,
12, 1834–5, 1840

West Indies
vesper bats, *2*, 226
West Virginia
opossums, *10*, 1522–3
Wiltshire Downs
rabbits, *12*, 1808–9
Wrangel Island
lupine foxes, *5*, 703
Wyoming
American black bears,
2, 244
beavers, *3*, 330
black-footed ferrets,
15, 2236
coyotes, *4*, 540
deer, *4*, 570
prairie dogs,
15, 2236

Y

Yangtze
dolphins,
5, 649, 651
Yemen

rhinoceroses,
13, 1949
Yucatan
vesper rats,
13, 1879
Yugoslavia
brown bears,
2, 287
Yukon Territory
collared pikas,
7, 950
hares, *7*, 950–1
snowshoe hares,
7, 950

Z

Zaire
aardvarks,
1, 12, 24
chimpanzees,
4, 480, 490, 494–5
leopards,
8, 1220
mongooses,

9, 1352
okapis, *6*, 819
white rhinoceroses,
13, 1951
Zambia
African buffalo,
3, 426
antelopes, *1*, 72, 76
elephants, *5*, 662
hippopotamuses,
7, 1010
lions, *9*, 1238
Zanzibar
eastern tree hyraxes,
1, 25
galagos, *5*, 753–4
Zanzibar red colobus
monkeys, *10*, 1435
Zimbabwe
black rhinoceroses,
13, 1951
cheetahs, *4*, 469
elephants,
5, 674, 677

Scientific names index

A

A. a. mexicana
   (Mexican pronghorn),
   12, 1769

A. a. peninsularis (Californian
   pronghorn), *12*, 1769

A. a. sonoriensis (Sonoran
   pronghorn), *12*, 1769

Acinonychinae (cheetah),
   12, 1772

Acinonyx (cheetah),
   4, 445

Acinonyx jubatus (cheetah),
   4, 449, 451

Aepyceros melampus
   (antelope), *1*, 58

Aepyprymnus rufescens
   (rufous rat kangaroo),
   13, 1855

Aetiocetidae (whale),
   15, 2242

Agorophiidae (whale),
   15, 2242

Ailurinae (red panda),
   11, 1589, *12*, 1826

Ailuropoda (giant panda),
   11, 1592

Ailuropoda melanoleuca
   (giant panda), *11*, 1589, 1595

Ailuropodinae (panda),
   11, 1589

Ailurus fulgens (red panda),
   11,1589, 1593

Alcelaphini (antelope),
   1, 55–6, 58, 62–3, 65–6, 68,
   70, 74

Alces alces (moose),
   4, 552

Alopex lagopus (arctic fox),
   5, 683

Amitermes meridionalis
   (magnetic termite),
   11, 1650

Anomaluridae (flying squirrel),
   14, 2127

Antechinus apicalis (dibbler),
   14, 2139

Antechinus bellus
   (fawn antechinus), *14*, 2156

Antechinus godman (Godman's
   marsupial mouse),
   14, 2156

Antechinus minimus
   (swamp antechinus),
   14, 2156

Antechinus swainsonii
   (dusky antechinus),
   14, 2150

Anthropoidea (higher primate),
   5, 735, *10*, 1407, 1459, 1485

Antidorcas (springbok),
   6, 763

*Antilocapra americana
   americana* (pronghorn),
   12, 1769

Antilocapra americana
   (pronghorn),
   12, 1745, 1748

Antilocapridae (pronghorn),
   12,1745

Antilocaprinae (pronghorn),
   12, 1745–6

Antilopinae (antelope),
   6, 757, 781

Antilopini (gazelle),
   6, 757, 760–1

aperia (wild cavy),
   6, 893

Aplodontia (beaver),
   3, 315

Aplodontia rufa
   (mountain beaver),
   3, 318

Aplodontidae (beaver),
   3, 315

Apodemus (mouse),
   13, 1910

archaeoceti (whale),
   15, 2241, 2242, *16*, 2320

Arctocebus (angwantibo),
   5, 731

Arctocephalus
   (southern fur seal),
   13, 1953

Artiodactyla (even-toed
   ungulate),
   1, xx, 55, *3*, 341,
   393, 419, 549, *6*, 757, 809,
   812, 835, *7*, 991, *11*, 1615,
   12, 1745

Ateles paniscus
   (black spider monkey),
   10, 1411

avellanarius (common
   dormouse), *7*, 919

B

B. lasius (Harris's olingo),
   12, 1847

Babyrousa babyrussa (babirusa),
   11, 1619

bairdi (Baird's tapir), *16*, 2447

Balaena (right whale),
   15, 2291

Balaena glacialis australis
   (southern right whale),
   15, 2293–4

Balaena glacialis (right whale),
   15, 2291, 2293–4, 2297

Balaena mysticetus
   (bowhead whale),
   15, 2292, 2294–5

Balaenidae (right and
   bowhead whale), *15*, 2291–2

Balaenoptera acutorostrata
   (minke whale), *16*, 2320

Balaenoptera borealis
   (sei whale),
   16, 2321

Balaenoptera edeni
   (Bryde's whale),
   16, 2321

Balaenoptera musculus
   (blue whale), *16*, 2321

Balaenoptera physalus
   (fin whale),
   16, 2320

Balaenoptera (rorqual),
   16, 2317

Balaenopteridae (rorqual),
   16, 2317

Basilosauridae (whale),
   15, 2241, *16*, 2320

Bassaricyon (olingo),
   12, 1823, 1826–7

Bassaricyon pauli
   (Chiriqui olingo),
   12, 1847

Bassariscus (ringtail and
   cacomistle), *12*, 1823–4

Bathyergidae (mole rat),
   9, 1355

Bathyerginae
   (dune mole rat),
   9, 1355, 1358, 1378

Birbalomys (mole rat),
   9, 1358

Bison athabascae (wood bison),
   3, 393, 396

Bison bison (plains bison),
   3, 393, 396–7

Bison bonasus
   (European bison),
   3, 393, 396

Bison latifrons (giant bison),
   3, 395

Bison occidentalis (bison),
   3, 396

*Blarina carolinensis
   shermani* (shrew),
   14, 2051

Blarina (short-tailed shrew),
   13, 1885

Blarinomys (shrew mouse),
   13, 1885

Boselaphini (antelope),
   1, 58, 64

Bos (true cattle or oxen),
   3, 419, 421, 423

Bovidae (cattle, goats, antelopes, etc.), *1*, 55, 58–9, *3*, 393–4, 397, 419, 423, *4*, 549, *6*, 757, 781, 809, 835, 838, *12*, 1745–6

Bovids (water buffalo), *4*, 553

Bovinae (cattle), *1*, 62, *3*, 393, 397, 419, 421, 423

Bovini (wild cattle), *3*, 393, 423

Bradypodidae (sloth), *14*, 2057

Bradypus (three-toed sloth), *14*, 2057–9

Bradypus tridactylus (pale-throated sloth), *14*, 2057, 2061, 2063

Bradypus ursinus (sloth bear), *3*, 292

Bradypus variegatus (maned sloth), *14*, 2057, 2061

Bubalus (Asian buffalo), *3*, 419–22

Bunolagus (bushman hare), *7*, 939

Bunolagus monticularis (bushman rabbit), *7*, 943

burchelli (plains zebra), *16*, 2447

Burramyidae (pygmy possum), *12*, 1719, 1723

C

caballus (domestic horse), *7*, 1017

Caenolestidae (shrew opossum), *10*, 1520

Callithricidae (marmoset and tamarin), *10*, 1485, 1489, 1494 1501

Callithrix jacchus (common marmoset), *10*, 1488, 1491

Callorhinus ursinus (northern fur seal), *13*, 1953, 1956, 1959 1970

Callosciurus (tree squirrel),

14, 2109, 2113

Caluromyinae (oppossum), *10*, 1511,1514, 1515

Caluromys lanatus (woolly opossum), *10*, 1515

camelus (camel), *3*, 341

Camelus bactrianus (Bactrian camel), *3*, 341, 344

Camelus dromedarius (dromedary), *3*, 344

canadensis (Canadian or North American beaver), *3*, 315

Canidae (dog), *4*, 523–4, 575, 578, *5*, 601, 605, 679, 682, 705, *8*, 1069, *16*, 2395, 2398

Canis (gray wolf and red wolf), *16*, 2397

Canis (lupine dog), *5*, 682

Canis adjustus (side-striped jackal), *8*, 1069, 1073

Canis aureus (golden jackal), *8*, 1069, 1073, 1075

Canis dingo (dingo), *16*, 2398

Canis familiaris (domestic dog), *4*, 575, *16*, 2398

Canis latrans (coyote), *4*, 523, 527, *16*, 2398

Canis lupus (gray wolf), *16*, 2395, 2399, 2401

Canis mesomelas (black-backed jackal), *8*, 1069, 1073

Canis rufus (red wolf), *16*, 2395, 2399

Canis simensis (Simien jackal), *8*, 1069, 1072

Canoidea (doglike form), *11*, 1563, 1589, 1667, *16*, 2395

capensis (badger), *1*, 107, 111

Caperea marginata (pygmy right whale), *15*, 2291, 2294

Capra (alpine ibex), *6*, 841

Caprinae (goat antelope), *6*, 835–8, 844

Caprolagus (hispid hare), *7*, 939

Caprolagus hispidus (hispid hare), *7*, 943

Carcharodon (whale), *15*, 2243

Carnivora (carnivore), *1*, xx, 107, *2*, 237, 263, *3*, 289, *4*, 445, 497, 523, 575, *5*, 601, 679, 705, *7*, 1043, *8*, 1069, 1199, *9*, 1225, 1251, 1303, 1329, *11*, 1563, 1589, 1667, *12*, 1771, 1823, *14*, 2005, *15*, 2161, 2213, *16*, 2369, 2395

Castor canadensis (Canadian beaver), *3*, 319

Castor fiber (European beaver), *3*, 318

Castoridae (beaver), *3*, 315

Cavia (cavy), *6*, 891, 893

Caviidae (capybara), *3*, 370

Caviomorpha (cavylike rodent), *3*, 367, 369–70, *6*, 887–8, *9*, 1355

Cavoidea (cavy, pacaran, pacas, agouti, acouchi, capybara), *6*, 887

Cebidae (cebid monkey), *10*, 1407, 1489

Cebus apella (brown capuchin), *10*, 1411

Cebus capucinus (white-faced capuchin), *10*, 1413

Cephalophinea (duiker), *6*, 757, 760

Ceratotherium simum (white rhinoceros), *13*, 1927, 1930, 1933

Cercocebus torquatus (white mangabey), *10*, 1463

Cercopithecinae (guenon, macaque, and baboon), *10*, 1459, 1462

Cercopithecoidea (Old World monkey), *10*, 1433–7, 1459

Cercopithecus aethiops (vervet), *10*, 1463

Cervidae (deer), *4*, 549

Cervoidea (deerlike animal), *4*, 549

Cervus elaphus (red deer), *4*, 553

Cervus schombergki (deer), *4*, 570

Cetacea (whale and dolphin), *1*, xxi, *5*, 627, 629–31, *15*, 2239, 2241, 2265, 2291, 2295, *16*, 2317, 2320, 2338, 2343

Cetotherium (whale), *15*, 2243

Chaetomys subspinosus (thin-spined porcupine), *12*, 1717

Cheirogaleidae (dwarf and mouse lemur), *8*, 1173

Chinchilloidea (chinchilla,viscacha, pacarana), *6*, 887, 889, 891

Chiroptera (bat), *1*, xx, *2*, 133, 136, 159, 185, 196, 210

Choeropsis (pygmy hippo), *7*, 991

Choloepus didactylus (Linne's sloth), *14*, 2057, 2060

Choloepus hoffmanni (Hoffmann's sloth), *14*, 2057, 2060

Choloepus (two-toed sloth), *14*, 2057–9

Chrysochloridae (golden mole), *10*, 1381, 1384

Chrysocyon brachyurus (maned wolf), *4*, 523, 526

Colobinae (colobine), *10*, 1433–6, 1462

Colobus (colobus monkey), *10*, 1433, 1436

Condylarths (aardvark), *1*, 3–4, 6

Conepatus (hog-nosed skunk), *16*, 2372–3

Craseonycteridae (sheath-tailed bat), *2*, 188

Cricetinae (hamster),
  7, 913
Cricetulus triton
  (ratlike hamster), *7*, 932
Cricetus (hamster), *7*, 919
Cricetus cricetus
  (common European
  hamster), *7*, 916, 933
Crocidura desperata (shrew),
  14, 2055
Crocidura odorata goliath
  (shrew), *14*, 2031, 2051
Crocuta crocuta
  (spotted hyena),
  7, 1043, 1047, 1049
Crusafontia (mammal),
  1, xviii, xix
Cryptomys hottentotus
  (common mole rat),
  9, 1359
Cryptoprocta ferox (fossa),
  4, 499–500
Cryptoproctinae (fossa), *4*, 497
Ctenodactylidae (gundi),
  9, 1355, 1359
Ctenodactylus vali
  (desert gundi), *9*, 1377
Cuon alpinus (dhole),
  4, 575, 578
Cyclopes tetradactyla
  (silky anteater), *1*, 29, 33
Cynognathus (mammal),
  1, xviii
Cynomys (prairie dog),
  14, 2087
Cystophora cristata
  (hooded seal),
  13, 1982

D

Dasypodidae (armadillo),
  1, 81
Dasyproctidae (agoutis
  and acouchi), *6*, 889
Dasyuridae (cat-, rat-,
  and mouselike forms),
  14, 2135, 2139
Dasyuromorphia
  (marsupial carnivore),
  14, 2135–7, 2139

Dasyurops maculatus
  (spotted-tail quoll),
  14, 2151
Dasyurus (quoll), *14*, 2139
Dasyurus geoffroyi
  (western native cat),
  14, 2146
Dasyurus viverrinus
  (eastern native cat),
  14, 2145
Daubentoniidae (aye-aye),
  8, 1173, 1177
Delphinidae
  (oceanic dolphin family),
  5, 627, 631, *15*, 2265
Delphinoidea (dolphin),
  15, 2265–6
Dendrohyrax (tree hyrax), *1*, 6
Dendrolagus (tree kangaroo),
  8, 1151
Dermoptera (flying lemur),
  1, xx
Desmaninae (desman),
  10, 1383
Desmatophocidae
  (marine carnivore),
  13, 1956
Desmodontidae
  (vampire bat), 2,162–3
Dicerorhinae
  (two-horned rhinoceros),
  13, 1927, 1931
Dicerorhinus sumatrensis
  (Sumatran rhinoceros),
  13, 1927, 1930
Diceros (black rhinoceros),
  13, 1927
Diceros bicornis
  (black rhinoceros),
  13, 1930
Didelphidea (opossum),
  10, 1511, 1514
Didelphids (South American
  marsupial),
  14, 2139
Didelphimorphia
  (opossum and extinct
  relatives), *10*, 1511
Didelphinae (opossum),
  10, 1511, 1514, 1515
Didelphis virginiana

  (Virginia opossum),
  10, 1515, 1517
dinomyids (terrible mouse),
  3, 370
Dinomyoidea (pacarana),
  6, 890
diprotodon (giant grazing
  wombat), *16*, 2424
Diprotodonta (marsupials with
  only two lower incisors),
  8, 1121, 1147, *12*, 1719,
  13, 1849
Doedicurus (armadillo), *1*, 84
Dolichotis patagona (mara),
  6, 890, 910
Dorcatherium (chevrotain),
  12, 1749
Dorudontinae (whale), *15*, 2241
Dremomys (red-cheeked
  squirrel), *14*, 2119
dremotheres (deer), *4*, 550
dromedarius (dromedary),
  3, 341
Dugong dugon (dugong),
  9, 1280
Dugongidae (dugong), *9*, 1277
Dusicyon (fox),
  5, 679, 688, 705
Dusicyon australis
  (Falkland Islands wolf),
  5, 681
Dusicyon fulvipes (fox), *5*, 682

E

E. fuscocapillus (southern
  mole-vole), *15*, 2191
E. talpinus (northern mole-
  vole), *15*, 2191
Echymipera
  (spiny bandicoot), *16*, 2430
Edentata (armadillo, sloth,
  and anteater), *1*, xx, 81, 83,
  14, 2057, 2059
Edwardi (short-finned pilot
  whale), *15*, 2276
Elasmotherium
  (rhinoceros), *13*, 1929
Elasomdontomys obliquus
  (cavy), *6*, 910
Elephantoidea (elephant),

  5, 653
Elephas (Asian elephant),
  5, 653, 657
Eliomys quercinus
  (garden dormouse), *7*, 920
ellobiini (mole-vole), *15*, 2187
Ellobius (mole-vole), *15*, 2191
Emballonuroidea
  (sheath-tailed bat),
  2, 185–6, 188, 214
Emballonuroidea
  (mouse-tailed bat), *2*, 191
Enaliarctidae
  (marine carnivore), *13*, 1956
Enhydra lutris (sea otter),
  11, 1567
Eohippus (dawn horse), *7*, 1020
Eomanis waldi (pangolin),
  1, 85
Equidae (horse, zebra, and ass),
  7, 1017, *16*, 2447
Equus asinus
  (African wild ass),
  7, 1017, 1021
Equus burchelli (plains zebra),
  16, 2447, 2453
Equus burchelli quagga
  (quagga), *16*, 2468
Equus caballus (horse),
  7, 1019
Equus grevyi
  (Grevy's zebra),
  16, 2447, 2451
Equus hemionus
  (Asiatic wild ass),
  7, 1017, 1021
Equus przewalskii,
  7, 1020, 1023
Equus zebra (mountain zebra),
  16, 2447, 2450
Erethizon dorsatum (North
  American porcupine),
  12, 1696, 1699
Erethizontidae
  (New World porcupine),
  6, 887, *12*, 1693
Erignathus barbatus (bearded
  seal), *13*, 1982
Erinaceidae (hedgehog),
  7, 965–6
erinaceomorpha (hedgehog),

7, 965

Erinaceus europaeus
  (European hedgehog),
  7, 969, 971

Eschrichtiidae (gray whale),
  15, 2239–40

Eschrichtius robustus
  (gray whale), 15, 2239, 2243,
  2245, 2247

Eubalaena (right whale),
  15, 2293

Eucladoceros (deer), 4, 551–2

Eumegamys (capybara), 3, 370

Eumetopias (Steller's sea lion),
  13, 1953

Euphractus sexcintus, 1, 84

Eupleres goudoti (falanouc),
  4, 499

Euplerinae (falanouc), 4, 497

Eurhinodelphis (porpoise),
  5, 628

Eutamandua (anteater),
  1, 32

Eutamias (chipmunk), 14, 2087

Eutheria (placental mammal),
  14, 2083

F

F. aurata (African golden cat),
  14, 2005

F. caracal (caracal), 14, 2005

F. chaus (jungle cat), 14, 2005

F. lybica (African wildcat),
  14, 2005

F. margarita (sand cat),
  14, 2005, 2007

F. nigripes
  (black-footed cat), 14, 2005

F. serval (serval), 14, 2005

Felidae (cat),
  4, 445, 8, 1199,
    9, 1251, 12, 1771, 14, 2005

felid (cat), 4, 498

Felinae (cat),
  9, 1251, 1253, 12, 1772

Felis caracal (caracal), 14, 2008

Felis (cat),
  9, 1251, 1266, 14, 2005–6,
    2008, 15, 2165

Felis (small cat),

12, 1771–2, 1775

Felis concolor (puma),
  12, 1771, 1774, 1777, 1795

Felis lynx (lynx), 9, 1255

Felis manul (Pallas's cat),
  9, 1254

Felis serval (serval),
  14, 2009, 2011

Felis silvestris
  (Eurasian wildcat),
  9, 1255, 1257, 12, 1795

Felis yagouaroundi
  (jaguarundi),
  12, 1771, 1775

Feloidea (catlike form),
  4, 445, 8, 1095, 1199,
    9, 1225, 1329, 15, 2161

Fennecus zerda (fennec fox),
  5, 683

Feresa attenuata
  (pygmy killer whale),
  15, 2269

fiber (European beaver),
  3, 315

Fissipedia
  (land-living carnivore),
  9, 1225, 11, 1667

Fossa fossa, 4, 499

Fossinae (fanaloka), 4, 497

G

G. gorilla berengei
  (mountain gorilla),
  6, 861, 864, 865, 881

G. gorilla gorilla
  (western lowland gorilla),
  6, 861, 863, 864

G. gorilla graueri
  (eastern lowland gorilla),
  6, 861, 863, 864

Galago (galago), 5, 731

Galago crassicaudatus
  (greater galago), 5, 734

Galemys Desmana
  (desman), 10, 1385

Galidiinae
  (Madagascar mongoose),
  9, 1329, 1333

Genetta genetta
  (common spotted genet),

4, 501

Geniohyus (hyrax), 1, 6

Geocapromys ingrahami
  ingrahami (hutia), 6, 908

Geomyidae (pocket gopher),
  14, 2083

Geomys
  (western pocket gopher),
  14, 2094

Georychinae
  (common mole rat, Cape
    mole rat, silvery mole
    rat, and naked mole rat),
  9, 1355, 1359

Gigantohyrax (hyrax), 1, 6

Gigantopithecus (ape), 4, 473

Giraffa (giraffe), 6, 809, 815

Giraffa camelopardalis (giraffe),
  6, 809, 812, 815

Giraffidae (giraffe), 6, 809

glama (llama), 3, 341, 345

Glaucomys
  (New World flying squirrel),
  14, 2109, 2112

Gliridae seleviniidae
  (dormouse), 7, 913, 917

Globicephala macrorhynchus
  (short-finned pilot whale),
  15, 2268

Globicephala melaena
  (long-finned pilot whale),
  15, 2268

Globicephalidae
  (dolphin, killer, and pilot
    whale), 5, 629, 15, 2265–8

Glyptodon (armadillo),
  1, 84, 100

Glyptodont (armadillo-like
    creature), 1, 30, 14, 2060

guanicoe (guanaco), 3, 341, 345

Gulo gulo (wolverine),
  16, 2372, 2375

H

H. agilis (agile gibbon), 6, 785

H. brachyura yunnanensis
  (porcupine), 12, 1717

H. hoolock (hoolock gibbon),
  6, 786

H. klossii (kloss gibbon), 6, 786

H. lar (lar gibbon), 6, 785, 787

H. moloch (moloch gibbon),
  6, 786

H. muelleri (Müller's gibbon),
  6, 786

H. pileatus (pileated gibbon),
  6, 786

Hapalemurinae (gentle lemur),
  8, 1177

Helarctos (sun bear), 3, 292

Hemigalinae (palm civet, otter
    civet), 4, 497–8

Hemigalus derbyanus (banded
    palm civet), 4, 500

hemionus (wild ass), 7, 1017

Heptaxodontinae (cavy), 6, 910

Herpestes auropunctatus
  (Indian mongoose), 14, 2052

Herpestes edwardsi (Indian
    gray mongoose), 9, 1333

herpestes (mongoose), 9, 1332

Herpestinae (African and Asian
    mongoose), 9, 1329

hesperocyon (dawn dog),
  5, 707, 709

Hesperomyidae
  (rat and mouse),
  13, 1878, 1882

Hesperomyinae
  (New World rat and mouse),
  13, 1875–6, 1878–9, 1903

Heterocephalus glaber
  (naked mole rat),
  9, 1359, 1361

Heterohyrax (bush hyrax),
  1, 6–7

Heteromyidae
  (pocket mouse),
  14, 2083

Hexaprotodon (hippopotamus),
  7, 991

Hexaprotodon liberiensis
  (pygmy hippo), 7, 994

Hippopotamus amphibius
  (hippopotamus), 7, 995, 997

Hippopotamus terrestris
  (Brazilian tapir), 16, 2455

Hipposideridae
  (leaf-nosed bat), 2, 187

Hippotraginae (antelope),
  1, 55, 57, 64

Hippotragini (antelope), *1*, 55, 59, 62, 66, 69

Hippotragus leucophaeus (antelope), *1*, 78

Hominoidea (apelike form), *4*, 471

Hyaena brunnea (brown hyena), *7*, 1043, 1047

Hyaena hyaena (striped hyena), *7*, 1043, 1047

Hyaenidae (hyena), *7*, 1043–4

hyaenid (hyena), *4*, 498

Hydrochaeridae (capybara), *3*, 367

Hydrochaeris (capybara), *3*, 367

Hydropotes inermis (water deer), *4*, 553

Hyemoschus aquaticus (water chevrotain), *12*, 1745

Hylobates (lar gibbon), *6*, 789, 790

Hylobates syndactylus (siamang gibbon), *6*, 785–6

Hylobatidae (gibbon), *6*, 861, *11*, 1537, 1540

Hylobatinae (gibbon), *6*, 783

Hylochoerus meinertzhageni (giant forest hog), *11*, 1619

Hylopetes (flying squirrel), *14*, 2109

Hyracoidea (hyrax), *1*, xx

Hyracotherium (dawn horse), *7*, 1020

Hysignathus monstrosus (hammer-headed bat), *2*, 137

Hystricidae (Old World porcupine), *12*, 1693

Hystricomorpha (cavy and porcupine rodent), *3*, 319, *9*, 1355, *12*, 1693, *14*, 2085

Hystrix (crested porcupine), *12*, 1717

Hystrix cristata (crested African porcupine), *12*, 1697, 1717

Hystrix indica (Indian porcupine), *12*, 1704

I

Ichthyomyini (fish-eating rat), *13*, 1879

Ilingoceros (pronghorn), *12*, 1749

Imagotaria (walrus), *13*, 1956

indicus (Malayan tapir), *16*, 2447

Indricotherium coelodonta (rhinoceros), *13*, 1929

Indricotherium grangeri (rhinoceros), *13*, 1929

Indriidae (indri and sifaka lemur), *8*, 1173

Indri indri (indri), *8*, 1176

Insectivora (insect-eating mammal), *1*, xx, *7*, 965, 968, *10*, 1381, *14*, 2031, 2034

Irachypithecus (brow-ridged langur), *10*, 1433

Ischyromys (rodent), *13*, 1904

Isoodon obsoletus (mouse bandicoot), *16*, 2444

J

jubatus (cheetah), *4*, 445, 449

L

Lagomorpha (hare, rabbit, and pika), *1*, xxi, *7*, 939, 941–43, 949, 962, *12*, 1797–9, 1801, *13*, 1877

Lagorchestes (hare wallaby), *8*, 1151, 1155

Lagostrophus (hare wallaby), *8*, 1151

Lagostrophus fasciatus (banded hare wallaby), *8*, 1150

Lagothrix (woolly monkey), *10*, 1410

Lama (llama, alpaca, guanaco), *3*, 341

Lasiorhinus (hairy-nosed wombat), *16*, 2424

Lemmini (lemming), *15*, 2187, 2191

Lemmus lemmus (Norway lemming), *15*, 2191, 2193

Lemur catta (ring-tailed lemur), *8*, 1175–6, 1179

Lemur fulvus (brown lemur), *8*, 1175

Lemur fulvus rufus (red-fronted lemur), *8*, 1197

Lemuridae (lemur), *8*, 1173

Lemurinae (lemur), *8*, 1175

Lemur macaco (black lemur), *8*, 1197

Leontopithecus rosalia (golden lion tamarin), *10*, 1489

Lepilemurinae (sportive lemur), *8*, 1175, 1177

Leporidae (rabbit and hare), *7*, 939–40, *12*, 1797, 1800

Leptailurus (serval), *14*, 2008

Lepus (hare and jackrabbit), *7*, 939–40, 960–1, 963, *12*, 1800

Lepus europaeus (brown hare), *7*, 943, 945

Lobodon carcinophagus (crabeater seal), *13*, 1983

Loris (slender loris), *5*, 731

Lorisidae (galago), *5*, 731, 735

Loxodonta (African elephant), *5*, 653

Lumbricus terristris (earthworm), *1*, 120

Lutra (otter), *11*, 1563–4

Lutra (Hydrictis) maculicollis (spotted-necked otter), *11*, 1567

Lutra lutra (Eurasian otter), *11*, 1566, 1569

Lutrinae (otter), *11*, 1563, 1566

Lycaon pictus (African wild dog), *5*, 601, 603, 604

lynx (lynx), *12*, 1771

M

M. angustirostris (northern elephant seal), *13*, 1983

M. leonina (southern elephant seal), *13*, 1983

Macaca mulatta (rhesus macaque), *10*, 1462

Macroderma gigas (Australian false vampire bat), *2*, 205

Macroglossinae (fruit bat), *2*, 133, 135

Macropodidae, *8*, 1121, 1124, 1150

Macropus giganteus (gray kangaroo), *8*, 1125

Macropus rufus (red kangaroo), *8*, 1127

Macroscelididae (elephant shrew), *1*, xx, *14*, 2034

Macrotis (bilbies), *16*, 2421, 2425

malayanus (sun bear), *3*, 289

Mammalia (mammal), *11*, 1667, *14*, 2083

Mammuthus imperator (elephant), *5*, 656

Mandrillus sphinx (mandrill), *10*, 1463, 1465

Manidae (pangolin), *1*, 81

Manis temminickii (pangolin), *1*, 85

Marmosa (opossum), *10*, 1512

Marmota (marmot), *14*, 2086

Marsupialia (marsupial), *1*, xx, *8*, 1121, 1147, *10*, 1511, *12*, 1719, *13*, 1849, *14*, 2135, *16*, 2421

Martes flavigula (yellow-throated marten), *9*, 1307

Martes martes (pine marten), *9*, 1307, 1309

Martes pennanti (fisher), *9*, 1306

maximus (elephant), *5*, 653

Megachiroptera (fruit bat), *2*, 133–4, 159, 163, 213

Megadermatidae (African yellow-winged bat), *2*, 197

Megaladapidae (sportive lemur), *8*, 1173

Megaloceros (deer), *4*, 551–2

Megalohyrax (hyrax), *1*, 6

Megalomys (rice rat), *13*, 1898

Megalonychidae
(two-toed sloth), *14*, 2057

Megaptera novaeangliae
(humpback whale),
16, 2317, 2320

Megatherium (ground sloth),
14, 2060

melaena (long-finned
pilot whale), *15*, 2276

Meles meles (badger), *1*, 110

Melinae (badger), *1*, 110

Mellivora (badger), *1*, 107

Mellivora capensis (badger),
1, 111

Mellivorinae (badger),
1, 107, 111

Melododon (badger), *1*, 108

Melursus (sloth bear), *3*, 292

Mephitinae (skunk),
16, 2369, 2373

Mephitis (striped skunk),
16, 2372–3

Merychippus (horse), *7*, 1018

Merycopotamus
(hippopotamus), *7*, 992

Mesocricetus auratus
(golden hamster), *7*, 930

Mesohippus (horse),
7, 1018

Miacoidea (civet), *4*, 497

Microcavia australis
(mountain cavy), *6*, 896

Microcebus spp.
(mouse lemur), *8*, 1175

Microchiroptera (small bat),
2, 134, 159–60, 185–6, 210–1

Microtinae
(lemmings and vole),
15, 2187

Microtini (vole), *15*, 2187, 2190

Microtus agrestis
(field vole), *15*, 2190

Mirounga (elephant seal),
13, 1983

Molossidae (free-tailed bat),
2, 195

Monachinae (southern seal),
13, 1979, 1982

Monachus (monk seal),
13, 1983

Monodelphis domestica
(short–tailed opossum),
10, 1529

Monodontidae (white whale),
16, 2343, 2346

Monotremata
(echidna and platypus),
11, 1641, 1644–5

Morganucodon (mammal),
1, xviii

Mormoopidae
(leaf–chinned bat),
2, 159, 162

Moschidae (musk deer),
4, 549

Muntiacus muntjacs
(Indian muntjac),
4, 553

Muridae (rat, mouse, and
allies), *7*, 913, *13*, 1875,
1879, 1901

Murinae (Old World rat
and mouse), *9*, 1355,
13, 1876, 1901–2, 1905,
1917–8, 1923

Murina robinsoni
(mouse opossum), *10*, 1527

Muscardinus
(common dormouse), *7*, 919

Mus musculus (house mouse),
13, 1905

Mustela erminea (ermine),
15, 2216

Mustela nivalis
(common weasel),
15, 2216–7, 2219

Mustela putorius
(European polecat),
15, 2216

Mustela vison
(american mink),
9, 1306

Mustelidae (weasels and their
allies), *1*, 107–11, *9*, 1303,
11, 1563, 1566,
15, 2213, *16*, 2369

Mustelinae (weasels and their
allies), *9*, 1303, *15*, 2213,
16, 2369, 2373

Myocastor coypus (coypu),
3, 370

Myocastoridae (capybara),
3, 367

Myomorpha (mouselike
rodent), *3*, 319, *7*, 913, 916,
13, 1901, *14*, 2085,
15, 2187

Myrmecobiidae (numbat),
14, 2139

Myrmecobius fasciatus
(squirrel-sized numbat),
14, 2149

Myrmecophaga tridactyla
(giant anteater), *1*, 29

Myrmecophagidae (anteater),
1, 29, 33

Mystacinidae
(short-tailed bat),
2, 159, 162

Mysticeti (baleen whale),
15, 2239, 2265–6, 2291,
16, 2317, 2320, 2343

mysticetus (bowhead whale),
15, 2291

Myzopodidae
(sucker-footed bat), *2*, 206

N

N. narica (white–nosed coati),
12, 1825

N. nelsoni (island coati),
12, 1825

Nandinia binotata (African
palm civet), *4*, 501

Nasalis (proboscis monkey),
10, 1433, 1439

Nasua (coati), *12*, 1823, 1827

Nasua nasua (coati), *12*, 1825

Nasuella (mountain coati),
12, 1823

Nasuella olivacea
(mountain coati), *12*, 1825

Neofelis (clouded leopard),
12, 1772

Neofelis nebulosa brachyurus
(Formosan clouded
leopard), *8*, 1202

Neofelis nebulosa
(clouded leopard),
8, 1199, 1202

Neomys anomalus
(southern water shrew),
14, 2033

Neophoca (Australian sea lion),
13, 1953

Neotragini (dwarf antelope),
6, 757, 781

Nesolagus (Sumatran hare),
7, 939

Nesolagus netscheri
(Sumatran rabbit), *7*, 943

Ningaui timealeyi
(Pilbara ningaui), *14*, 2150

Noctilio leporinus
(greater bulldog bat), *2*, 163

Noctilionidae (bulldog bat),
2, 163

Notomys (Australian
hopping mouse),
13, 1916

Notoryctidae (marsupial mole),
14, 2139, 2158

Nyctereutes procyonoides
(raccoon dog), *4*, 575, 579

Nycticebus (slow loris),
5, 731, 735

Nyctimene major (tube-nosed
fruit bat), *2*, 137

Nyctomys sumichrasti
(vesper rat), *13*, 1879

O

Ochotona (pika), *7*, 939

Ochotona hyberborea
(northern pika), *7*, 942

Ochotona princeps
(American pika), *7*, 942

Ochotonidae (pika),
7, 939–41, *12*, 1797

Octodontoidea (degus and other
octodonts, chinchilla-rat,
tuco-tuco, spiny rat, hutia,
coypu), *3*, 367, *6*, 887,
889–90, 898

Odobenidae (walrus),
13, 1953, 1956, 1979

Odobenus rosmarus
(walrus), *13*, 1957, 1959

Odontoceti (toothed whale),

5, 627, *15*, 2265–6,
   16, 2343–4
Okapia (okapi),
   6, 809
Okapia johnstoni (okapi),
   6, 809, 813
Orcinus orca (killer whale),
   15, 2269, 2271
ornatus (spectacled bear),
   3, 289, 295
Ornithorhynchidae (platypus),
   11, 1641
Ornithorhynchus anatinus
   (platypus),
   11, 1641, 1645, 1647
Orthogeomys (taltuza),
   14, 2094
Orycteropus afer (aardvark),
   1, 7
Oryctolagus cuniculus
   (European rabbit),
   12, 1801, 1803, 1818
Oryzomyini (rice rat),
   13, 1878, 1898
Otaria (southern sea lion),
   13, 1953
Otariidae (eared seal),
   13, 1953, 1956, 1979, 1983
Otocyon megalotis
   (bat-eared fox), *5*, 683
Ovibos moschatus (musk ox),
   6, 838
Oxymycterus (burrowing
   mouse), *13*, 1878

P

pacos (alpaca), *3*, 341, 345
Paenungulata (sirenian),
   9, 1279
Palaeocastor (beaver),
   3, 316
Palaeolagus (rabbit), *12*, 1800
Paleotragus (giraffe), *6*, 812
Pan paniscus
   (pygmy chimpanzee),
   4, 471, *4*, 475
Panthera (big cat),
   8, 1199, 1201, 1095,
   12, 1772
Panthera leo (lion), *8*, 1202,

9, 1225, 1228, 1231,
   15, 2164
Panthera leo persica
   (Asiatic lion),
   9, 1246
Panthera onca (jaguar),
   8, 1095, 1099, 1101, 1202,
   15, 2164
Panthera pardus (leopard),
   8, 1203, 1205, *15*, 2164
Panthera pardus orientalis
   (Anatolian leopard),
   8, 1203
Panthera tigris altaica
   (Siberian tiger),
   15, 2161, 2163, 2167
Panthera tigris amoyensis
   (South China tiger),
   15, 2161
Panthera tigris balica
   (Bali tiger), *15*, 2164
Panthera tigris corbetti
   (Indochinese tiger),
   15, 2161, 2164
Panthera tigris sondaica
   (Javan tiger), *15*, 2164
Panthera tigris sumatrae
   (Sumatran tiger),
   15, 2161, 2164
Panthera tigris (tiger),
   8, 1202, *15*, 2165
Panthera tigris tigris
   (Bengal tiger),
   15, 2161, 2164, 2167
Panthera tigris virgata
   (Caspian tiger), *15*, 2164
Panthera uncia
   (snow leopard), *8*, 1203
Pantherinae (large cat),
   9, 1225, *12*, 1772
Pan troglodytes
   (common chimpanzee),
   4, 471, 474, 477
Paradoxurinae (palm civet),
   4, 497–8, 507, 519
Paramys (near mouse),
   7, 914
Parapithecus
   (small monkey), *6*, 862
pardus (leopard), *8*, 1199
Pecora (cattlelike animal),

4, 549
Pedetes capensis
   (springhare), *14*, 2098
Pedetidae (springhare),
   14, 2083
Peponocephala electra
   (melon-headed whale),
   15, 2268
Peponocephalidae (whale),
   15, 2265
Perameles gunnii
   (eastern-barred bandicoot),
   16, 2425
Peramelidae (bandicoot),
   16, 2421
Perissodactyla
   (odd-toed ungulate),
   1, xx, *7*, 1017,
      13, 1927, 1931, *16*, 2447
Perodicticus (potto),
   5, 731, 735
Peromyscus maniculatus
   (deer mouse),
   13, 1881, 1897–8
Perorcytes (bandicoot),
   16, 2430
Petauridae (glider),
   12, 1719, 1723
Petaurista (flying squirrel),
   14, 2109
Petaurista petaurista
   (giant flying squirrel),
   14, 2112
Phacochoerus aethiopicus
   (warthog), *11*, 1618
Phalangeridae (cuscus and
   brush-tailed possum),
   12, 1719, 1723
Phascolarctos cinereus
   (koala), *8*, 1147, 1150,
   1153
Phascolonus (wombat),
   16, 2424
Phenacodontids, *1*, 4
Phenacodus, *1*, 4
Phocarctos (Auckland sea lion),
   13, 1953
Phoca vitulina (common seal),
   13, 1982, 1985
Phocidae (true seal),
   13, 1979

Phocinae (southern seal),
   13, 1979, 1982
Phocoenidae (porpoise),
   5, 627, 631
Phocoidea (seal), *13*, 1983
Pholidota (pangolin),
   1, xx, 81, 83, *14*, 2057
Phyllostomatoidea
   (leaf-nosed bat), *2*, 159,
      162–3, 166, 168, 176
Phyllostomatoidea
   (vesper bat), *2*, 183, 214
Phyllotini (leaf-eared mouse),
   13, 1879
Physeteridae (sperm whale),
   16, 2343, 2347
Physeter macrocephalus
   (sperm whale), *16*, 2349
Piliocolobus (red colobus
   monkey), *10*, 1433
pinchaque (mountain tapir),
   16, 2447
Pinnipedia (eared seal,
   true seal, and walrus),
   1, xxi, *13*, 1953,
   1969, 1979
Pipistrellus pipistrellus
   (vesper bat), *2*, 213
Pithecia pithecia
   (guianan saki), *10*, 1411
Platanistidae (river dolphin
   family), *5*, 627, 630
Platybelodon (elephant),
   5, 656
platyrrhine (New World
   monkey), *10*, 1409
Plecotus auritus (vesper bat),
   2, 214, 219–20
Pliohippus (one-toed horse),
   7, 1019
Podomys (Florida mouse),
   13, 1895
Poebrotherium (camel), *3*, 344
Polyprodontia (bandicoot,
   marsupial carnivore, and
   American opossum),
   14, 2135
Pongidae (orangutan,
   chimpanzee, and gorilla),
   4, 471, *6*, 783, 861,
      11, 1537, 1540, 1543

Pongo pygmaeus (orangutan), *11*, 1537, 1541, 1543, 1559

Pongo pygmaeus albelii (Sumatran orangutan), *11*, 1537, 1539, 1546, 1559

Pongo pygmaeus pygmaeus (Bornean orangutan), *11*, 1537, 1539, 1546

Postschizotherium (hyrax), *1*, 6

Potamochoerus porcus (bushpig), *11*, 1619

Potamotherium (badger and otter), *1*, 111, *11*, 1564

Potoroidae (rat kangaroo), *13*, 1849, 1853

Potos (kinkajou), *12*, 1823, 1827

Praomys natalensis (multimammate rat), *13*, 1918

Presbytis (leaf-monkey langur), *10*, 1433, 1437

Primate (primate), *4*, 471, *6*, 783, *10*, 1407, 1433, 1485

Proboscidea (elephantlike form), *1*, xx, 653, 655

Procamelus (camel), *3*, 344

Procavia (rock hyrax), *1*, 6–7

Procaviidae (hyrax), *1*, 3

Procolobus (colobus monkey), *10*, 1433, 1436

Procolobus badius (red colobus monkey), *10*, 1436, 1439

Proconsul africanus (ape), *6*, 862

Procoptodon (mammal), *1*, xix, *8*, 1125

Procyonidae (raccoon), *11*, 1589, *12*, 1823–4, 1828, 1843

Procyoninae (raccoon), *12*, 1823, 1826–7

Procyon (raccoon), *12*, 1823

Procyon lotor (common raccoon), *12*, 1823, 1826, 1829

Procyon maynardi (raccoon), *12*, 1833

Profelis (African golden cat and caracal), *14*, 2008

Propithecus tattersalli (golden crowned sifaka), *8*, 1196

Propthicus verreauxi (Verreaux's sifaka), *8*, 1179, 1183

Proscalopinae, *10*, 1383

Prosimii (lower primate), *8*, 1173, *10*, 1485

Prosqualodon (toothed whale), *15*, 2268, *16*, 2346

Proteles cristatus (aardwolf), *7*, 1043, 1046

Protocetidae (whale), *15*, 2241

Protohydrochaeris (capybara), *3*, 370

Pseudaelurus (early cat), *8*, 1199, 1202, *9*, 1229

Pseudalopex culpaeus (colpeo fox), *5*, 682

Pseudocheiridae (ring-tailed possum), *12*, 1722

Pseudorca crassidens (false killer whale), *15*, 2269

Pseudoryx nghetinhensis (wild cattle), *3*, 421

Pteromys (Old World flying squirrel), *14*, 2109, 2112

Pteropodidae (fruit bat), *2*, 133

Pteropodinae (fruit bat), *2*, 133, 135, 137

Pteropus poliopcephalus (gray-headed flying fox), *2*, 136, 137

Ptilodus (mammal), *1*, xix

Pygathrix (douc langur), *10*, 1433, 1439

Q

Quemesia gravis (guemi), *6*, 910

R

Ramapithecus (ape), *11*, 1540

Rattus norvegicus (brown rat), *13*, 1894, 1905, 1907

Rattus rattus (common rat), *13*, 1894

Ratufa (giant squirrel), *14*, 2113

Ratufa (tree squirrel), *14*, 2109

Redunca (reedbuck), *1*, 59

Reduncini (antelope), *1*, 55, 59, 62, 64, 68, 76

Reithrodontomys (harvest mouse), *13*, 1894

Reithrodontomys megalotis (western harvest mouse), *13*, 1894

Rhachianectes glaucus (gray whale), *15*, 2247

Rhinocerinae (one-horned rhinoceros), *13*, 1927, 1931

Rhinoceros sondaicus (Javan rhinoceros), *13*, 1927, 1931

Rhinoceros unicornis (Indian rhinoceros), *13*, 1927, 1931

Rhinocerotidae (rhinoceros), *13*, 1927

Rhinolophoidea (vesper bat), *2*, 185–6, 188, 189, 214

Rhinopithecus roxellana (golden monkey), *10*, 1454

Rhinopithecus (snub-nosed langur), *10*, 1433, 1437

Rodentia (rodent), *1*, xxi, *3*, 315, 367, *6*, 887, *7*, 913, *9*, 1355, *12*, 1693, *13*, 1875, 1901, *14*, 2083, 2085, 2109, *15*, 2187

Rousettus aegyptiacus (fruit bat), *2*, 137

rufa (mountain beaver), *3*, 315

Ruminantia (cud chewer), *4*, 549, *6*, 809, 835, *7*, 994

Rupicapra rupicapra (chamois), *6*, 839

S

Sagatherium (hyrax), *1*, 6

Saguinus oedipus (cotton-top tamarin), *10*, 1489

Saiga tatarica (saiga), *6*, 838

Sarcophilus harrisii (Tasmanian devil), *14*, 2135

Satanellus hallucatus (northern native cat), *14*, 2145

Scandentia (tree shrew), *1*, xxi, *14*, 2034

Sciuridae (squirrel), *14*, 2083, 2087–8, 2109, 2113, 2118

Sciuromorpha (squirrel-like rodent), *3*, 315–6, 319, *14*, 2083, 2085, 2087, 2109

Sciurus (tree squirrel), *14*, 2109

Sciurus vulgaris (red squirrel), *14*, 2113, 2115

Semnopithecus (hanuman langur), *10*, 1433, 1436

Simias (pig-tailed langur), *10*, 1433, 1437

Sirenia (sea cow and manatee), *1*, xxi, *9*, 1277–8

Sivacanthion (Old World porcupine), *12*, 1694

Sivapithecus (ape), *4*, 473, *11*, 1540

Sivatherium (giraffe), *6*, 812

Smilodon (saber-toothed tiger), *15*, 2164

Sminthopsis longicaudata (long-tailed dunnart), *14*, 2150, 2159

Solenodon cubanus (Cuban solenodon), *14*, 2031

Solenodon paradoxus (Hispaniola solenodon), *14*, 2031

Solenodontidae
(solenodon), *14*, 2031
Sorex (shrew), *14*, 2031
Sorex minutus (pygmy shrew),
14, 2035
Soricidae (shrew),
14, 2031
Soricomorpha
(shrewlike insectivore),
14, 2034
Spalacidae (blind mole rat),
9, 1355, 1358
Speothos venaticus
(bush dog), *4*, 523, 527
Spermophilus (ground
squirrel), *14*, 2086,
2113
Sphiggurus spinosa
(South American tree
porcupine), *12*, 1696
Spilogale (spotted skunk),
16, 2372–3
Squalodontidae (whale),
15, 2242
stegodon (elephant), *5*, 656
Steneofiber (beaver),
3, 319
Stenidae (coastal dolphin
family), *5*, 627, 630
Strepsicerotini (antelope),
1, 55, 58, 59, 64, 68, 70
subungulate (sirenian),
9, 1279
Suidae (wild pig),
11, 1615, 1619
Suina (hippopotamus),
7, 991, *11*, 1615
Suncus ater
(Bornean musk shrew),
14, 2051
Suncus etruscus
(Etruscan shrew),
14, 2033
Suricata suricatta (meerkat),
9, 1329, 1333, 1335
Sus scrofa (wild boar),
11, 1619, 1621
Sylvilagus (cottontail),
12, 1800
Sylvilagus brasiliensis
(forest rabbit),

12, 1818
Synceros (African buffalo),
3, 419, 423

T

T. m. latirostris (Florida
manatee), *9*, 1281
Tachyglossidae (echidna),
11, 1641
Tachyglossus aculeatus
(short-nosed echidna),
11, 1645, 1662
Talpa europaea
(European mole),
10, 1385
Talpidae (mole, desman,
and shrew-mole),
10, 1381–3, 1387, 1390
Tamandua mexicana
(anteater), *1*, 29
Tamandua tetradactyla
(anteater), *1*, 29
Tamias (chipmunk),
14, 2087
Tamiasciurus (American red
squirrel), *14*, 2113
Tamiasciurus (tree squirrel),
14, 2109
Tapiridae (tapir),
16, 2447
Tapirus (tapir),
16, 2447–8, 2451
Tarsiidae (tarsier),
5, 731, 734
Tarsipedidae (rat kangaroo),
13, 1849
Tarsipes (honey possum),
13, 1849, 1852
Tarsius spectrum
(spectral tarsier), *5*, 734
Taurotragus (antelope),
1, 59
Tayassuidae (peccary),
11, 1615, 1619
Tayassu tajacu (collared
peccary), *11*, 1618
telicomys (capybara),
3, 370
Tenrecidae (tenrec),
7, 965

Tenrecomorpha
(tenrec-type insectivore),
7, 965, *10*, 1384, *14*, 2034
Terrestris (Brazilian tapir),
16, 2447
Theria (live-bearing mammal),
14, 2083
Thomomys (eastern
pocket gopher), *14*, 2094
Thylacinidae (Tasmanian wolf
or tiger), *14*, 2139
Thylacoleo carnifex (marsupial
lion), *14*, 2154
Thylacomyidae (bilbies),
16, 2421
Thyropteridae
(disc-winged bat), *2*, 188
Thibetanus (Asian black bear),
3, 289
tigris (tiger),
15, 2161
Titanotylopus (camel), *3*, 344
Trachypithecus (brow-ridged
langur), *10*, 1436
Tragelaphus (antelope), *1*, 58
Tragulidae (pronghorn),
12, 1745
Tragulus hyemoschus
(chevrotain), *12*, 1748
Tragulus javanicus
(lesser Malay chevrotain),
12, 1745
Tragulus meminna (Indian
spotted chevrotain), *12*, 1745
Tragulus napu (greater Malay
chevrotain), *12*, 1745
Tremarctinae (small bear),
3, 292
Tremarctos ornatus
(spectacled bear),
2, 240, *3*, 292, 295
Tremarctos (small bear),
3, 289
Trichechidae (manatee),
9, 1277
Trichechus (manatee),
9, 1277
Trichechus inunguis (Amazonian
manatee), *9*, 1277, 1281
Trichechus manatus manatus
(Antillean manatee),

9, 1281
Trichechus manatus
(West Indian manatee),
9, 1277, 1281, 1283
Trichechus senegalensis
(West African manatee),
9, 1277, 1281
troglodytes (chimpanzee),
4, 471
Tubulidentata (aardvark),
1, xx, 5
Tylopoda, *7*, 995

U

U. a. arctos (European bear),
2, 263, 266
U. a. horribilis (grizzly bear),
2, 263
U. a. middendorffi
(Kodiak bear), *2*, 263
U. a. yesoensis
(Hokkaido bear), *2*, 263
uncia (leopard), *8*, 1199
Ursavus (brown bear), *2*, 264
Ursidae (bear), *2*, 237, 263, *3*,
289, *11*, 1589, 1667
Ursinae (bear), *11*, 1667
ursinus (sloth bear), *3*, 289
Ursus (bear),
2, 237, 263–4, *3*, 289, 291
Ursus americanus (American
black bear), *2*, 237, 241, 267
Ursus americanus floridanus
(Everglades bear), *2*, 259
Ursus americanus luteolus
(bear), *2*, 259
Ursus arctos (brown bear),
2, 240, 263, 264, 266–7
Ursus arctos californicus
(grizzly bear), *2*, 284
Ursus arctos nelsoni
(grizzly bear), *2*, 284
Ursus arctos piscator
(brown bear), *2*, 285
Ursus elemensis (dawn bear),
2, 240
Ursus malayanus (sun bear),
2, 241, *3*, 292
Ursus maritimus (polar bear),
2, 241, 267, *11*, 1667,

WILDLIFE RESERVES AND PARKS

A

Abruzzo National Park,
6, 846–7
Amboseli National Park,
8, 1223, 13, 1946
Ampijeroa Forest Reserve,
8, 1183
Ankara Special Reserve,
8, 1184
Anzihe Reserve, 11, 1613
Arctic National
Wildlife Refuge,
11, 1691

B

Banff National Park,
14, 2105
Bardia 15, 2185
Barguzin 9, 1327
Barnardi Wildlife
Sanctuary,
11, 1637
Barwon Park, 12, 1817
Basse Casamance
National Park,
6, 781
Berenty Nature Reserve,
8, 1183, 1196
Bialowieza National
Park,
3, 402, 404–5, 412, 415
Brazzaville Zoo (Congo),
6, 885
Bronx Zoo,
3, 415, 12, 1769
Bukit Raja Reserve,
11, 1549

C

Camp Leakey, 11, 1561
Central Park Zoo,
6, 830
Chimpanzoo, 4, 495

Chinchilla National Reserve,
6, 911
Cincinnati Zoo,
14, 2029
Cockscomb Basin Wildlife
Sanctuary,
8, 1117, 1119
Colombo Zoo, 8, 1222
Corbett National Park,
4, 508–9
Coto Doñana National Park,
9, 1270, 1273
Custer State Park,
12, 1768

D

David Fleay's Park,
11, 1651
Davies Creek National Park,
13, 1873
Denali National Park,
2, 286
Drill Rehabilitation and
Breeding Center,
10, 1483

E

Ecuadorean Park Service
and Fundacion Natura,
3, 362
Etosha National Park, 1, 92,
6, 819, 9, 1249, 14, 2020

F

Fengtongzhai Reserve,
11, 1613
Frankfurt Zoo, 1, 27
Franklin-Lower Gordon
Wild Rivers National Park,
14, 2154
Frozen Zoo,
4, 2029

G

Garamba National Park,
13, 1951
Gemsbok National Park,
7, 1065
Gibson Desert Nature
Reserve, 14, 2159
Glacier National Park,
2, 258, 272
Gombe National Park,
4, 486–7, 495
Gonarhezhou National
Park,
13, 1948
Grand Teton National Park,
4, 540

H

Hanover Zoo, 12, 1769
Hattah-Kulkyne
National Park,
8, 1142
Hobart Zoo,
14, 2154
Hope Zoo, 6, 909
Howletts Zoo (England),
6, 885
Huangshuihe Reserve,
11, 1613
Hwange National Park,
13, 1951

I

Itatiaia National Park,
4, 547

J

Jaú National Park,
8, 1116, 1119
Jersey Wildlife
Preservation Trust,
6, 909, 10, 1508

K

Kafue National Park,
5, 614, 9, 1238
Khalid Wildlife Research
Center,
6, 781
Khosh-Yeilagh Wildlife
Reserve (Iran), 4, 468
Kosciusko National Park,
14, 2150

L

Lal Suhanra National Park,
6, 781
London Zoo,
9, 1249, 11, 1610, 1612
Lowry Park Zoo, 9, 1301

M

Mahale Mountains
National Park,
4, 495
Manas Wildlife Sanctuary,
11, 1637–9
Masai Mara Reserve,
16, 2456
Miami Seaquarium, 9, 1301
Missouri Botanic Garden,
8, 1195
Mountain Lion Preservation
Foundation, 12, 1793
Mountain Zebra National Park,
16, 2468
Mt. Iglit Game Preserve,
3, 440

N

Nairobi National Park, 4, 466
National Cameloid Center,
3, 362
National Parks Board of
South Africa, 16, 2471

National Wildlife
   Research Center,
   8, 1223
National Zoological Park,
   12, 1706
New Mexico Zoo,
   12, 1769
Ngorongoro
   Conservation Area,
   9, 1236, 1247

P

Pampa Galeras
   National Vicuña
   Preserve, *3*, 362
Parc National des Volcans
   (Rwanda), *6*, 884
Philadelphia Zoo, *11*, 1554
Poco das Antas
   Biological Reserve,
   10, 1506–7, *14*, 2081
Podocarpus National Park,
   3, 363
Port Lymne Zoo (England),
   6, 885
Pouting Reserve, *11*, 1561

Q

Queen Elizabeth
   National Park,
   7, 1002, 1012
Queensland National
   Parks and Wildlife
   Service, *16*, 2442

R

Reserves Natural Integrale,
   8, 1195
Rio de Janeiro Primate Center,
   10, 1506, 1508
Rio Platano
   Biosphere Reserve,
   8, 1119
Royal Chitwan
   National Park,
   3, 313, *15*, 2184
Ruaha National Park,
   6, 817
Ruwenzori Park,
   9, 1339

S

Sakkarbaug Zoo,
   9, 1249
Salonga National Park,
   4, 494–5
Salvador Zoo,
   14, 2081
Sao Paulo Botanical Gardens,
   14, 2066
Sapo National Park,
   7, 1015
Serengeti National Park,
   5, 611, 622, *6*, 820, *8*, 1209,
   9, 1236–7, *16*, 2457
Serra da Canastra
   National Park,
   4, 547
Sokoke Reserve,
   9, 1352

Southern Ocean Refuge,
   15, 2313
Southern Sanctuary
   (Antarctica),
   16, 2339
Stora Sjöfallet
   National Park,
   16, 2392
Strict Reserves of Bemahara
   and Namoroka,
   8, 1184
Sundarbans Tiger Reserve,
   15, 2172–3, 2184

T

Tangjiahe Reserve,
   11, 1611
Tijuca National Park,
   14, 2081
Tikal National Park,
   8, 1119
Topeka Zoo,
   11, 1538
Torres del Paine
   National Park,
   12, 1794
Tsavo National Park,
   5, 672, *6*, 766, *8*, 1221
Twycross Zoo,
   6, 805, 807

U

Ujong Kulon National Park,
   3, 431, *13*, 1948–9

V

Vu Quang Nature Preserve,
   3, 441

W

Wanglang Panda Reserve,
   11, 1610
Washington National Zoo,
   10, 1506
Way Kambas National Park,
   13, 1948
Whipsnade Zoo Park,
   13, 1950
Wolong Nature Reserve,
   10, 1454, *11*, 1611–3
Wood Bison National Park,
   3, 415–6

Y

Yellowstone National Park,
   2, 237, 258, 261, 287, *3*, 400,
   403, 406, 414, 417, *4*, 570,
   12, 1768, 1795

ORGANIZATIONS

African Wildlife Foundation
1717 Massachusetts Avenue, NW
Washington, DC 20036
Phone: (202) 265-8394
Fax: (202) 265-2361

Mission: To increase the sustainable contribution of natural resources to local and national economies and to promote the sound protection and management of these resources by the people of Africa, by working to build the capacity of African individuals and institutions to effectively manage their natural resources, especially wildlife and wildlife habitats

Programs: Training of professionals, public education, institutional strengthening, and scientific research; programs and activities in protected areas management, environmental awareness, policy development and implementation, conservation science, support for species and habitats of prime ecological significance, and community based approaches to conservation; neighbors as Partners Program works to ensure that local people and communities adjacent to parks and other protected areas derive some tangible benefit from their proximity; Conservation of Biodiverse Resource Areas works to implement this five-year project and help Kenya Wildlife Service establish a Community Wildlife Service unit to implement and coordinate community-based programs; Protected Area Conservation Strategy; World Conservation Union (IUCN) meetings; Mweka College of African Wildlife Management; International Gorilla Conservation Program; Amboselli Elephant Research Project; Planning and Assessment for Wildlife Management

American Cetacean Society
P.O. Box 2639
San Pedro, CA 90731-0943
Phone: (213) 548-6279

Mission: To protect whales, dolphins, porpoises, and their environments through research, education, and conservation

Programs: Whale-watching trips; educational programs

Australian Conservation Foundation
340 Gore Street
Fitzroy, Victoria 3065
Australia
Phone: (613) 416-1455
Fax: (613) 416-0765

Founded 1967. Research, information, and advocacy. Interests include natural environment and wildlife; forestry; resources, industry, and employment; and land management

Australian Littoral Association
P.O. Box 49
Moorooka, Queensland 4105
Australia

Concerned with aquatic life, water quality, and coastal zone management

Australian Trust for Conservation Volunteers
P.O. Box 423
Ballarat, Victoria 3350
Australia
Phone: (6153) 327-490
Fax: (6153) 332-290

Undertakes practical conservation projects on a national basis, such as protecting endangered animals, tree planting, erosion control, and seed collection

Bat Conservation International, Inc.
P.O. Box 162603
Austin, TX 78716-2603
Phone: (512) 327-9721
Fax: (512) 327-9724

Mission: To promote conservation of bats and their habitats worldwide and to educate the public about the vital ecological and economic roles of bats, as part of the more general goal of preserving the diversity and health of life on earth

Programs: North American Bat House Research Project sets up bat houses and makes careful observations to learn more about bat roosting requirements; Adopt-A-Bat Program

Birdlife International
P.O. Box 57242
Washington, DC 20037-7242
Phone: (202) 778-9563
Fax: (202) 293-9342

Mission: To prevent the extinction of any bird species in the wild, to monitor the conservation status of all bird species and important bird habitats worldwide, to identify and secure adequate conservation of critically important sites for the conservation of bird diversity, and to promote worldwide interest in, and concern for the conservation of birds and the environment.

Programs: Field action programs, based on research, to identify the threats to birds and their habitats; conservation program in the Palas Valley in Pakistan to protect the Western Trapogan pheasant and its habitat; conservation at Kao Nor Chuchi in southern Thailand to protect the Gurney's Pitta; conservation program in Europe that includes about thirty countries, combining international activities with national campaigns and actions, and working under a unified strategy; conservation programs in Ghana, Turkey, Madeira, Cameroon, Spain, and Nigeria

Canadian Wildlife Federation
2740 Queensview Drive
Ottawa, Ontario
K2B 1A2
Phone: (613) 721-2286
Fax: (613) 721-2902

Mission: To promote the conservation of fish and wildlife, and their habitats; to foster understanding of natural processes; to ensure adequate stocks of fish and wildlife; to provide education programs and sponsor research; to work with legislators, government agencies, and other nongovernmental agencies

Programs: The Federation's education programs include National Wildlife Week, Project W.I.L.D., Endangered Species, and Habitat 2000. It is also helping develop a new National Recreational Fisheries and Aquatic Environments Programme. Advocates on conservation and environmental issues, provides numerous conservation awards

Center for Marine Conservation
1725 DeSales Street, NW
Washington, DC 20036
Phone: (202) 429-5609
Fax: (202) 872-0619

Mission: To protect marine wildlife and their habitats, prevent over-exploitation, and conserve ocean and coastal resources through policy research, science-based advocacy, education, regional citizen coalitions, and interaction with governments and industries, with an emphasis on sustainable fisheries, prevention of solid waste pollution, conservation of species, and management of marine-protected areas around the world

Programs: International Conservation Network helps governments, industries, and nongovernmental conservation organizations work together. International Beach Cleanup Campaign; Citizen Pollution Patrol Program; Marine Debris Action Plan; Clean Ocean Campaign; Storm Drain Stenciling Campaign; and Sea Grassroots Activist Program

Conservation International
1015 18th Street, NW, Suite 1000
Washington, DC 20036
Phone: (202) 429-5660
Fax: (202) 887-5188

Mission: To conserve ecosystems, biological diversity, and the ecological processes that support life on earth, with special emphasis on building local capacity. Temperate and tropical rainforest conservation, and indigenous peoples' rights are the organization's main areas of focus

Programs: Marketing development communications; scientific programs; conservation biology; conservation economics; gender and social policy; legislative affairs

Defenders of Wildlife
1244 19th Street, NW
Washington, DC 20036
Phone: (202) 659-9510
Fax: (202) 833-3349

Mission: To further a comprehensive approach to habitat protection that will preserve intact wildlife communities that support a wide variety of plant and animal life. The Defenders are committed to the belief that this conservation principle, known as biological diversity, is the framework upon which all environmental protection strategies must be built.

Programs: Protection and restoration of endangered species; protection of marine mammals; preservation of biological diversity; banning the importation of wild-caught birds; promotion of watchable wildlife viewing areas

Federation of Ontario Naturalists
355 Lesmill Road
Don Mills, Ontario M3B 2W8
Canada
Phone: (416) 444-8419

Mission: To improve understanding of Ontario's natural areas and wildlife, to conserve and protect Ontario's biodiversity and quality of life, and to help in the restoration of important natural habitats and endangered wildlife

Programs: Ontario Rare Breeding Bird Programme is Canada's largest research project on rare, threatened, and endangered species. Ontario Mammal Atlas Project maps the distribution of Ontario's mammal species; Wildlife Programme; Forest Management Programme

International Environmental Law Centre
280 Pitt Street, Suite 82
Sydney, NSW 2000
Australia
Phone: (612) 261-3599

National Audubon Society
700 Broadway
New York, NY 10003-9562
Phone: (212) 979-3000
Fax: (212) 979-3188

Mission: To conserve and restore natural ecosystems, focusing on birds and other wildlife for the benefit of humanity and the earth's biological diversity

Programs: Protecting the Arctic National Wildlife Refuge from oil development; assisting concerned citizens to protect wetlands in their communities; mapping the ancient forests of the Pacific Northwest and lobbying for legislation that will create an ancient forest reserve system; fighting water developents on the Platte River; fighting for strengthened Endangered Species Act; protecting important habitat for migratory birds; lobbying for population policies that encourgage utilities to switch to solar energy; improving the environment of the Everglades ecosystem

National Wildlife Federation
1400 16th Street, NW
Washington, DC 20036
Phone: (202) 797-6800
Fax: (202) 797-6646

Mission: To educate, inspire, and assist individuals and organizations of diverse cultures to conserve wildlife and other natural resources while protecting the earth's environment, and to promote a peaceful, equitable, and sustainable future

Programs: Class Project; Naturequest Program; leadership training; Nature Scope Guides; Nature Scope Workshops; Teen Adventure; Wildlife Camp

Nature Conservancy
1815 North Lynn Street
Arlington, VA 22209
Phone: (703) 841-5300

Mission: To preserve plants, animals, and natural communities that represent the diversity of life on Earth by protecting the lands and waters they need to survive. To save ecologically-significant lands, the organization first identifies significant natural areas that need to be set aside, then protects those areas through gift, purchase, cooperative agreements, landowner education, or by assisting or advising government

Programs: Manages more than 1,300 reserves and other natural areas through restoration techniques such as prescribed burnings, reforestation, fencing, and the removal of alien species. The Conservancy's Pacific Program is working to identify and protect threatened areas in Indonesia, Melanesia, and Micronesia. In Latin America, the Conservancy's Conservation Program works to help provide infrastructure, community development, professional training, and long-term funding for legally protected but underfunded areas throughout the continent. Total acres protected in the United States since 1953: 6.9 million; outside the United States: 20 million

Nature Conservancy of Canada
110 Eglinton Avenue, West
Toronto, Ontario
M4R 2G5
Canada
Phone: (416) 932-3202
Fax: (416) 932-3208

Mission: Dedicated to preserving biological diversity through purchasing and protecting ecologically significant natural areas and places of special beauty and educational interest

Programs: Ongoing land acquisition program; Natural Land Donations Programme

Rainforest Action Network
450 Sansome Street, Suite 700
San Francisco, CA 94111
Phone: (415) 398-4404
Fax: (415) 398-2732

Mission: To preserve the world's rainforests through activism on issues including the logging and importation of tropical timber, cattle ranching in rainforests, the activities of international development banks, and the rights of indigenous rainforest peoples. Sponsors letter-writing campaigns, boycotts, and demonstrations; conducts grassroots organizing in the USA; builds coalitions; and collaborates with other environmental, scientific, and grassroots groups. Works to educate the public about the effects of tropical hardwood logging, and promotes ecologically sound plantations

Rainforest Alliance
65 Bleeker Street
New York, NY 10012-2420
Phone: (212) 677-1900
Fax: (212) 677-2187

Mission: To conserve the world's endangered tropical rainforests by developing and promoting economically viable and socially desirable alternatives to tropical deforestation. The Alliance works in concert with local peoples to develop forest products and businesses that offer long-term stable income for native people

Programs: Banana Project; Timber Project; Smart Wood Certification Program; Amazon Rivers Project; Catalysts Grant Program

Royal Australasian Ornithologists Union
21 Gladstone Street
Moonee Ponds
Victoria 3039
Australia
Phone: (613) 370-1422

The Wilderness Society
900 17th Street, NW
Washington, DC 20006-2596
Phone: (202) 833-2300
Fax: (202)429-3958

Mission: To advocate the protection and sound management of federal public lands and other natural landscapes. The Wilderness Society works on the conservation of biological diversity and promotes development of a land ethic

The Wildlife Conservation Society
c/o New York Zoological Society
185th Street & Southern Boulevard
Bronx, NY 10460
Phone: (212)220-5100

Mission: To work for the better understanding and protection of endangered species and ecosystems through an innovative combination of the resources of wildlife parks with the world's largest staff of nongovernmental field scientists

Programs: The Society operates five wildlife parks (four zoos and one aquarium) in the New York area and 150 international conservation projects in forty-five countries. Friends of Zoos Program–the Nairobi office supervises African programs; educational programs

Wild Life Preservation Society of Australia
8 Reiby Road
Hunters Hill, NSW 2110
Australia
Phone/Fax: (612) 817-3705

Founded 1909. Watchdog and advisory group concerned with protection of fauna and flora

Wildlife Preservation Trust International, Inc.
3400 West Girard Avenue
Philadelphia, PA 19104-1196
Phone: (215) 222-3636
Fax: (215) 222-2191

Mission: To support the propagation of rare and endangered species in captivity, the reintroduction of rare and endangered species to their native habitats and the restoration of these habitats, to research these species in captivity and in the wild; to educate all persons (particularly those from developing countries living in close association with rare and endangered species) concerning the value of wildlife; to professionally train zoologists and conservation biologists, particularly those from developing countries of the world; to formulate strategies and policy activities for the conservation of endangered species and their habitats

Programs: The Trust has ongoing conservation programs underway in different areas, including Madagascar, Mauritius, Brazil, Columbia, Central America, and the United States. Assists in the operation of the International Training Center for the Conservation and Captive Breeding of Endangered Species, which trains conservation workers; holds annual members luncheons in different cities, and offers membership tours of different regions of the world in which the group is active

The Wildlife Society
5410 Grosvenor Lane
Bethesda, MD 20814-2197
Phone: (301) 897-9770
Fax: (301) 530-2471

Mission: To enhance the scientific, technical, managerial, and educational capability and achievement of wildlife professionals in conserving diversity and sustaining productivity of wildlife resources ; to develop and promote sound stewardship of wildlife resources and environments; to undertake an active role in preventing human-induced environmental degradation; and to increase awareness and appreciation of wildlife values

Programs: Working Groups, forums for members of the Society with common professional interests to network and exchange information. Working Groups includes Biological Diversity, College and University Wildlife Education, Geographic Information Systems and Remote Sensing, Habitat Restoration, Native Peoples' Wildlife, Population Ecology and Management Sustainable Use of Ecosystem Resource, Wildlife Damage Management, Wildlife Economics, Wildlife Toxicology

World Conservation Union (IUCN)
1400 16th Street, NW
Washington, DC 20036
Phone: (202) 797-5454
Fax: (202) 797-5461

Mission: IUCN is a union of sovereign states, government agencies, and nongovernmental organizations working to promote scientifically based action that will link development and the environment; to provide leadership and promote a common approach for the world conservation movement; and to ensure that human use of natural resources is appropriate, sustainable, and equitable.

Programs: Ongoing efforts working for species conservation, responsible wetlands use, ecology, environmental strategies, forest conservation, parks and protected areas

World Wide Fund for Nature (WWF)
1250 24th Street, NW
Washington, DC 20037-1175
Phone: (202) 293-4800
Fax: (202) 293-9211

Mission: To participate in the international drive to rescue endangered animals from extinction; to curb illegal trade in rare species; to establish and protect national parks and reserves; to help meet the needs of local people without destroying natural resources; to train and equip rangers, guards, and antipoaching teams; and to promote scientific research to develop long-range conservation programs. Over the past three decades, WWF has sponsored more than 3,000 conservation projects in 140 wildlife-rich countries.

Programs: The Fund's Special Rescue program has helped stop the brutal slaughter of some of the world's most critically threatened animals, including Latin America's jaguar, the African elephant, the Asian snow leopard, and India's Bengal tiger. Their Wildlands and Human Needs Program helps people improve the quality of their lives without destroying their own natural resources. The Fund also operates training programs to form park rangers and antipoaching teams, conservation educators who travel to schools, churches, markets, and workplaces in Third World countries. Campaigns for major international agreements, legislation, and treaties on endangered species and habitats

World Wide Fund for Nature—Australia
G.P.O Box 528
Sydney, NSW 2001
Australia
Phone: (612) 247-6300
Fax: (612) 247-8778

Affiliate of the World Wide Fund for Nature (WWF International)

Yukon Conservation Society
P.O. Box 4163
Whitehorse, Yukon Territory
Y1A 3T3
Canada

Mission: To ensure the sound management of the Yukon's natural resources through advocacy, education, and research; to encourage change that is sensitive to the uniquely fragile northern environment

Programs: Conservation education; guided nature appreciation hikes; school programs; public meetings; Ted Parnell Scholarship for students pursuing any aspect of environmental studies